# *Project Management Made Simple and Effective*

## Daniel C. Yeomans, PMI-PMP, PMI-RMP, PMI-ACP, CSM, CMQ/OE

Contributors: Peter Rogers and Alex Wright

© 2016 Daniel C. Yeomans, PMI-PMP, PMI-RMP, PMI-ACP, CSM, CMQ/OE

All Rights Reserved.

No part of this publication may be reproduced, stored in a retrieval system, or transmitted, in any form or by any means, electronic, mechanical, photocopying, recording, or otherwise, without the written permission of the author.

This edition published by
Dog Ear Publishing
4010 W. 86th Street, Ste H
Indianapolis, IN 46268

www.dogearpublishing.net

ISBN: 978-145754-981-6

This book is printed on acid-free paper.

Printed in the United States of America

# Dedication

This book is dedicated to:

- Every individual who has ever had a great idea that they couldn't turn into reality.

- Every employee who was asked to deliver a project on time, at budget, and within scope who did not achieve their objectives.

- All my wonderful students thirsting for project management knowledge at Northwest University, Bellevue College, and Green River College.

- My friends and colleagues from multiple corporations who had the faith in me to share their project management challenges and allow me to help them develop frameworks that enabled success.

- The United States Air Force, who involuntarily placed me into the project management career field in 1977. At the time, I was an unhappy camper. In retrospect, thank you.

- All my friends in the Air Force Sergeants Association.

- Cynthia Holmberg, my long-time friend and associate. Much of what I've learned about project management was based on our discussions and cooperation.

- My good friend and associate, Peter Rogers. We have worked together for more than 15 years, shared ideas, and grown together. Peter is a big contributor to this book.

- Alex Wright, a great project manager and friend who shares a lot of wisdom in the pages that follow.

- Dustin Grosse for inviting us into companies and organizations he has managed. Dustin embraces innovation. He allowed us to deploy what we know, as well as to experiment with many new things. We wish every executive was as open to real innovation.

- My family and friends who put up with me every day. I know that is a challenge!

# Project Management Quotes: The Importance of Project Management

"Project managers function as bandleaders who pull together their players each a specialist with individual score and internal rhythm. Under the leader's direction, they all respond to the same beat."
**L.R. Sayles**


"Of all the things I've done, the most vital is coordinating the talents of those who work for us and pointing them towards a certain goal."
**Walt Disney**


"In poorly run projects, problems can go undetected until the project fails. It's like the drip…drip…drip of a leaky underground pipe. Money is being lost, but you don't see it until there is an explosion."
**Joy Gumz**


"In Nestlé's experience, and also in my personal experience within supply chain and operations, we regularly observe that great projects are delivered by the most outstanding project management skills -the people who can see and anticipate the risk, prepare for contingency before hitting the problem, understand stakeholder management, and have the communication skills to manage stakeholder expectations, critical path and project planning, etc. In summary, outstanding project managers are a "must have" ingredient to any successful product innovation, and Nestlé is increasingly recognizing our project managers because they bring competitive advantage to our organization."
**S. King, Nestlé**


"Simplicity boils down to two steps: Identify the essential. Eliminate the rest."
**Leo Babauta**


**Authors' Note:** We have tried to provide the essentials and avoid everything else. It is unlikely that you will use everything in this book on any one project. Consider it all, then adopt and adapt to the needs of your project. This is part of the art of project management. Feel free to contact us at any time you have a question. Our Group P17 mail address is Contact@p17group.com.

# Table of Contents

Introduction ................................................................................................................................. xv
About the Author ...................................................................................................................... xvii
    Daniel C. Yeomans ............................................................................................................. xvii
About the Contributors ............................................................................................................. xix
    Peter Rogers ...................................................................................................................... xix
    Alex Wright ........................................................................................................................ xx
Chapter 1: Introduction to Project Management: What You Need to Know ............................. 1
    Problem 1: Lack of Planning and Ineffective Project Management ..................................... 2
    Figure 1.1 PDCA Model ....................................................................................................... 2
    Problem 2: Deficiencies in Project Selection and Prioritization ........................................... 3
    Figure 1.2 Project Portfolio Planning Approach .................................................................. 3
    Problem 3: Inadequate Stakeholder Management .............................................................. 4
    Problem 4: Poor Scope Definition and Management ......................................................... 5
    Problem 5: Ineffective Estimates and Unrealistic Schedules .............................................. 6
    Problem 6: Poor Budget Planning ....................................................................................... 6
    Problem 7: Ineffective Change Management and Control ................................................. 6
    Problem 8: Lack of Resource Planning ................................................................................ 7
    Problem 9: Poor Communications Management and Team Dynamics .............................. 8
    Problem 10: Failure to Manage Risk and Poor Execution ................................................... 8
    Chapter 1 Summary ........................................................................................................... 10
    Peter's Corner: Chapter 1 Edition ...................................................................................... 11
    Chapter 1 Food for Thought .............................................................................................. 12
Chapter 2: Initiating the Project: Getting Off on the Right Foot .............................................. 13
    Figure 2.1 Project Manager's Triangle .............................................................................. 14

## Table of Contents

Project Charter Format ........................................................................................................... 15

Figure 2.2 Project Charter Template ..................................................................................... 16

The Balanced Scorecard Model .............................................................................................. 17

Figure 2.3 Balanced Scorecard Model ................................................................................... 18

The Balanced Scorecard Model Defined .............................................................................. 19

Project Charter Keys to Success ............................................................................................. 19

Managing Stakeholders .......................................................................................................... 20

Figure 2.4 Stakeholder Management Process ...................................................................... 20

Project Stakeholders Defined ................................................................................................. 21

    The Project Team ................................................................................................................ 21

    Other Stakeholders ............................................................................................................. 22

The Stakeholder Register ........................................................................................................ 23

Figure 2.5 Stakeholder Register ............................................................................................. 24

Stakeholder Management: Closing Thoughts .................................................................... 26

Figure 2.6 Stakeholder Management Plan ........................................................................... 27

Changing Commitment Levels .............................................................................................. 28

David McClelland's 3 Needs Theory .................................................................................... 29

Figure 2.7 The 3 Needs Theory .............................................................................................. 30

Chapter 2 Summary ................................................................................................................. 32

Peter's Corner: Chapter 2 Edition ......................................................................................... 33

Chapter 2 Food for Thought ................................................................................................... 36

Chapter 3: Planning Scope: The Gift that Keeps on Giving .............................................. 37

    Project Scope Overview ..................................................................................................... 38

    Defining Project Requirements ......................................................................................... 39

    Figure 3.1 Project Requirements Overview .................................................................... 39

    Project Requirement Types: The FURPS Model ........................................................... 42

    Figure 3.2 FURPS Model .................................................................................................... 42

    Requirements Feasibility and Prioritization Matrix ...................................................... 43

    Figure 3.3 Requirements Feasibility and Prioritization Matrix ................................... 43

Figure 3.4 Requirements Feasibility and Prioritization Matrix Process ..................................... 45

Figure 3.5 Requirements Feasibility and Prioritization Matrix Scoring ..................................... 45

Next Step: The Scope Statement ..................................... 47

Figure 3.6 Project Scope Statement Template ..................................... 48

Figure 3.7 Typical Project Phase Approaches ..................................... 49

Figure 3.8 DMAIC Project Scope Statement Example ..................................... 50

Scope Statement: Closing Thoughts ..................................... 50

Developing a Comprehensive Scope Statement: Alex's 7 Qs ..................................... 51

Figure 3.9 The 7 Qs ..................................... 51

The Work Breakdown Structure (WBS): The Cornerstone of Project Planning ..................................... 52

Figure 3.10 Sample WBS Using DMAIC Approach ..................................... 52

WBS Variations ..................................... 54

Figure 3.11 WBS Variations ..................................... 54

The Work Breakdown Structure (WBS) Dictionary ..................................... 55

Figure 3.12 WBS Dictionary Example (DMAIC Process) ..................................... 56

Special Topic: Multi-Phase Project Planning (Project Chunking) ..................................... 56

Figure 3.13 Multi-Phase Project Planning (Project Chunking) with PDCA Approach ..................................... 57

Multi-Phase Project Planning (Project Chunking) Summary ..................................... 57

Chapter 3 Summary ..................................... 59

Peter's Corner: Chapter 3 Edition ..................................... 60

Chapter 3 Food for Thought ..................................... 61

Chapter 4: Planning the Schedule: "I Want It Yesterday!" ..................................... 63

The Project Time Management Process ..................................... 63

Step 1: Review the Work Breakdown Structure (WBS) ..................................... 64

Step 2: Determine Dependencies ..................................... 64

Figure 4.1 Project Dependencies ..................................... 65

Dependency Categories ..................................... 65

Step 3: Estimate Work Packages, ..................................... 67

Figure 4.2 PERT Time Management Illustration ..................................... 67

## Table of Contents

Figure 4.3 PERT Application ............................................................................................. 69

Step 4: Consider Leads and Lags ...................................................................................... 69

Figure 4.4 Leads and Lags ................................................................................................. 70

Step 5: Develop a Project Network Diagram ................................................................. 70

Figure 4.5 Project Network Diagram Sample with DMAIC Approach ...................... 71

Project Network Diagram: Clarifying Comments ........................................................ 72

Step 6: Calculate the Critical Path ................................................................................... 73

Step 7: Balance the Schedule ............................................................................................ 73

Chapter 4 Summary ........................................................................................................... 75

Peter's Corner: Chapter 4 Edition .................................................................................... 76

Chapter 4 Food for Thought ............................................................................................. 77

Chapter 5: Planning the Budget: Spend a Little to Make a Lot ....................................... 79

CAPEX and OPEX Funding/Cost Categories ............................................................... 79

Project Cost Categories ...................................................................................................... 80

Figure 5.1 Cost Categories ................................................................................................. 80

Defining Budget Requirements ........................................................................................ 81

Figure 5.2 Budget Template Sample ................................................................................ 81

Sample Budget Template Clarifying Notes .................................................................... 82

Estimating Project Costs .................................................................................................... 83

Figure 5.3 Resource Breakdown Structure Template ................................................... 83

Resource Breakdown Structure Highlights ................................................................... 83

Depreciation ........................................................................................................................ 84

Figure 5.4 Calculating Value of Depreciation ................................................................ 84

Project Funding Requirements ......................................................................................... 85

Figure 5.5 Project Funding Requirements ...................................................................... 86

Chapter 5 Summary ........................................................................................................... 87

Peter's Corner: Chapter 5 Edition .................................................................................... 88

Chapter 5 Food for Thought ............................................................................................. 89

Chapter 6: Managing Change: Change Is Inevitable ......................................................... 91

Effective Project Change Management: A Proven Process ........................................................... 91

Figure 6.1 Project Change Management Process ...................................................................... 92

The Change Timeline ................................................................................................................... 94

Figure 6.2 Change Timeline ......................................................................................................... 94

The Project Change Request Form .............................................................................................. 96

Figure 6.3 Sample Project Change Request Form ..................................................................... 97

Project Change Request Form: The Essentials ............................................................................ 99

Project Change Log ...................................................................................................................... 101

Figure 6.4 Project Change Request Log Example .................................................................... 101

Chapter 6 Summary ..................................................................................................................... 104

Peter's Corner: Chapter 6 Edition .............................................................................................. 105

Chapter 6 Food for Thought ....................................................................................................... 106

Chapter 7: Project Human Resource Management: The People Make the Difference ........................ 107

Introduction to Project Resource Management ......................................................................... 107

Building the Team: The Tuckman Model and Situational Leadership Merge ........................ 109

Figure 7.1 Tuckman Team Building Model and Situational Leadership ................................ 110

    Step 1: Form ............................................................................................................................ 110

    Step 2: Storm ........................................................................................................................... 111

    Step 3: Norm ........................................................................................................................... 111

    Step 4: Perform ....................................................................................................................... 112

The Staffing Management Plan ................................................................................................... 113

Figure 7.2 Staffing Management Plan and RACI Template .................................................... 113

Figure 7.3 Responsibility Assignment Matrix (RAM) Example ............................................... 116

Project Human Resource Management: Final Thoughts ........................................................... 117

Managing the "Virtual Team" ..................................................................................................... 118

The Team Charter ......................................................................................................................... 120

Figure 7.4 Team Charter Format ................................................................................................ 120

Chapter 7 Summary ..................................................................................................................... 123

Peter's Corner: Chapter 7 Edition .............................................................................................. 124

## Table of Contents

Figure 7.5 Emotional Intelligence (EQ) Model ........................................ 125

Chapter 7 Food for Thought .................................................................. 127

### Chapter 8: Project Communications: The 90% Rule ........................ 129

Figure 8.1 Communications Model ...................................................... 129

Why Plan for Communications: The Grapevine Effect ....................... 131

Figure 8.2 Grapevine Visual ................................................................. 132

The Communications Management Plan ............................................ 133

Figure 8.3 Communications Management Plan Template ................. 134

Communications Management Plan: Key Success Factors ................ 136

What to Communicate ......................................................................... 137

Figure 8.4 Potential Project Communications Activities ..................... 137

Project Communications Plan Appendices ........................................ 138

Overcoming Communications Issues: The Communications Management Plan "Plus" ................ 139

Figure 8.5 Communications Management Plan Plus ......................... 139

Chapter 8 Summary ............................................................................. 142

Peter's Corner: Chapter 8 Edition ....................................................... 143

Chapter 8 Food for Thought ................................................................ 145

### Chapter 9: Managing Risk: "Manage Risk, or It Will Manage You" ........................ 147

PIER-C: A Risk Management Methodology ....................................... 147

Figure 9.1 The PIER-C Approach ........................................................ 148

PIER-C Step 1: Plan ........................................................................... 150

Figure 9.2 Risk Management Plan Format ......................................... 151

Risk Management Plan Highlights ..................................................... 151

Figure 9.3 Probability and Impact Rating System Examples ............. 153

Figure 9.4 Probability and Impact Matrix .......................................... 155

Figure 9.5 Risk Breakdown Structure (RBS) Sample ......................... 157

PIER-C Step 2: Identify ...................................................................... 159

Figure 9.6 Standard Risk Register Template ...................................... 160

Building the Risk Register .................................................................. 160

Figure 9.7 Risk Metalanguage ..................................................................................................... 161

Additional Risk Identification Tools ......................................................................................... 162

    SWOT Analysis ......................................................................................................................... 162

Figure 9.8 SWOT Analysis .......................................................................................................... 163

    Delphi Technique .................................................................................................................... 163

Figure 9.9 Delphi Technique ...................................................................................................... 164

PIER-C Step 3: Evaluate .............................................................................................................. 164

PIER-C Step 4: Respond .............................................................................................................. 167

Figure 9.10 Risk Response Generation Process ....................................................................... 167

Risk Response Strategies ............................................................................................................. 169

Figure 9.11 Risk Response Strategies Defined ......................................................................... 169

PIER-C Step 5: Control ................................................................................................................ 172

Figure 9.12 Project Risk Management Control Process .......................................................... 173

Figure 9.13 Risk Management Matrix ....................................................................................... 174

Chapter 9 Summary ..................................................................................................................... 176

Peter's Corner: Chapter 9 Edition .............................................................................................. 177

Chapter 9 Food for Thought ....................................................................................................... 179

Chapter 10: Project Planning: Putting it all Together ............................................................... 181

    Figure 10.1 Project Initiation and Planning Sequence ....................................................... 182

        Step 1: Initiating ................................................................................................................ 183

        Step 2: Stakeholder Planning .......................................................................................... 183

        Step 3: Scope Planning ..................................................................................................... 184

        Step 4: Time and Cost Planning ..................................................................................... 185

        Step 5: Support Planning ................................................................................................. 187

        Step 6: Risk Planning ....................................................................................................... 188

        Step 7: Project Planning ................................................................................................... 188

    Figure 10.2 Five-Step Presentation Process ......................................................................... 191

    Five-Step Presentation Process: Final Thoughts ................................................................ 195

    Figure 10.3 Emergenetics Approach to Gaining Project Approval and Commitment ...... 196

## Table of Contents

    The Analytical Stakeholder ............................................................................................................. 197

    The Social Stakeholder .................................................................................................................... 197

    The Structural Stakeholder ............................................................................................................. 198

    The Conceptual Stakeholder ........................................................................................................... 198

Identifying the Emergenetics Attributes ................................................................................................ 199

    Analytical Phrases ........................................................................................................................... 199

    Social Phrases ................................................................................................................................... 200

    Structural Phrases ............................................................................................................................ 200

    Conceptual Phrases ......................................................................................................................... 201

Chapter 10 Summary ................................................................................................................................. 202

Peter's Corner: Chapter 10 Edition ......................................................................................................... 203

Chapter 10 Food for Thought .................................................................................................................. 205

Chapter 11: Project Executing, Monitoring and Controlling, and Closing: Achieving Results ............ 207

Project Execution, Monitoring and Controlling, and Closing: Scope, Time, and Cost ........................ 207

    Managing Scope .............................................................................................................................. 207

    Managing Time ................................................................................................................................ 208

    Managing Cost ................................................................................................................................. 209

Figure 11.1 Tracking Schedule and Budget Using EVM Methodology ............................................... 210

Figure 11.2 Calculating Earned Value (EV) Using 50/50 Progress Reporting Method ...................... 211

Project Execution, Monitoring and Controlling and Closing: The Support Plans ............................. 212

Decision Making: The "OARP" Model .................................................................................................. 215

Figure 11.3 OARP: A Decision Making Framework ............................................................................. 215

    The OARP Process .......................................................................................................................... 216

Status Reporting: How to Get It Right .................................................................................................. 216

Figure 11.4 Project Status Report Sample ............................................................................................... 218

    Status Reporting 101: The Report and More ............................................................................... 219

Effective Meeting Management ............................................................................................................... 221

    Is a Meeting Necessary? .................................................................................................................. 221

Figure 11.5 Meeting Determination Checklist ....................................................................................... 221

The Ten Commandments of Meeting Management ............................................................................ 222

Figure 11.6 Ten Commandments of Meeting Management .............................................................. 222

The Meeting Agenda ........................................................................................................................ 224

Figure 11.7 Meeting Agenda Templates ............................................................................................ 224

Figure 11.8 Meeting Minutes Template ............................................................................................ 226

Managing the Meeting ..................................................................................................................... 227

Managing Project Stakeholders ............................................................................................................ 228

Project Closure ....................................................................................................................................... 230

Conducting Lessons Learned ........................................................................................................... 231

Figure 11.9 Lessons Learned Template ............................................................................................. 232

Chapter 11 Summary ............................................................................................................................. 233

Peter's Corner: Chapter 11 Edition ....................................................................................................... 234

Chapter 11 Food for Thought ............................................................................................................... 236

Website Access Code for Templates and Examples ........................................................................... 237

APPENDIX A: A Portfolio Approach ................................................................................................. 239

APPENDIX B: Project Charter Example ............................................................................................. 241

APPENDIX C: Stakeholder Register and Management Plan Examples ......................................... 245

APPENDIX D: Scope Planning Tools Examples ............................................................................... 247

APPENDIX E: Schedule Planning Tools Examples .......................................................................... 251

APPENDIX F: Budget Planning Tools Examples .............................................................................. 253

APPENDIX G: Project Communications Management Plan Example ........................................... 255

APPENDIX H: Project Risk Register Example .................................................................................. 257

APPENDIX I: Project Plan Pitch Sample ........................................................................................... 259

APPENDIX J: Project Status Report Sample .................................................................................... 261

Glossary of Terms and Index ................................................................................................................ 262

# Introduction

Project management is critical in both business and life. Project management is an essential competency and is embraced by nearly all successful firms and organizations. Successful projects turn great ideas into reality. Unsuccessful projects result in lost customers, reduced revenue, inefficient processes, and frustrated employees.

Recent reviews reveal that between 40% and 80% of all projects fail[1]. Some projects fail to satisfy scope. Others fail to satisfy the timeframe when project deliverables are needed. Others deliver scope on time but at the expense of cost, quality, or other success factors. Our book investigates common project management problems and provides practical solutions.

Many consequences occur because of failed projects. Businesses must continue to rapidly move forward with new products or services, to quickly adjust to meet demands, to effectively market their goods, and more. These goals depend on effective project management. When project management fails, businesses often follow.

The purpose of this book is three-fold. First, we—I am delighted to act as lead auhor and incorporate the wisdom of Peter and Alex-- simplify project management to enable you to satisfy project success criteria. The triple constraints — time, cost, and scope — will control you unless you control them. This book is for those new to project management, as well as those with experience. Our insights and tips are easy to understand and really work. We walk you through a proven project management framework and provide recommendations at each step along the way.

Second, we present a common sense approach keying on application rather than theory. Each process, method, and tool that is provided clearly states how, when, and where to use the technique to your advantage. We provide a toolbox of tools and techniques available for download that you can adapt to your project management environment. We aim to improve your effectiveness. We don't want your project to be one of the 40% to 80% that fail.

---

[1] www.pmi.org

# Introduction

Third, we highlight examples you can understand and apply from day one. This book is published as an 8-1/2 by 11-inch document. We made the book this size for a purpose. Use this book as a source document for your everyday project management activities, write notes, add highlights, and apply what we share. Use the book as a primary text for a course or simply as a reference book. Share the book with other project managers and aid their efforts to succeed. Each chapter is stand-alone and provides value. You can open the book to any chapter and get what you need.

We refer to "You" throughout this book. You are the one who must manage projects successfully. You are responsible for delivering projects on time, at budget, and within scope, plus other project success criteria. Because *you* are accountable, and because we want *you* to be successful, this book is for **YOU**.

# About the Author

## Daniel C. Yeomans

Daniel C. Yeomans brings more than forty years of project management experience to his client work. He is a highly proficient and acknowledged expert as a senior project manager, process manager, business analyst, and trainer, delivering over 4,000 seminars and classes in his extensive career. Dan began his project management career in 1977 while in the United States Air Force. His passion and knowledge were recognized in 1985 when the Air Force named him their "Project Manager of the Year." Dan has managed a portfolio of projects that includes infrastructure development and modification, process development and improvement, course development, Information Technology, and more.

Dan develops project management training curriculum to satisfy the needs of multiple corporations through his work with the P17 Group. He also develops materials and teaches project management for Northwest University, Bellevue College, and Green River College, teaching at both the college and corporate levels. He is also responsible for helping thousands of students attain the coveted Project Management Professional (PMP) certification through the Project Management Institute (PMI).

Dan's expertise has taken him through the doors of such companies as Microsoft, American Express, T-Mobile, Nordstrom, AT&T Wireless, Western Wireless, FEMA, US Air Force, and Lucent Technologies. An avid learner, Dan holds an MBA from St. Martin's College and a BA in Management from McKendree College. Professional designations include Project Management Professional (PMI-PMP®), Risk Management Professional (PMI-RMP®), and Agile Certified Practitioner (PMI-ACP ®) certifications from the Project Management Institute (PMI ®); Certified Scrum Master (CSM) from the Scrum Alliance; and a Certified Manager of Quality/Organizational Excellence Certified (CMQ/OE ®) from the American Society of Quality. Dan is also a qualified Emergenetics® Associate. In his spare time, Dan loves all sports.

Contact: dan@p17group.com

# About the Contributors

## Peter Rogers

Peter Rogers combines a strong academic background with his high-impact development expertise to bring out the best in people, their teams, and their organizations. Peter challenges people to choose what and where they want to be and enables them to thrive in the ecosystems that they impact and mold to their purposes. Peter draws heavily from his advanced degrees in biological and management sciences, policy, and economics as he works with people to frame solutions to the most daunting challenges.

Drawing on over thirty years of experience, with over twenty of those years as a consultant to Microsoft and other Fortune 100 companies, Peter typically works with leaders and managers in the space between strategy development and strategy implementation to ensure that organizations allocate their resources to the work that will deliver on their goals and strategies. He ensures that leaders' visions resonate with those who are tasked with delivering on those visions, and he causes unproductive behaviors and work to be removed from systems.

Prior to forming P17, Peter was instrumental in the startup and success of two companies. In a third company, Cell Therapeutics, he served as head of strategic projects and helped to take the company public on NASDAQ. Peter has been an adjunct professor and guest lecturer at Florida International University and several other colleges and universities. A sought-after speaker, he has spoken at Project World and other conferences. Peter has two advanced degrees from the University of Washington. He earned an MA in Business Economics, and a Master of Marine Affairs (MMA).

Peter actively seeks opportunity and is an advocate of the importance of change, risk, and adventure. He is an avid sailboat racer and finds that being of service brings the most meaning to his life.

Contact: peter@p17group.com

About the Contributors

## Alex Wright

As a development coach, Alex Wright has more than fifteen years of experience at multiple Fortune 100 companies coaching senior directors, general managers, presidents, and their teams worldwide. His background includes the successful delivery of global systems and support for Human Resources, Leadership Development, Finance, Operations, and Treasury systems. Alex combines his years of business success with a personal passion for unlocking leadership and team potential. His award-winning work has been recognized in industry journals such as *Treasury and Risk Magazine*, and *Directions on Microsoft*.

Alex's coaching is distinguished by the use of Emotional Intelligence, consistency, and kindness to get the most out of people. He's found that even in today's technology-rich work environment, success in business is still based on functional interpersonal relationships.

From his earliest days as a cable TV personality, to living in a remote Eskimo fishing village on the Alaskan tundra, to surviving a near-fatal parachute malfunction, Alex values measured risk-taking and embraces change for growth, both of which he calls prerequisites for getting the most out of people and realizing one's own potential. Alex received his education from the University of Washington, with a focus on English and Communications. He has a degree in Computer Information Systems from Bellevue College and multiple Leadership Development certifications.

Contact: alex@p17group.com

# Chapter 1: Introduction to Project Management: What You Need to Know

Project management is both an art and a science. The art of project management involves dealing effectively with the variety of project stakeholders you may encounter. By definition, a stakeholder is anyone who is interested in or impacted by a project. Project management is also a science. It is important to define and follow a standard framework or process that will meet the needs of your project and allow for standardized—great—results.

Projects fail for many reasons. As we stated before, statistics and a variety of studies cite a 40% to 80% failure rate. Chapter 1 will provide an overview of why projects fail. This chapter will also provide an introduction of what the follow-on chapters in this book will share. During my time in the Air Force, I learned an important lesson from my leaders: "Never share a problem unless you have a solution." This chapter will discuss the problems, along with a few solutions. By the time the book is complete, however, we will provide easy and understandable solution recommendations to many of the problems that are shared.

We have researched the many reasons why projects fail and condensed the listing into our top ten. We also designed our book around these ten problems to provide guidance, best practices, and easy-to-use tools and techniques you can use to overcome them. Here is our list, along with how we can help.

1. Lack of Planning and Ineffective Project Management
2. Deficiencies in Project Selection and Prioritization
3. Inadequate Stakeholder Management
4. Poor Scope Definition and Management
5. Ineffective Estimates and Unrealistic Schedules
6. Poor Budget Planning
7. Ineffective Change Management and Control
8. Lack of Resource Planning
9. Poor Communications Management and Team Dynamics

10. Failure to Manage Risk and Poor Execution

## Problem 1: Lack of Planning and Ineffective Project Management

Many organizations use a project management methodology that echoes the Nike Corporation's slogan, "Just Do It." This slogan works well for Nike. Unfortunately, it does not work well in managing projects. Just Do It will normally result in your project being part of the 40% to 80% that fail.

Figure 1.1 shows a planning approach that every project manager needs to embrace. This planning approach, sometimes referred to as the Deming Cycle, is PDCA. Plan, Do, Check, and Act, that's PDCA. Successful project managers always "plan" first. They "do" or execute only what is in the plan. They "check" during the project execution to ensure the plan is being followed, and if there are variances, they "act" to fix them. Every successful project management framework follows the PDCA methodology. This is true for both traditional project management models, such as Waterfall, and Agile project management models, such as Scrum. It should be noted that Agile models include a "PDEL" segment within the PDCA process. Plan, Do, Evaluate, and Learn, that's PDEL.

### Figure 1.1 PDCA Model

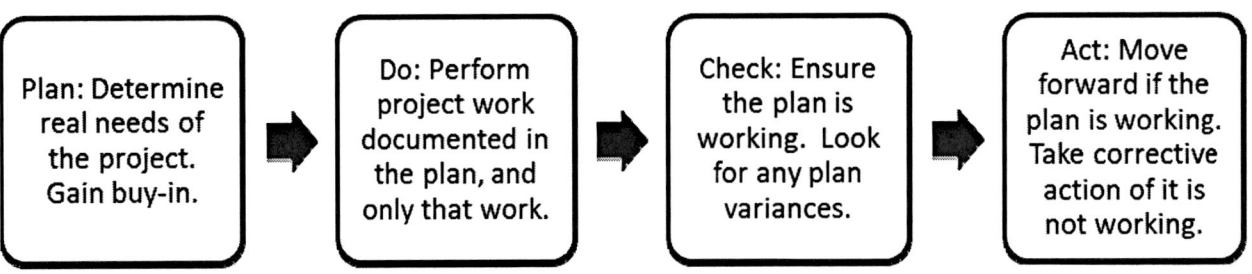

Note: Look for this checkmark icon throughout the book. It provides important clarifying notes to support what we've shared with you. The intent of this book is to provide a proven planning methodology you can use to plan and implement a project from start to finish. Chapter 10 will summarize everything we share and show you how and when to use each tool and technique we provide. In addition, we will provide an overview of how to effectively present a Project Charter and/or Project Plan to management.

## Problem 2: Deficiencies in Project Selection and Prioritization

Many organizations take a piecemeal approach to identifying and approving projects. They look at individual projects without seeing how each project fits in the overall big picture. As a result, projects are randomly approved, the project portfolio grows at unsustainable rates, and each project is Priority One. This is an almost guaranteed path to failure. A portfolio approach to identifying and prioritizing project requirements can reduce this deficiency.

Figure 1.2 shares a visual that shows how the portfolio approach works. In addition, we provide a sample of a potential corporate portfolio in Appendix A.

> *Project Management Tip: Take a holistic approach to determine which projects should be implemented. The portfolio approach reduces risk and boosts results.*

### Figure 1.2 Project Portfolio Planning Approach

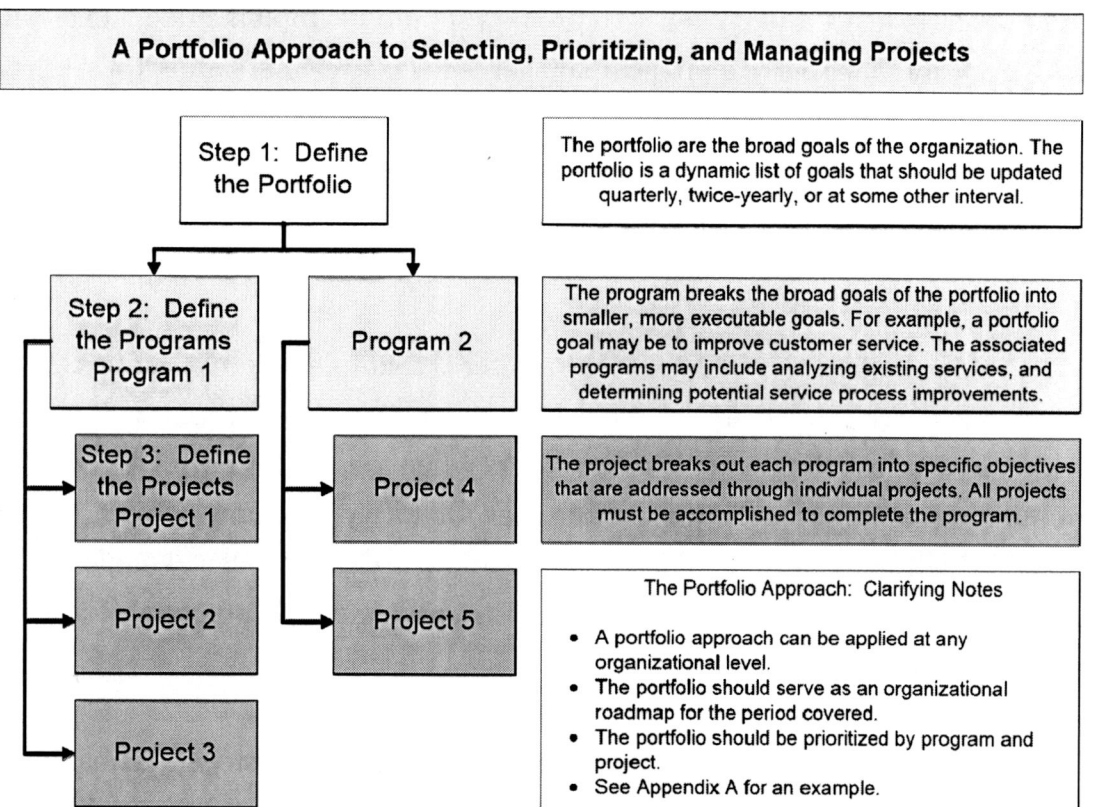

## Problem 3: Inadequate Stakeholder Management

Managing stakeholders from the project's beginning to end is essential. Either you can manage stakeholders, or they will manage you. Failure to effectively manage stakeholders will result in conflict—the dysfunctional type.

In Chapter 2, we introduce three simple tools you can apply to help manage stakeholders and set realistic expectations for the project. We can summarize our goals here by using a building analogy from Alex. If you want to build a 40-story building, you have to start by digging a 40-story hole. People watching your project impatiently wait for visible progress. They want it done now! You need to let them know that first, we need to big a hole before we build. If we try to build a 40-story hole without a solid foundation, we will fail. The moral of this story is simple: start slow, ensure everyone is on board with what the project really entails, and avoid rushing into execution until you are prepared to do so. With that, these tools are:

- **Project Charter:** A Project Charter is an important first step when a project is born. It defines, at a high level, what the project will deliver. This is a critical first step that sets expectations, confirms the project is needed, and provides for a go or no-go decision. You may have heard the saying, "All projects should be implemented." Let's kill that myth up front. The role of a project manager is to ensure value-added projects are implemented. On the other hand, a Project Charter can serve as a means to let management and Sponsors know that an idea that may have looked good on paper is not as feasible as initially thought. There may be times when a Project Charter serves as a means to disapprove a project as well.

- **Stakeholder Register:** A Stakeholder Register is a simple tool that defines the key stakeholders in a project, along with expectations for each stakeholder. It is important to identify and collaborate with stakeholders when a project is born. A good rule of thumb is to identify stakeholders before they identify you. Many projects have been kicked off without effective initial collaboration with the project stakeholders. The result is generally frustration, confusion, resistance, and high potential for project failure.

- **Stakeholder Management Plan:** Sometimes you need to classify stakeholder levels of commitment and develop strategies intended to ensure they are committed at the proper levels. This tool is one that is not shared with the general stakeholder public.

However, it provides the project manager with a means to gauge and adjust stakeholder commitment levels.

## Problem 4: Poor Scope Definition and Management

Scope is arguably the most important aspect of any project. Scope requirements drive time, cost, and all other project considerations. Poor scope management results in poorly defined requirements, unmanageable and false expectations, disappointed stakeholders, and negative impacts to the company's bottom line. Many project managers define scope on day one and attempt to make the project a success. The best practice, however, is to use progressive elaboration. This method allows you to define scope incrementally by beginning with a high-level definition and adding detail as you plan. At the end of the day, each project is ultimately measured by the value of the product and/or service you delivered—or failed to deliver. This is one aspect of project management that you need to get right.

Chapter 3 of this book will provide a number of key tools and techniques designed to help you manage scope and prevent scope creep. Some of the key tools we will introduce include:

- **Requirements Feasibility and Prioritization Matrix:** Requirements are normally collected in a manner that involves only a little analysis, which means that all requirements are listed as Priority One. The Requirements Feasibility and Prioritization Matrix is a tool that allows you to quantitatively analyze and score requirements in a manner that allows for feasibility analysis, prioritization, and identification of key risks impacting success.

- **Scope Statement:** The Scope Statement defines a project's scope in detail. We make this step easy. We provide a number of common project methodologies you can leverage to lay out your project in a manner that guides success. When complete, the Scope Statement will define a feasible implementation process and identify key activities that must occur to make each step of the project process successful. In addition, it will provide a roadmap to those who test the final deliverables in terms of what success truly looks like.

- **Work Breakdown Structure (WBS):** The WBS is arguably the most important project management document you will create. We make this step easy as well. We wil' you how to build a functional WBS that allows you to plan, manage, and cor project effectively. We will also share how to keep your WBS simple by outlining activity attributes and details on a WBS Dictionary.

## Problem 5: Ineffective Estimates and Unrealistic Schedules

Planning a schedule that realistically meets the realities of the project and is also acceptable to stakeholders is most challenging. Too often, project managers attempt to put 16 ounces into a 12-ounce cup and fail miserably. Chapter 4 of this book is dedicated to using the functional WBS developed in Chapter 3, planning for dependencies, and developing a realistic schedule. A realistic schedule open the door for effective discussions with decision makers and Sponsors to find trade-offs that may be necessary if the schedule needs to be adjusted. We will share best practices in estimating that can work for both time and cost planning. In addition, we will highlight one key tool in this section, the Project Network Diagram.

- **Project Network Diagram:** A Project Network Diagram uses the project's WBS to lay out a chronological plan to effectively complete all activities on time. The Project Network Diagram considers various dependencies, defines the project's Critical Path, and shows where Float may be available if the schedule needs help to stay on track.

## Problem 6: Poor Budget Planning

Planning a budget that realistically meets the realities of the project and is also acceptable to stakeholders is very challenging. In Chapter 5, we will share budget planning basics to assist you in this critical planning function. We will define various types of project costs, apply estimation techniques discussed in Chapter 4 to budget preparation, and provide a process that works. We will highlight the following tools in this chapter as well:

- **Project Budget Template:** This template provides a simple, step-by-step process to address all key project costs. In addition, it shows how to effectively forecast project funding requirements.

- **Resource Breakdown Structure:** This simple tool allows you to effectively estimate resources required to complete all project work using your WBS.

## Problem 7: Ineffective Change Management and Control

A common quote echoed by many experienced project managers is, "You can manage change, or change will manage you." Poor change management leads to scope creep, which often leads to project failure. We focus on change management and control in Chapter 6 of this book.

We will begin the chapter with an overview of how people react to change. We will provide tips on how to influence the factors that lead to change. In addition, we will provide two valuable tools you can use to manage change, as follows:

- **Change Request Form:** This form was developed to be easy to complete, to define all key information required to process a change request, and to allow for the right approval or rejection decision.

- **Project Change Request Log:** This simple tool tracks well with the Change Request Form described above. It allows the project manager to track each change and provides a status update for all stakeholders submitting a change.

## Problem 8: Lack of Resource Planning

Chapter 7 of this book will address what is arguably the most important resource a project manager must manage—people. The project team must be managed properly to ensure the greatest potential for success. This includes ensuring they understand and commit to their assigned roles. This includes establishing when each individual is required to support the project and coordinating personnel resource requirements with the Functional Managers who control the resources you need. This management becomes more complex when managing virtual teams.

We will share valuable tools that allow you to manage the human resources you need to ensure both the needs of the project team, and the project, are satisfied as follows:

- **Staffing Management Plan:** The Staffing Management Plan uses the WBS to ensure you and all project stakeholders understand when and what human resources are required to support the project. It allows the project manager to ensure the right people are available when needed, allows Functional Managers to better understand when their personnel need to be available to support the project, and ensures the project team is on-boarded and off-boarded in an efficient manner.

- **Responsibility Assignment Matrix (RAM):** Defining roles and responsibilities is critical. Stakeholders need to understand where they fit in the project and what is expected from them. Two common methods are use of a RACI or RAM. RACI stands for Responsible, Accountable, Consult, and Inform. We highlight the RACI tool in Chapter 2. A RACI is a great tool to use to share roles and responsibilities in your Stakeholder Register, or it may be used as a stand-alone document. A RAM, however, often supplements the RACI and drills down on actual responsibility, execution, and approval requirements. We share a format and example in Chapter 7.

## Problem 9: Poor Communications Management and Team Dynamics

Effective communication is the glue that holds the project together and keeps the team members all moving in the same direction. The success of almost every task a project manager performs is impacted by communications in some way, shape, or form. Chapter 8 of the book will highlight the communications challenges a project manager faces. We will share the challenge of the "grapevine" and provide a number of tips to improve your overall communications effectiveness. In addition, the following tool will be shared:

- **Communications Management Plan:** This simple planning format allows you to create a "Rhythm of the Project," set stakeholder communications expectations, and anticipate and address potential communications challenges.

## Problem 10: Failure to Manage Risk and Poor Execution

Risk is defined as any event that can impact your project, either negatively or positively. A common quote is, "You can manage risk, or risk will manage you." Every project has unknown factors that can lead to either negative or positive consequences. In Chapter 9, we will share best practices in risk management that will help you identify both opportunities and threats. We will highlight best practices in risk planning, identification, and prioritization. We will highlight critical project management tools, as introduced below:

- **Risk Management Plan:** A Risk Management Plan sets the stage for all risk management activities that follow. This simple plan provides guidance and information to the members of your risk management team.

- **Risk Register:** A risk register is an essential project management tool to help identify, document, and manage project risks. And—it is easy to put together and maintain. We will share a Risk Register template that can serve your project needs. It may be used in an operational environment as well.

Many project managers are able to successfully put together a project plan. Unfortunately, the plan soon becomes outdated and stakeholders fail to follow the plan. Despite their best efforts, the project fails. In Chapter 11, we will discuss best practices in project execution and control. In addition, we will highlight some simple tools you can adopt to help you stay on track once the project plan is approved. The tools we will highlight include:

- **Earned Value Management (EVM):** EVM is a methodology that all who desire certification in project management must learn. However, EVM is being adopted by more and more organizations as a means to determine the budget and schedule status for a project. We will introduce this concept to familiarize you with how it works. You may find this method useful for managing projects and a great study reference for certification testing☺. Also referred to as Earned Value Technique, or EVT.

- **Decision Making Matrix:** We will provide direction on how to effectively make decisions using an OARP model. OARP stands for Owner, Approver, Reviewers, and Participants. This model establishes a solid process you can use to ensure all decisions are properly collaborated and implemented.

- **Status Report:** Status reporting is a huge headache for most project managers. We will simplify the process, share a very simple yet effective status reporting format, and hopefully make this important aspect of project execution and control easier for you.

- **Meeting Agenda and Minutes:** An associate of mine joked many years ago that the acronym PM, which most people will define as Project Manager, actually meant "Perpetual Meetings." It is a fact of life: project management success will be greatly impacted by the effectiveness, or ineffectiveness, of the meetings you conduct. We will provide a sample agenda and minutes format that works. In addition, we will share best practices in effective meeting management that will help you moving forward.

- **Lessons Learned:** All projects should be evaluated to determine what went well, what can be improved, and what to change to take your project management from good to great. Lessons Learned are still often referred to as a "Post Mortem." We will complete Chapter 11 with an overview of the process and encourage you to adopt it as your own.

## Chapter 1 Summary

Project Management is challenging. As a result, the majority of projects fail. Many great books discuss project management competency in an effort to help overcome these challenges and succeed. For example, the Project Management Institute's *Project Management Body of Knowledge (PMBOK Guide) ®, 5th Edition*[2], provides a wealth of information and best practices. This publication is *the* book to purchase if you are seeking certification in the project management field. However, the focus of our book is to provide best practices and, of course, teach you how to effectively manage a project.

We believe you will find this book organized in a way that gives you a greater chance of project management success. It is organized in a way that walks you through key project management steps in the order in which they need to occur. We provide you with simple, easy-to-follow guidance plus share simple-to-use tools and techniques proven to be effective and provide examples of each. At the end of the book, we provide a code you can use to go to our website, www.p17group.com, to download the full set of tools and techniques we share. Thanks again for purchasing this book. We look forward to any feedback you may share.

---

[2] www.pmi.org

## Peter's Corner:  Chapter 1 Edition

Have any of your projects failed because you used the wrong process or tool?

In my experience, the root cause of project failure is almost always people.

"They are the problem... if they did what they were supposed to, the project would have been a success"

It is easy to point fingers at others. It is much harder to point at ourselves, to admit that we are responsible for part of the mess. The mess is easy to identify. We must determine how we contributed to the mess and what we could have done (and will do next time) to prevent it. This is the work of project leadership — to own the problem, to get the team to own the problem, and to prevent it from happening again.

Many projects are accomplished in a haphazard way that usually results in failure. Dan, Alex, and I have brainstormed what it takes be successful and will share our experiences in this book.  Thanks for choosing this book. We will justify the choice!

Here is one final point before I close.  Remember, we are in this together. We will succeed and fail together.

## Chapter 1 Food for Thought

1. Why do you feel many of your organization's projects fail? Which tools and techniques do you believe might be helpful to improve chances of project success? In which areas do you feel your organization needs to improve its focus?

2. How well does your organization follow the PDCA model? Do you feel adhering to PDCA could improve project management effectiveness?

3. How does your organization select and prioritize projects? How do you believe taking a portfolio approach may help improve your efforts to achieve success?

4. Choose one of the 10 problems we shared for project failure. Which problem is most prevalent in your organization or in your life?

5. Peter's Deep Thought Challenge:

*Reflections:*

Think of a project with your involvement that failed or was not fully successful. What could YOU have done diffferently* to make this project more successful**?

| |
|---|
| 1. |
| 2. |
| 3. |

*Differently is intentionally misspelled. ☺

**Does your response include how you will guide, influence, or work with others to achieve success?

# Chapter 2: Initiating the Project: Getting Off on the Right Foot

Initiating the project correctly is absolutely critical. You have likely heard the phrase, "first impressions are lasting." This is true in life and is also a key to effective project management. During the initiating stage, you need to satisfy a number of objectives.

The first thing you need to do when assigned as a project manager is to create a document called a Project Charter. Any key stakeholder can prepare the Project Charter. Oftentimes, a Project Charter may be driven by an approved Business Case Analysis (BCA). When this is the case, it is imperative that the project manager ensures the Project Charter captures and builds upon the information documented in the approved BCA.

Peter and I teamed with our associate, Alex Wright, to develop a book on how to develop and present effective business cases.[3] If you need to develop great business cases, we are confident this book can help. See the full title below☺.

It is highly recommended that the Project Manager participate in development of the Project Charter. This document defines a project at a high level. Approval of the Project Charter is referred to as "Pre-Baseline." Here are three primary reasons why a Project Charter adds value.

- Some projects are initiated in response to a management directive. When this is the case, the Project Charter serves as a tool to ensure that communication is clear. Without a Project Charter, you risk initiating a project that does not meet the real needs of management. That is a poor way to start.

- A Project Charter can also be written to evangelize a bottom-up project. In this instance, the goal is to capture the attention of management and successfully gain project approval. In this case, the Project Charter serves a dual purpose as both a business case and as a means to establish what the project will deliver at a high level.

---

[3] *Turn Great Ideas Into Reality: Develop and Present a Winning Business Case*, Yeomans, Rogers, and Wright.

- Sit down for this. A Project Charter can also serve as a means of letting management know that a project should not move forward. The goal of a good project manager is to move good projects forward and stop bad projects from continuing. Too often, project managers accept projects that are doomed to failure.

> *Project Management Tip: Never begin a project without a Project Charter!*

The primary goal of a project manager is to manage the "triple constraints," the Project Manager's Triangle. The Project Charter is the first step to ensure you deliver the project on time, within budget, and with the right scope. Figure 2.1 provides a quick visual you need for your awareness.

### Figure 2.1 Project Manager's Triangle

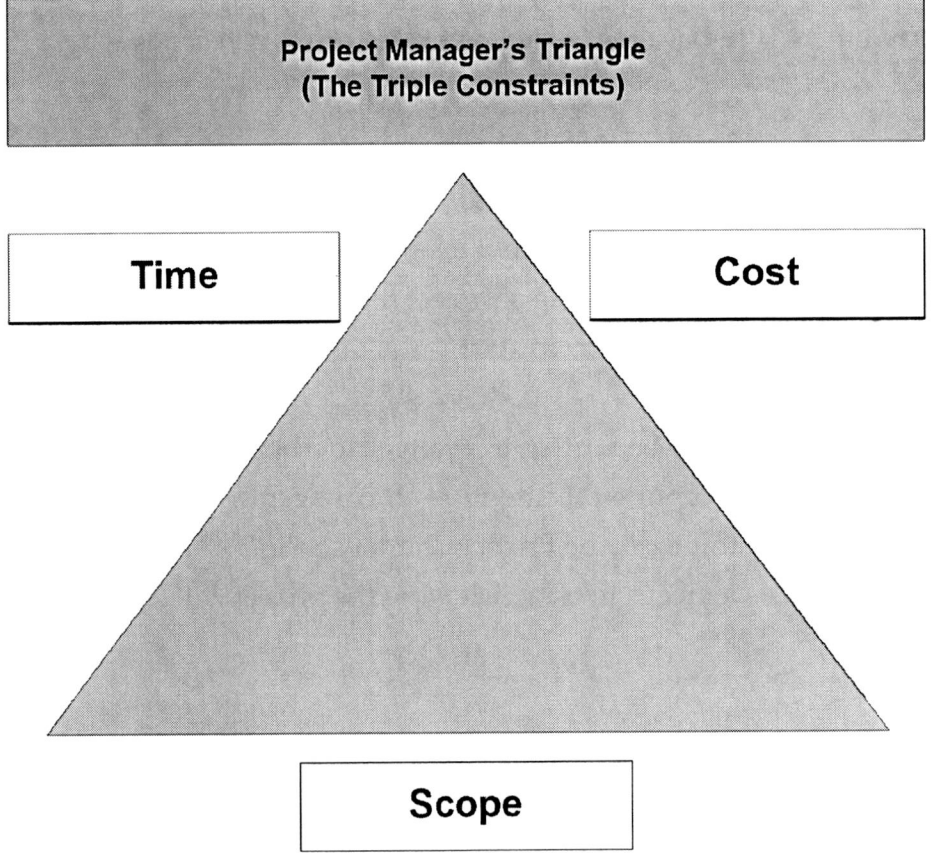

Creating a Project Charter also enables the project manager to be more successful by satisfying three critical needs.

- First, a Project Charter authorizes a project manager to perform the work required to be successful. Trying to manage a project without authority is difficult, at best.

- Second, a Project Charter authorizes a project manager to expend resources for project planning. It gives you the authority you need to reach out to Functional Managers to gain access to the Subject Matter Experts (SMEs) you need to help you manage the project.

- Finally, a Project Charter helps you gain the formal sponsorship you need in the early stages of the project.

Before we share a proven Project Charter template, let's review the Problems listed in Chapter 1. Problem #1 was "Lack of Planning and Ineffective Project Management." The Project Charter is designed to ensure all key stakeholders understand and sign off on the project at a high level. The Project Charter is *not* designed to provide all project details. In contrast, it is designed to ensure all key stakeholders agree with high-level scope, cost, timelines, and risk *before* you begin more detailed planning.

Problem #2 discussed "Deficiencies in Project Selection and Prioritization." The Project Charter serves as a means to review each proposed project, evaluate the envisioned value, and prioritize the project relative to other projects. In addition, as we stated earlier, the Project Charter may also serve as a means of killing a project that shouldn't be implemented.

Problem #3 referenced "Inadequate Stakeholder Management." A Project Charter is a great way to set initial stakeholder expectations and get everyone on the same page, at least initially.

## Project Charter Format

Figure 2.2 provides a format you can use to complete a Project Charter. An example of a completed Project Charter is included in Appendix B. As a reminder, this template is a simple Microsoft Word document that is available for download at our website. We will use the information in this Project Charter to build a sample project using the total set of tools and techniques we highlight as an example for you to follow. Appendix C and beyond will build upon Appendix B.

**Figure 2.2 Project Charter Template**

| Charter Item | Comments |
|---|---|
| Project Name | Give the project an identifying name. |
| Project Goal | What is the overarching goal of your project? What is your product or service? |
| Project Value Proposition and Benefits | What is the value of this project? What are the benefits to the business?<br><br>**Note**: Many groups use the Balanced Scorecard Model as a means to quantify a business need. Consider financial, process, employee, and customer impacts. See Figure 2.3 for additional clarification. |
| Problem or Opportunity Statement | Why does this project need to be accomplished now? Who or what is driving this project? |
| Proposed Solution(s) | Describe your solution to the problem. You may list alternative solutions, but choose only *one*. |
| Project Priorities | What is your priority to accomplish Time, Cost, and Scope objectives? Prioritize each as 1, 2, and 3. |
| Return on Investment (ROI) | Are there financial benefits? If so, predict returns at a high level. You may use soft benefits here, as well. Note that only high level cost and benefits are required in a Project Charter. |

| | |
|---|---|
| Project Schedule | What are the approximate start and end dates? |
| Assumptions or Constraints | Assumptions: Something we believe to be true but must validate. Identify them.<br><br>Constraints: Situations/events that may limit this project such as regulations, dependencies, economic conditions, capacity, etc. List these as well. |
| Risks (Potential) | What *potential* events could pose threats or opportunities to successful project completion?<br><br>(Cause, Event, Impact) |
| Resources Required | Who needs to be part of the team to succeed? May include roles, skills, positions, etc. |
| Project Manager | Who does the Sponsor name as the project manager? Entry provides essential authority. |
| Approval Authority/Sponsor | Who in the organization must approve this project and authorize planning to begin? |

## The Balanced Scorecard Model

Every project should show value. Decision makers may choose your project at the expense of not choosing others. When choices are necessary, opportunities to achieve benefits from projects not chosen are foregone. It is critical to show that your project offers greater opportunity than others in a competitive environment. The best way to achieve this goal is to show as much value as possible. Let decision makers know why your project is a must!

Robert S. Kaplan and David P. Norton[4] created a model called the Balanced Scorecard®. This model has been adopted by CEOs and other corporate leaders around the world because it identifies objectives a business organization or corporation needs to satisfy to sustain a business and grow. The Balanced Scorecard is an excellent way to show multiple reasons for "Why" a project should be undertaken. Figure 2.3 shows the four interlocking components of the Balanced Scorecard.

## Figure 2.3 Balanced Scorecard Model

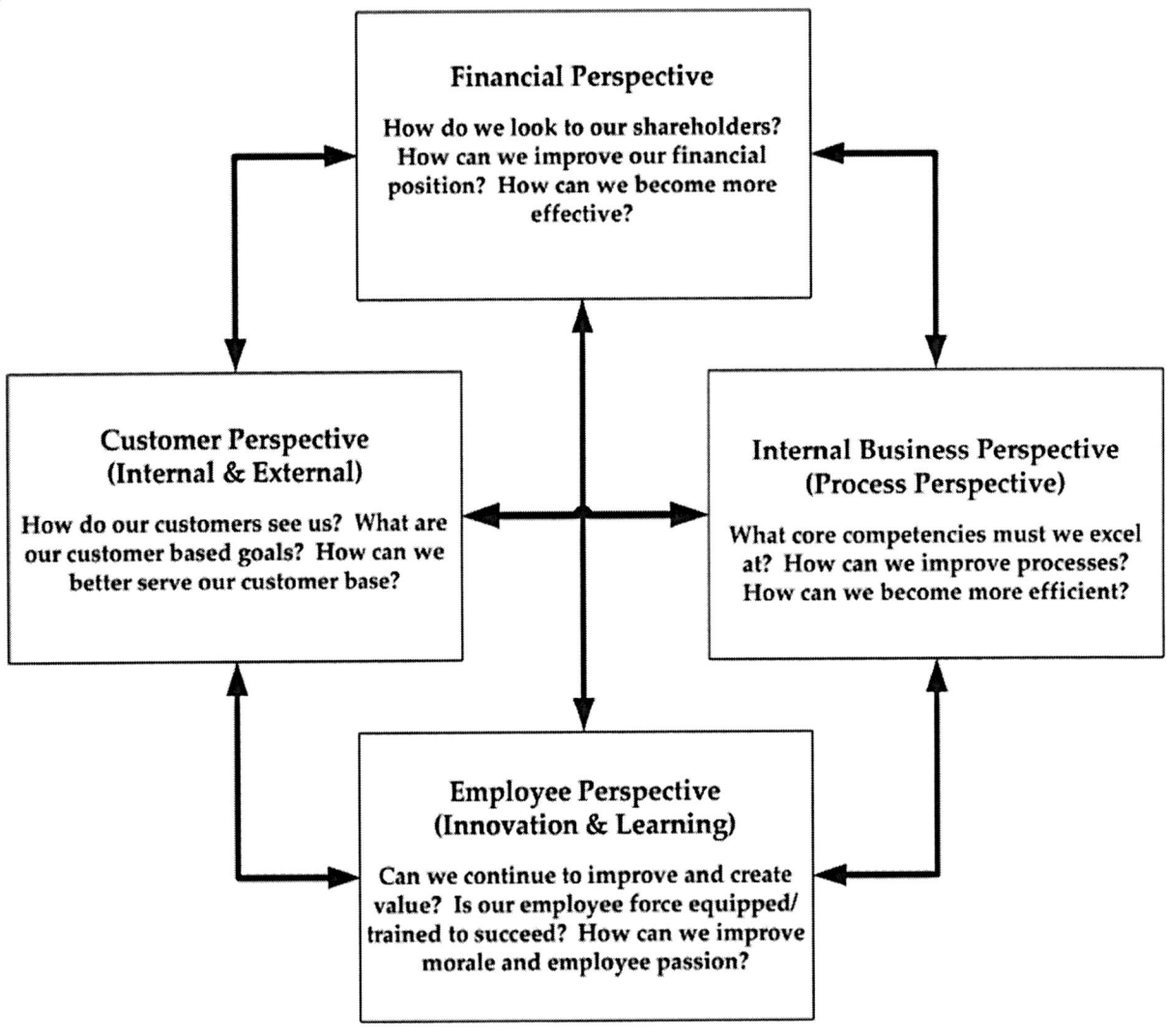

---

[4] <u>Harvard Business Review on Measuring Corporate Performance</u>, Harvard Business School Press

## The Balanced Scorecard Model Defined

The Balanced Scorecard model's components include a financial perspective, internal business or process perspective, employee or innovation and learning perspective, and a customer perspective. All perspectives must be satisfied and balanced for a business to thrive. You should not sacrifice one or two perspectives to improve a single perspective. This will result in short-term gain for long-term pain.

Some projects may enhance one of the four components. However, others may enhance multiple components. If you want to increase the chances that your project will be approved, the more components your project supports, —the better. If you don't want a project to be disapproved, show how your project objectives fail to support any of these perspectives, or support them minimally compared to competing projects.

## Project Charter Keys to Success

There are some keys to success to remember when developing and staffing a Project Charter. Understanding and adhering to the tips below will improve your overall success in effectively initiating your project.

1. A Project Charter is authorized and should be issued, or communicated, by a Sponsor, Project Management Office, or Portfolio Steering Committee when available. It is recommended that the Project Sponsor approve the Project Charter in writing (Signature).

2. All projects should have a Project Charter, even those accomplished by an external vendor or seller.

3. A Project Sponsor should be at a level appropriate to funding for the project.

4. Project Charters are normally broad. There is no need to change them as a project progresses unless scope is altered dramatically.

5. Always ensure a Project Charter is complete before progressing to the next steps in the project planning sequence.

6. Approval of the Project Charter is referred to as the "Pre-Baseline." The approved Project Charter formally initiates the project and allows you to formally enter the project planning stage.

7. Some Project Sponsors may not agree with calling this document a Project Charter. If that is the case, change the name to project feasibility study, business case analysis, or whatever works.

## Managing Stakeholders

In project management, a stakeholder is defined as anyone who is either "interested or impacted" by a project. Problem #3 we referenced in Chapter 1 was "Inadequate Stakeholder Management." Development of a Project Charter is a great way to address this problem. A second way is creation of a tool called a Stakeholder Register. In this section, we provide an example of this tool and provide guidance on how to make it work for you.

Effective stakeholder management begins from the very moment a project is envisioned and continues through the final project signoff and transition of deliverables. A number of key stakeholder management objectives are listed in Figure 2.4, which provides a step-by-step approach we recommend you follow.

### Figure 2.4 Stakeholder Management Process

| Step | Action | Things to Remember |
|---|---|---|
| 1 | Identify All Key Stakeholders | <ul><li>If a stakeholder is not identified, they will surface sometime during the project. If you don't identify them, they may identify you.</li><li>A list of stakeholders should be created, shared, and validated. It becomes part of the project records early in the project. This is a key first step.</li><li>A Stakeholder Register is a great tool that allows you to effectively address the objectives of this step.</li></ul> |
| 2 | Determine Stakeholder Requirements and Expectations | <ul><li>Clearly identify all requirements and ensure that the requirements satisfy stakeholder expectations.</li><li>Be ready to deal with conflicting expectations.</li><li>Project management is a lot like "herding cats." Determine expectations, explore expectations, and determine which can be—and can't be—met.</li><li>Manage expectations with effective communications throughout the project.</li></ul> |

| Step | Action | Things to Remember |
|---|---|---|
| 3 | Manage Stakeholder Influence | • Stakeholder expectations will often change as the project evolves. Changes will be requested.<br>• Influence, influence, influence. Stakeholder commitment levels will change as the project progresses as well. A supportive stakeholder may become resistant due to project status, changes, etc. You need to keep your fingers on the pulse of each stakeholder to ensure they are committed in the right way.<br>• Communicate, communicate, communicate. Ensure stakeholders are informed of changes, current status, and reminded of what is, and what is not, in scope. |
| 4 | Define—and Redefine—Key Roles and Responsibilities | • Stakeholders need to understand the specific expectations you have for them. In a few pages, we introduce a RACI tool. RACI is a great way to share these expectations.<br>• Stakeholder roles will change as the project progresses. It is critical that the project manager is aware of these changes, communicates these changes, and updates applicable documentation in a timely manner. |

> *Project Management Tip: Manage stakeholders closely, or they will manage you!*

## Project Stakeholders Defined

You need to identify and manage a number of key stakeholders. Here is a list of some of the key stakeholders that can make or break a project. The naming conventions we share are widely used in the world of project management.

**The Project Team**

- **Project Manager:** Responsible for project deliverables and managing expectations. Controls the project processes.

- **Project Management Team:** Develop key project management documentation. Manage extended team members. The project management team provides the project manager with the management expertise he or she needs to effectively plan and manage a project. Sometimes referenced as the Core Team.

- **Extended Team:** Team members on-boarded to perform specific work on the project. A best practice is to let extended team members know when they are needed on the project and when their services are no longer required. We will discuss this later in the book when we introduce a simple but effective Staffing Management Plan.

**Other Stakeholders**

- **Customer/User:** Uses the product or service developed by the project. Keep these very important stakeholders in the loop. Both of these terms are used in this book.

- **Seller/Business Partners:** External partners who contribute in some manner or are dependent on the project.

- **Sponsor:** Funds the project. Authorizes expenditure of funds and use of personnel resources. Provides project manager with the authority he or she needs to manage the project effectively.

- **Project Management Office (PMO):** Organization often directly or indirectly responsible for a project. <u>Note</u>: Not all firms/organizations have a PMO.

- **Functional Managers:** Managers who provide authorized personnel resources you need for your project. <u>Note</u>: These are sometimes referred to as Resource Managers.
- **Influencers:** Stakeholders or others who can influence project results positively or negatively. The "influencers" may or may not be legitimate stakeholders with an interest in the project or who are impacted by the project. *An influencer may be the associate who has nothing better to do than to share opinions on projects in the break room. Some of them may have positive comments to share: leverage their enthusiasm☺. Others, however, may be negative. Identify and neutralize.*

- **Portfolio Manager:** Responsible for high-level governance of programs and projects. See Chapter 1; remember the portfolio approach we shared?

- **Operations Manager:** Incorporates project deliverables into operations. It is very important that a project manager identifies a transition plan to ensure the product or service created by the project is supported and managed after the project ends. Too often, project managers become operations managers because they fail to plan for the transition.

- **Project Champion:** Possesses high levels of expertise and knowledge. Often provides key go or no-go input. A Project Champion is often management's "go-to" person for advice. They may or may not be high up in the organizational chain of command.

## The Stakeholder Register

Now it is time to share a simple tool that you can use throughout the project to identify stakeholders, define and manage expectations, manage stakeholder influence, and define roles and responsibilities. This tool is called a Stakeholder Register. The initial Stakeholder Register should be developed in conjunction with the Project Charter shared earlier in this chapter. Both the Project Charter and Stakeholder Register should be presented to decision makers for a determination if the project is a go or no-go. Figure 2.5 presents a project Stakeholder Register for review. We will clarify what needs to be entered into the Stakeholder Register after you review the template.

### Figure 2.5 Stakeholder Register

| Stakeholder Register |||||||||
|---|---|---|---|---|---|---|---|
| **Stakeholder Segment:** |||||||||
| Name | Organization | Role | R | A | C | I | Comments |
|  |  |  |  |  |  |  |  |
|  |  |  |  |  |  |  |  |
|  |  |  |  |  |  |  |  |
|  |  |  |  |  |  |  |  |
|  |  |  |  |  |  |  |  |

| RACI Terms Defined | | |
|---|---|---|
| | R | Responsible for doing work on the project |
| | A | Accountable for outcomes |
| | C | Consult as Subject Matter Expert |
| | I | Inform as the Project Progresses |

Version:

The Stakeholder Register simply and effectively defines key stakeholders; where they reside in the organization; identifies the role the stakeholder is expected to play; categorizes the stakeholder's involvement using the RACI methodology, which we'll touch upon in a bit; and provides any comments to further clarify the stakeholders role.

**Note:** Once the Stakeholder Register is complete and approved by the Project Sponsor, ensure a copy is shared with everyone on the list. Ask for confirmation that they are both aware and willing to commit to the roles they have been assigned. Do not assume that simply sending the completed Stakeholder Register to stakeholders will gain their support.

An example of a completed Stakeholder Register is shared in Appendix C.

Now, let's break out the entry criteria.

- **Stakeholder Segment:** Documenting all stakeholders in a single document would be difficult to manage and would create information overload for those who review it. A best practice is to break out the Stakeholder Register into multiple tabs to represent a key segment of the project's stakeholders. For example, you may have one Stakeholder Register that addresses the Sponsor and leadership team. Another may address external partners and customer/users. A third tab may be used for the project team. Most Stakeholder Registers (including the one Peter and I will share) use Microsoft Excel or an equivalent spreadsheet methodology that allows you to maintain a single file with multiple tabs. Of course, for a smaller project, less is needed. In some cases, a single Stakeholder Register may suffice for the entire project.

- **Name:** You have a few choices here. If you know the name of the actual stakeholder, fill it in here. However, there may be times when early in a project you have no name. In this case, a simple To Be Determined (TBD) or role designator such as "Development SME" will suffice. When used this way, the Stakeholder Register serves a dual purpose. First, it documents the need for a key stakeholder. Second, it now serves as a means to identify a need or gap to management before formal project planning kicks off.

- **Organization:** For small projects, this column may not be needed. For larger projects, however, this entry is essential. Many large projects require stakeholders from multiple organizations or firms. Here is where you share this information with your project stakeholders.

- **Role:** Briefly define the role the stakeholder is expected to play. Less is more. Strive for a brief explanation. For example, SME, Dev, Test, etc. You can use the comments section of the Stakeholder Register to elaborate.

- **RACI:** The RACI methodology is a commonly used way to define who does what on a project. Here are a few rules to remember:

  - A stakeholder may have multiple RACI roles. For example, a Developer may have an "R" to develop a new product design and a "C" to provide technical expertise to the Project Team on a new technology being used.

- o Only have one "A" for each row or item in the RACI. For example, don't have two people accountable for a single task.

- o The Stakeholder Register will change. As you can see in the example, version control is critical. Roles and people will change.

- **Comments:** Add clarifying comments as needed to further ensure all stakeholders are clear on their roles and responsibilities. If necessary, provide links to other project documents when further clarification may be available.

## Stakeholder Management: Closing Thoughts

Saying that good stakeholder management is essential is a massive understatement. Solid stakeholder management is essential to success. We want to share another potential tool you may wish to consider. It is called a Stakeholder Management Plan by some project management practitioners. This concept was conceived by the Project Management Institute (PMI) and is broadly defined in the *Project Management Body of Knowledge*. It is a simple tool we created that can be constructed using a Microsoft Word document or a spreadsheet.

<u>Note:</u> The Stakeholder Management Plan shared in Figure 2.6 should not be shared with the majority of project stakeholders. It is an internal management tool used by the project manager to define commitment gaps. If shared with a broad audience, information in this document could result in unwanted dysfunctional conflict.

# Figure 2.6 Stakeholder Management Plan

| Stakeholder Management Plan ||||
|---|---|---|---|
| Name | Current State | Desired State | Strategy |
|  |  |  |  |
|  |  |  |  |
|  |  |  |  |
|  |  |  |  |

**Recommended Level of Commitment Designators**

| | |
|---|---|
| U | **Unaware:** Stakeholder is unaware of the project. |
| N | **Neutral:** Stakeholder has yet to determine level of support. |
| R | **Resistant:** Stakeholder does not support the project. |
| S | **Supportive:** Stakeholder agrees with the project. |
| L | **Leading:** Stakeholder is supportive and actively engaged in project. |

**Note:** An example of a completed Stakeholder Management Plan is shared in Appendix C.

Now, let's break out the entry criteria.

- **Name:** Enter the key stakeholder by name. Remember, this plan is not shared. All stakeholders do not need to be annotated in this plan. Select only those stakeholders whose commitment is critical but potentially subject to change.

- **Current State and Desired State:** Your overarching goal is to match the current and desired states. Once you do so, you may want to continue to track the stakeholder so you can sustain the match.

- **Stakeholder Coding:** Recommended coding is based on the RACI assignments in Figure 2.5. To clarify the coding:

    o **Unaware:** This stakeholder is not aware the project exists or does not understand the value proposition of the project.

- **Neutral:** This is a stakeholder who has no real view of the project's value, either negative or positive. In addition, they have yet to make a commitment to either support, or not support, the project.

- **Resistant:** This stakeholder is opposed to the project in some way. They may support the intent of the project but disagree with features selected to implement. On the other hand, they may be against implementation of the project in its totality. You need to identify and neutralize the "Resistors" if your project is one you believe needs to move forward. On the other hand, remember that all projects do not need to be implemented. Move the good projects forward, and stop the bad ones. You may enlist the support of Resistors if your recommendation is to have the project killed or delayed.

- **Supportive:** This is a stakeholder who is happy with the project and supports it. A supporter is not necessarily tasked to do more than give voice support or provide guidance and/or expertise. Chances are good that this individual is reflected on your Stakeholder Register as a "C" or an "I".

- **Leading:** This is the highest level of commitment. A stakeholder who needs to be leading is one who not only needs to be supportive, but also needs to take a variety of actions to support the project. In most cases, a leading stakeholder commitment is required for those with an "A" or "R" on the Stakeholder Register.

- **Strategy:** Here is where you need to put on your thinking cap. How can you move the stakeholder to your desired state or keep the stakeholder from slipping back into a contrary state of commitment?

## Changing Commitment Levels

Peter and I could write a whole other book on the topic of changing commitment levels. When I first became a project manager, a sign was presented to me that proudly proclaimed, "The Psychologist Is In." We have stated before—and will state again—that project management is a science *and* an *art*.

Completing a Stakeholder Register and Stakeholder Management Plan using the formats shared is the science regarding stakeholder management. The art of project stakeholder management is to understand the needs and motivations of each stakeholder and to work with these stakeholders for the benefit of the project. This doesn't mean you have to succumb to every request. If you do, the project will become chaotic to the point where you find yourself in the 40% to 80% failure group. It *does* mean, however, that you need to have the conversation and reach an outcome that supports, or is at least neutral for the project.

Alex uses a very powerful tool to change commitment levels to the positive. He tells key stakeholders, "We are going to be a huge success, and I will not be shy about your valuable contributions when we deliver." Imagine someone telling you that they cannot wait to brag about your good work to peers and managers! Very powerful—always makes an impact. Positive motivation is always better than negative challenges or escalation. The project manager needs to set expectations and be transparent. A project manager who is positive and is an "open book" creates a healthy environment.

Before we summarize this important chapter and turn our attention to Peter's Corner and our Food for Thought sections, I want to share the motivational theory that has provided me with the greatest results when I needed to influence and gain commitment.

<u>Note:</u> Here are some words of wisdom from Alex. We naturally spend time with those people we like and who share our beliefs. With stakeholders, we actually get the most value spending time with problematic stakeholders. This practice allows us to ensure their opinions stay in-check. It may prevent them from spreading false rumors, and it goes a long way to minimize the damage to your project they can cause. One loud and uncooperative stakeholder who drones and complains can undo a lot of good will from the many positive stakeholders connected to your project.

## David McClelland's 3 Needs Theory

David McClelland[5] stated in his work that a team member needs three things to be happy and productive; achievement, affiliation, and empowerment. In all of us, one, two, or all three may be important. Everyone is quite different. However, we are all motivated or driven by certain factors. If you consciously approach increasing commitment levels using these three motivators, chances are quite good something will resonate with the individual.

---

[5] *Theory of Needs*, David Clarence McClelland, 1917 - 1998

Many project managers make the mistake of assuming commitment. This is a poor assumption. As a project manager, get to know each of the key project stakeholders to the greatest extent possible. Appeal to their needs, and commitment will likely follow. Refer to Figure 2.7 below for a quick visual of the 3 Needs Theory.

> *Project Management Tip: Never overlook "Diversity of Thought." All stakeholders are not the same!*

**Figure 2.7 The 3 Needs Theory**

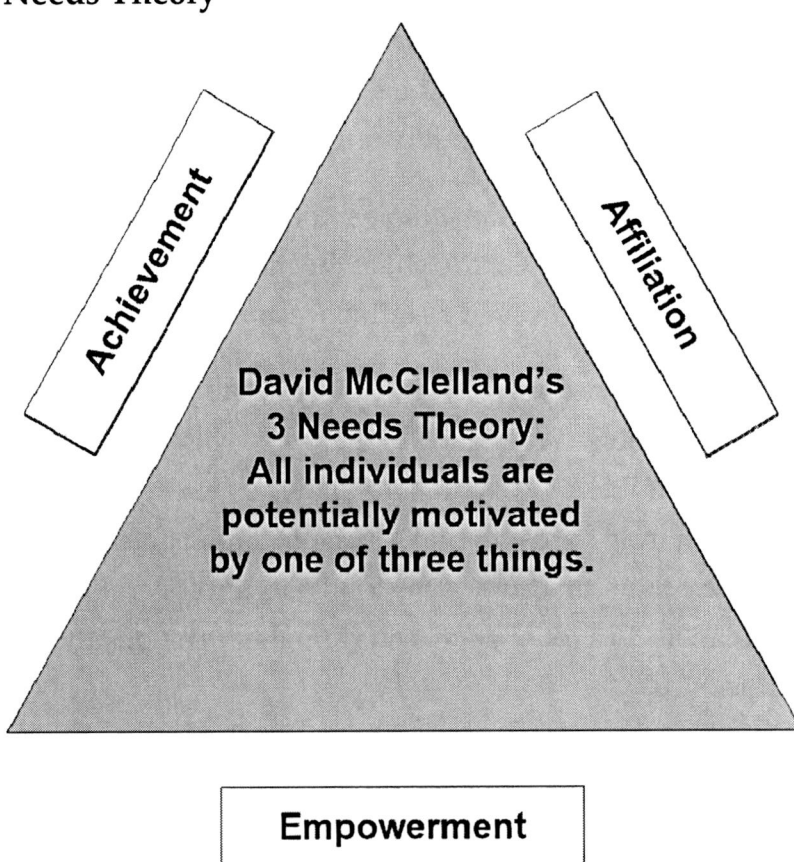

The three areas McClelland cites as motivational are a sense of achievement, feelings of affiliation, and empowerment, the satisfaction that ideas will be heard and acknowledged. For the project manager, the goal is to address these areas in all team members to generate and maintain commitment.

- **Achievement:** The project manager realizes that achievement differs for everyone. One team member may look at achievement as passing a certification test. Another may most value finishing the project on time. Others may value positive feedback from a customer. Learn what achievement means for each team member. Don't assume it!

- **Affiliation:** Have you ever felt you were on the outside looking in? The project manager ensures each team member feels they are a valued part of the team. In addition, the project manager ensures each team member truly believes they add value.

- **Empowerment:** People are motivated when they feel empowered. All team members need to believe that their feedback, thoughts, and ideas are welcome. The project manager empowers the team to be creative, to trust others, and to share ideas whenever practical. Every idea may not be adopted. However, sometimes just being heard can be the difference between productive or non-productive team members.

> *Alex's Project Management Tip: Always try to "educate and influence." Take the time to explain things as best you can, be transparent, and allow people to understand the thinking behind your actions and decisions. You may not change your decision. However, stakeholders will feel better about the project's direction because they understand your thought process. And when you take time to educate, others follow suit, and information is better proliferated and shared with all.*

## Chapter 2 Summary

How you initiate a project is critical. As we stated in the Chapter 2 introduction, first impressions are lasting. When a project is born, many stakeholders have a variety of views regarding exactly what the project will produce. It is imperative that the project manager shares his or her vision of success at a high level and gains consensus from all key stakeholders. In project management, an important process and key concept is *progressive elaboration*, which means that the scope of a project should be defined in stages. The Project Charter defines scope at a high level. It is imperative that all stakeholders agree with the project goals and objectives at a high level before moving forward into detailed planning.

Stakeholder management is the second key to success. Stakeholder involvement and commitment levels can make or break a project. Identify stakeholders up front. Once you do, ensure you share your expectations and ask for validation from them regarding their roles. If needed, develop individualized strategies designed to bring current commitment levels in line with desired commitment levels.

Development of a Project Charter and Stakeholder Register will take a bit of time. However, these high-level planning activities will help ensure the project gets off on the right foot and pave the way for greater success potential. A Stakeholder Management Plan may be a value-added time investment if you have key stakeholders whose current commitment is not at the desired level.

Take a few moments to consider our Food for Thought items. But first, it's time for the second edition of Peter's Corner.

## Peter's Corner: Chapter 2 Edition

*"I have a dream…"*

Do you know who said this famous phrase comes?

Hint 1: A speech in the United States.

Hint 2: Delivered in 1963.

Answer: See the end of this Corner.

Portray the Project Charter as a *dream,* a dream that you want all key stakeholders to buy into, embrace, and support.

A dream is not reality, is it? But the dream is for the project to *become a reality.*

The next phase, planning, is figuring out if and how the team can deliver the *dream.* Is the dream feasible? Can the dream become real?

Many times key stakeholders approve the Project Charter (Pre-Baseline stage) and believe that the project is a done deal. Just go do it! They set the Project Charter – the *dream –* including the scope, timeline, and cost, in concrete. You want to avoid this, because your project is at an important step in the process.

Starting up a project is one of the most important milestones in your planning process. If the project does not start well, then it will take a lot of effort to get the project on the right track. "Go slow now to go fast later" or, "Invest now for dividends later."

A key stakeholder is someone who can really help or hurt the project. Notice I refer to a person, not a group or organization. This is personal – about people and relationships and power – not about some nefarious group organization. So take out your people skills and have *real conversations* with key stakeholders. *Real conversations* are face-to-face or over the phone, via Skype, Facetime, etc. A real conversation is *not* email, instant messaging, voicemail, and the like.

Engage with those Naysayers who may hurt the project sooner rather than later. One Naysayer can create more damage than the help of seven supporters. Deeply listen to the Naysayer. Usually, they tell us something that we are denying, avoiding, or ignoring. They may tell us something we don't know, something that is in one of our blind spots. By the end of the *real conversation* with the Naysayer, you should have moved the Naysayer to commit to comply with their RACI role and what the project needs from them. Ideally, you move them to be Supportive.

Think about adding a column to your Stakeholder Management Plan for "Owner." You or a member of the core project management team should *own* the *health* of the *stakeholder relationship*. This means that the owner is accountable for assuring that the [key] Stakeholder provides to the project what the project needs and what they agreed to provide. Have you ever witnessed a stakeholder who is committed in the beginning, but then their commitment wanes? This can be disastrous for a project. Think about having Owners report on the health of their stakeholder relationships at each recurring project team meeting. Focus on those relationships that are not where they need to be. Never assume that stakeholders are doing what they said they would do. A key part of project management is monitoring and control (more on this later).

**The Verbal Contract**: During the *real conversation with the key stakeholder(s)*, discuss and agree on the stakeholder's role(s). Talk about what they will deliver, what success looks like, etc. Tell them what they can expect from you during the project, such as you will keep them informed, you will help them to remove obstacles, etc. Finally, *tell them what you expect from them. This includes behaviors*. Remember, the art of project management includes behaviors and setting operating norms (see Chapter 7, Project Team Charter). A Verbal Contract is created when they know what they can expect from you and what you expect from them. Enforce it throughout the project. Call them out when they are not living the Contract. This is what leadership is about.

Finally, remember radio station WII-FM, or, "What's In It For Me?" Humans are selfish. So preferably in advance of, or definitely during, *the real conversation* with the [key] stakeholder, find out what aspect of the project, or what part of the stakeholder's role in the project, would motivate the stakeholder to be supportive. Sometimes this is the only way to get a stakeholder on board.

Earlier, Dan mentioned that we could write a book on managing stakeholders. He is correct. This is a huge topic and is critical to a successful project. We encourage you to further explore this area and to continue to get better at managing stakeholders. Talk with experienced project managers. Visit www.pmi.org. There are many great articles and tips available to PMI members.

Here's one more thought. If you are not getting the necessary stakeholder participation, you have the authority to "pause the project." This is a great way to get people's attention. When you pause the project and let people know they are the reason behind the pause, they may suddenly become very motivated. Be careful though. The motivation they share may be directed positively or negatively toward the project.

Here's the answer to the *dream* question. Martin Luther King's famous 1963 speech is commonly known as, "I Have a Dream."[6]

---

[6] March on Washington for Jobs and Freedom on August 28, 1963

## Chapter 2 Food for Thought

1. Many projects fail. How can adopting a Project Charter as a mandatory step help reduce chances of failure?

2. Have you ever been involved in a project where you were not kept "in the loop?" How did you react? How could the situation have been handled better?

3. What motivates you? If a project manager was applying McClelland's 3 Needs Theory, which of the three techniques would best resonate with you, and why?

4. Have you ever encountered a team member who was not committed? What did you do to gain the desired level of commitment? Did it work?

5. We completed an overview of initiating the project. What are three things you believe are the key points of the chapter? Going forward, what will you do differently when initiating a project?

6. Peter's Deep Thought Challenges:

*Reflections*

- Recall a medium to large project that did not have a Project Charter. What effect did the lack of a Project Charter have on *you*, the planning and execution of the project, and its outcome?

- Recall a project with an unsupportive key stakeholder, preferably one who was a Naysayer or Saboteur. How did this person affect the project and its outcome? What could *you* have done differently to cause this person to be supportive?

# Chapter 3: Planning Scope: The Gift that Keeps on Giving

If you ever apply for certification in project management, you will learn that the definition of a successful project is one that is completed on time, within budget, and satisfied the customer's needs with the right scope. This is a great definition. A project manager should strive to complete the three key constraints of time, cost, and scope, as planned. Now, let's get real. If you miss a schedule, you'll likely be forgiven in the long term. If you exceed budget, you will likely be forgiven as well. If you mess up the scope, however, you will be long remembered. Scope is *the* primary reason for a project. And while we strive for projects that are on time, within budget, and with the right scope, if you can only get one right, nail the scope.

This chapter is critically important. We have the Project Charter in hand. We now need to progressively elaborate the scope in the Project Charter and define it at a level of detail that will allow us to successfully implement the project.

The PMI has a superb definition for project quality attributed to Crosby, Juran, and Deming. Their definition is, "conform to requirements and fit for use." This chapter will focus on these concepts. We want you to be able to effectively define the product or service the project will provide. In addition, we want you to go beyond the requirements. At the end of the day, we want you to provide the customer with something that adds value.

We can summarize scope planning success as follows: When you are complete, you know precisely what the project will produce, you have a game plan to get you there, and all key stakeholders are on board with the plan. In addition, once the project kicks off, you are able to control the scope, manage change, and discourage scope creep. Here's a quote from Walt Disney that truly describes the overarching goal of the project manager when it comes to planning scope. Enjoy!

> *"Of all the things I've done, the most vital is coordinating the talents of those who work for us and pointing them towards a certain goal."* — Walt Disney

## Project Scope Overview

As we stated earlier, scope is the most important component of project planning you need to get right. We also shared Problem #4, "Poor Scope Definition and Management," as a key problem you need to conquer. With that said, here is a quick breakout of the objectives you need to achieve in this critical planning area. The good news? It's not as difficult to get this right as you might think.

1. **Define Project Requirements:** Defining exactly what the project will produce (in scope) and, sometimes more importantly, what the project will not produce (out of scope) is job one. Let us warn you that at the first requirements planning meeting, everyone will want everything, and all requirements will be Priority #1. Your job is to work with all the key stakeholders and gain consensus on what the project will, and will not, deliver. We will highlight a Requirements Feasibility and Prioritization Matrix designed to help you quantify requirements and determine what needs to be part of the project.

2. **Break Out the Requirements into Detail:** Once you define requirements and have consensus on what is in scope, you need to develop a plan to turn the requirements into the actual product or service envisioned in the Project Charter. The PMI refers to this detailed document as a "Scope Statement." We will use that naming convention in our book and provide a simple template you can use to satisfy this need as well. Before you go any further in the scope planning process, this Scope Statement needs to be shared with key stakeholders to ensure their expectations are managed.

3. **Define Key Project Activities:** The next step in scope is to develop a Work Breakdown Structure (WBS). This critical project management step is a foundational planning deliverable that will be used to address additional planning requirements for time, cost, quality, communications, procurement, and risk. We will walk you through this process and make it easy for you.

4. **Define Activity Attributes:** It is not possible to list all activity attributes in the WBS. A WBS Dictionary is a tool that supplements the WBS and allows you to share the details stakeholders require to complete their assigned responsibilities. We will share an example of a WBS Dictionary and show you how it works.

## Defining Project Requirements

You have the approved Project Charter in your hands. Next, you need to further define the requirements for the project and determine the true nature of the product or service you will produce. Step 1 is having an understanding of the types of requirements you need to define. Figure 3.1 shares an overview of typical requirement categories that need to be identified.

**Figure 3.1 Project Requirements Overview**

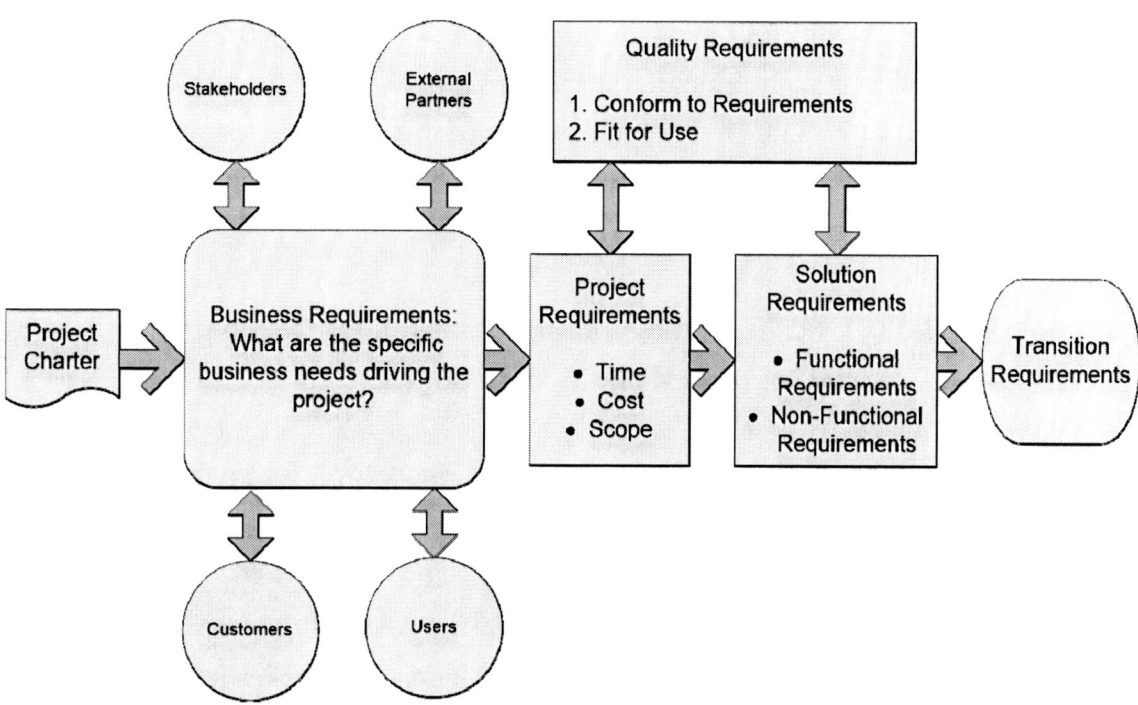

The Project Charter drives the requirements definition process. *Do not* include requirements that are not traceable back to the Project Charter. You need to define and consider a variety of requirements types. Here is a quick overview of each requirement type shown in Figure 3.1.

- **Business Requirements**: Business requirements are normally the primary driver or purpose of a project. Business requirements can be generated from any internal organization such as Finance, Operations, Marketing, Information Technology (IT), etc.

- **Stakeholder Requirements**: Your project may very well impact a stakeholder group or groups. You need to evaluate the impact on stakeholders, including customers, users, external partners, etc., when planning a project. You may need to include updated process maps, instructions, change management steps, training, etc.

- **Project Requirements**: The project requirements define the scope, time, and cost goals. Prioritize each one of the triple constraints. For example, if time is the number one priority, define the schedule goals as the primary consideration. Scope and cost will then be prioritized as two and three. When you develop solution requirements, you may determine that you can't meet all three goals as defined. When that occurs, you must negotiate with stakeholders to determine how to adjust the project to meet the stated goals. It is often said that when it comes to the idealistic scope, time, and cost scenario, you can usually meet one, often meet two, but rarely achieve all three without some adjustments. Some basics:

  - **Time Is Priority One:** If meeting the stated schedule is the top priority, you may need to reduce scope or request additional resources.

  - **Cost Is Priority One:** If meeting cost/budget considerations is driving the project, you may need to reduce scope or extend the schedule.

  - **Scope Is Priority One:** If meeting scope requirements is the number one priority, you may need to adjust the schedule or request additional resources.

- **Solution Requirements:** Solution requirements are those activities required to achieve the project's documented business and stakeholder objectives. Develop this detailed game plan while keeping the Project Requirements in mind. During this step, you want to achieve three primary objectives:

  - **Identify all Functional Requirements:** The Functional Requirements document the operations and activities that a system must be able to perform. Functional requirements define the behavior of the product or service the project is envisioned to provide. They could include how data is entered into a system; workflows; physical design criteria; etc.

- o **Identify all Non-Functional Requirements**: Non-Functional requirements specify criteria that can be used to judge the operation of a system, rather than specific behaviors. They are contrasted with functional requirements that define specific behavior or functions. Examples of non-functional requirements may include security, performance, reliability, etc.

- o **Build the Ideal First**: Define all requirements needed to satisfy business and stakeholder requirements at the 100% level. If the 100% solution meets the project requirement criteria for time, cost, and scope, have a party! If it looks like the desired time, cost, and scope objectives are not sufficient to satisfy the 100% solution, the negotiations and trade-offs as shared in the "Defining Project Requirements" section begin.

- **Quality Requirements**: Quality requirements are two-fold. First, you need measures to ensure you "conform to requirements." If a requirement is approved, you deliver it as planned. If a requirement is not approved, you don't deliver it unless a formal change request is processed and approved. Second, you need to ensure the final product or service is "fit for use." Simply stated, whatever you deliver must provide value to the business and/or stakeholders. Quality requirements are generally understood and accommodated through proactive Quality Assurance (QA) and Quality Control (QA) activities. QA and QC are defined during the Plan phase of PDCA. QA oocurs during the Do phase, and QC is part of the Check phase.

- **Transition Requirements**: PMI defines three key project characteristics. Projects are temporary, unique, and achieved through progressive elaboration. Transition requirements address the "temporary" attribute. It is imperative that you plan for transition of the product and/or service you are developing while you plan scope. Generally, transition planning steps are reflected in the Scope Statement we discuss in this chapter and are implemented during project closing. We will address this key activity again in Chapter 11.

> *Project Management Tip: Define all requirements needed to satisfy the Project Charter first. Then begin negotiating to balance time, cost, and scope objectives.*

## Project Requirement Types: The FURPS Model

The FURPS model[7] was conceived as a means to define functional and non-functional software requirements. While FURPS works great for software projects, it can be adapted as a means to categorize all project requirements. The FURPS model provides a five-step checklist that helps define what success looks like at the end of the project. You need to satisfy the five FURPS criteria for any project you deliver. As a quick summary, project deliverables need to provide the value required by the business and stakeholders; be easy to access; provide reliable and consistent results; provide results when needed; and be supportable after the project is complete.

Figure 3.2 provides a modified overview of the FURPS model we believe can be very useful to you. This model can be applied to any type of project.

### Figure 3.2 FURPS Model

| Category | Definition |
| --- | --- |
| F: Functionality | We defined functional requirements earlier. Functional requirements describe the behavior of the product or service you are producing. These are the measurable results the business or stakeholders expect the project to deliver. |
| U: Usability | Usability requirements are those needed to enhance the user experience. They may include specifications, documentation, instructions, Frequently Asked Questions (FAQs), aesthetics, or other human factors the project needs to deliver. |
| R: Reliability | Reliability requirements are generally non-functional. These are requirements you must include to minimize failure rates, ensure predictability of the functionality provided, or ensure accuracy of results from the product or service. |
| P: Performance | Performance requirements include ways to ensure project speed, efficiency, resource consumption (power, ram, cache, etc.), throughput, capacity, and scalability needs are satisfied. They may be both functional and/or non-functional. |
| S: Supportability | Supportability requirements generally support transition and post-operational needs. Requirements such as Service Level Agreements (SLA) that outline service specifics, maintenance and repair timeframes, and system test attributes qualify in this category. |

---

[7] Grady, Robert (1992). *Practical Software Metrics for Project Management and Process Improvement*

## Requirements Feasibility and Prioritization Matrix

You are now ready to gather your stakeholders together and determine the total requirements package for the project. As we shared earlier—beware. Everyone will want everything without regard to the reality of time, cost, and scope constraints. In your stakeholders' minds and hearts, each requirement will be Priority #1. You need to maintain passion and enthusiasm for the project, but you also must manage stakeholder expectations. At the end of the day, you need a prioritized list of requirements, a decision on which requirements are in scope—and more importantly, in some cases—which requirements are out of scope.

Figures 3.3, 3.4, and 3.5 provide a tool that you can use to drive the discussion. You first brainstorm to determine the total project requirements package. Then you quantify each requirement to determine which are feasible and which are not.

## Figure 3.3 Requirements Feasibility and Prioritization Matrix

| Requirements Feasibility and Prioritization Matrix | | | | | | | | | | |
|---|---|---|---|---|---|---|---|---|---|---|
| Requirement | Type | S | M | At | R | T | W | As | Y | Score |
| | | | | | | | | | | |
| | | | | | | | | | | |
| | | | | | | | | | | |
| | | | | | | | | | | |
| | | | | | | | | | | |
| | | | | | | | | | | |
| | | | | | | | | | | |

The Requirements Feasibility and Prioritization Matrix is relatively easy to use. Appendix D provides a completed example for a hypothetical project that you may refer to for further definition and clarity. Here is an overview of the tool.

**Note**: The Requirements Feasibility and Prioritization Matrix is actually a Microsoft Excel spreadsheet. As we shared before—but don't want you to forget—all tools and techniques shared in this book are available to you at www.p17group.com. Here is how you use this tool.

- **Requirement**: Annotate the requirement in specific terms. For example, develop an automated process to improve management of accounts receivables.

- **Type**: Categorize the requirement using any model that makes sense. The FURPS model works well for requirements that possess those attributes. Some projects may be categorized as simply Functional or Non-Functional. Others may use the model introduced in Figure 3.1. Categorize as Business, Stakeholder, Quality requirements, etc.

- **Scoring**: We recommend using a methodology to quantify the feasibility of each requirement using the SMARTWAY model. SMARTWAY is an extension of the common SMART model that may already be familiar to readers. If not, here's a great chance to expand your knowledge of this model and more. Each requirement is evaluated based on eight specific quantifiable considerations. Once finalized, each requirement has a score of 8 to 24. Figure 3.4 breaks out the scoring methodology.

Effective identification and prioritization of requirements is a make or break activity. If you want the project to be successful, this is one area you need to get right. The most effective use of the Requirements Feasibility and Prioritization Matrix follows a step-by-step/iterative approach as defined below:

- **Step 1**: Define all requirements supporting the project
- **Step 2**: Categorize each requirement and ensure all requirements are annotated
- **Step 3**: Score each requirement using the SMARTWAY method
- **Step 4**: Clarify all scores less than 3 and work with stakeholders to clarify requirements
- **Step 5**: Update scores for each requirement, based on follow-up analysis
- **Step 6**: Finalize scores and prioritize requirements based on feasibility
- **Step 7**: If possible, meet with the Project Sponsor and share your findings
- **Step 8**: Finalize in-scope and out-of-scope recommendations

Note: Remember that completion of the Requirements Feasibility and Prioritization Matrix is an iterative process. We verbalized the process above. Here is a visual of the process.

Figure 3.4 Requirements Feasibility and Prioritization Matrix Process

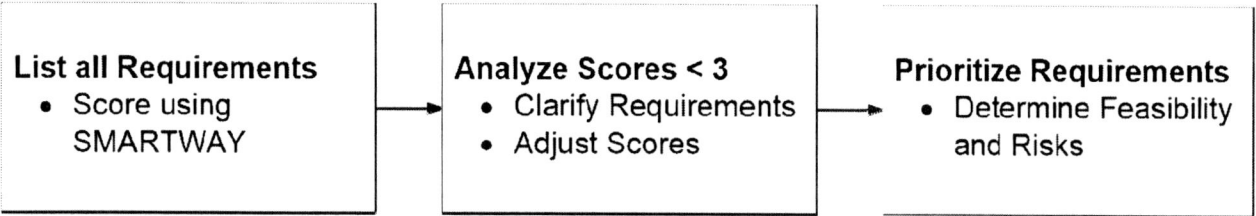

Figure 3.5 Requirements Feasibility and Prioritization Matrix Scoring

| Requirements Feasibility and Prioritization Matrix Scoring | |
|---|---|
| S: SPECIFIC | How well is the requirement defined and understood? Is the requirement ambiguous? |
| M: MEASUREABLE | Can you measure the final output? Can you envision what success looks like? Can you test the output? |
| At: ATTAINABLE | Are you confident the product or service can be implemented as defined? |
| R: RELEVANT | Does the requirement support the Project Charter? Do stakeholders support the requirement? |
| T: TARGET DRIVEN | Can this requirement be completed within the project's schedule goals? Is there traceability? |
| W: WORTH DOING | Does this requirement add value? Does it satisfy dependencies? Does it address constraints? |
| As: ASSIGNABLE | Do you have skill sets required to implement the requirement? Do you have capacity? |
| Y: YIELD RESULTS | What is your level of confidence you can add this requirement and complete it 100% successfully? |

| SCORING | |
|---|---|
| 3: HIGH | Satisfies all key criteria. Minimal risk factors. |
| 2. MODERATE | Some issues and risk factors. Moderate analysis required. |
| 1: LOW | Many issues and risk factors. In-depth analysis required. |

Let's end this section of Chapter 3 with a brief summary of how to use the results obtained by using the Requirements Feasibility and Prioritization Matrix:

- **Requirements Selection**: Scores will range from 8 to 24. The higher the score, the more feasible the requirement. When decisions need to be made—in particular, reducing scope to achieve realistic time and cost constraints, these results will help add sanity to the discussions. A requirement that scores 20 is far higher in priority and feasibility than a requirement that scores 15.

- **Risk Identification**: We have not discussed risk in great detail as of yet, but Peter and I promise we shall in the chapters that follow. Risk is any potential event that can impact your project either positively or negatively. Isn't that a paradigm breaker☺? Use the scoring to determine potential risk factors that need to be documented and addressed. As an example, you may have a requirement that is a "must have" that garners a low score of "1" in Measurable. You can document a risk using the common cause−event−impact methodology called "Risk Metalanguage".

    o **Cause**: Deliverable specifications are not clear

    o **Event**: May produce deliverables that are not "fit for use"

    o **Impact**: Wasted resources, customer dissatisfaction, and the need to address bugs and deficiencies at a high cost to the organization.

> *Project Management Tip: Use the Risk Metalanguage method to define risks. Cause-Event-Impact*

- **The Go or No-Go Decision**: Another repetition here, but it's worth repeating. The goal of a good project manager is to identify which projects should be approved and those that should not. Let's say there is a project whose requirements are so undefined and ambiguous that the Requirements Feasibility and Prioritization Matrix scores are very low overall. This is a very high-risk project. Perhaps the best decision may be to kill the project, or at least postpone the project until the information and clarifications required to increase the project's feasibility can be received.

## Next Step: The Scope Statement

You are now ready for the next scope planning step, development of a Scope Statement that describes with adequate detail how to turn requirements into tangible deliverables that conform to requirements and are fit for use. This is a critical step, and a step that usually is not done effectively by many project managers. The primary reason is that many project managers overanalyze this step and create documentation and plans that confuse and end up being quite unpractical. Our goal is to simplify the process and ensure we *don't* fail.

The ultimate objective of a Scope Statement is twofold. First, you need to define the project phases required to satisfy deliverables. Different types of projects can be satisfied by a variety of methodologies. Second, you need to identify the key deliverables that will happen during each phase.

At the end of the day, the Scope Statement provides a game plan for you to accomplish the requirements of the project. In this section, we will provide a complete example. We will provide an additional example in Appendix D that tracks to the sample project we have been using to provide you with a guide. Figure 3.6 shares a sample of a Scope Statement we will use for explanation.

> *Project Management Tip: All activities supporting a project should be defined using an action-result method. Each activity should have a measurable result that all agree upon. In addition, each activity identified should add value; if the activity was eliminated, the project would be incomplete.*

## Figure 3.6 Project Scope Statement Template

| Project Scope Statement |||||
|---|---|---|---|---|
| Phase | Phase | Phase | Phase | Phase |
|  |  |  |  |  |
| Deliverables by Phase (List in Chronological Order) |||||
|  |  |  |  |  |
|  |  |  |  |  |
|  |  |  |  |  |
|  |  |  |  |  |
|  |  |  |  |  |
|  |  |  |  |  |

The following entries are required to develop a Scope Statement that will satisfy the objectives we highlighted above.

- **Phase:** Every project is different. As a project manager, you need to evaluate the project objectives and determine a logical way to develop a roadmap that will lead you to success. Figure 3.7 shares some of the more common methods used to define the phases for a project.

## Figure 3.7 Typical Project Phase Approaches

| Phase Approach | Definition | Applicability |
|---|---|---|
| ADDIE | Analyze, Define, Develop, Implement, Evaluate | • Course development<br>• Training |
| DMADV | Define, Measure, Analyze, Design, Verify | • New product or service to meet specialized customer needs |
| DMAIC | Define, Measure, Analyze, Improve, Control | • Process development<br>• Process improvement |
| PEAK | Prospect, Engage, Acquire, Keep | • Sales campaigns<br>• New customer acquisition |
| PDCA | Plan, Do, Check, Act | • Most projects—the default<br>• Event planning, basic construction |
| PDEL | Plan, Do, Evaluate, Learn | • Multi-phase projects<br>• Research and development (R&D) |
| STP | Segment, Target, Position | • Marketing projects<br>• Voice of the customer projects |
| *SDLC (Software Development Life Cycle) | Envision, Requirements, Design, Build, Stabilize, Close | • Computer software<br>• Business applications |

<u>Note:</u> There are many variations of the SDLC. We chose a common iteration. The SDLC you are familiar with may differ slightly.

- **Deliverables:** Once you determine the optimal phase approach, you next need to define the key deliverables—those measurable project components you must produce—by each phase. In Figure 3.8 below, we define 23 key deliverables essential to completing a process development process using a process of Define, Measure, Analyze, Improve, and Control, or DMAIC. When it comes to defining deliverables in each phase, minimize the number of work packages you identify. Functionally group like activities under a single deliverable. For example, we could develop multiple tasks required to "Develop Process Maps." While identification of these tasks is important, the Scope Statement is *not* the place to break them down. Think high-level and your chances of success will soar.

## Figure 3.8 DMAIC Project Scope Statement Example

| Project Scope Statement ||||| 
|---|---|---|---|---|
| Phase 1 | Phase 2 | Phase 3 | Phase 4 | Phase 5 |
| Define Process | Measure Process | Analyze Process | Improve Process | Control Process |
| Deliverables by Phase (List in Chronological Order) |||||
| 1. Define Inputs and Outputs | 1. Measure Process Outputs | 1. Develop a Problem Statement | 1. Develop Project Charters | 1. Finalize Process Maps |
| 2. Develop SIPOC model | 2. Document Shortfalls | 2. Perform Root Cause Analysis | 2. Develop Project Plans | 2. Communicate Changes |
| 3. Develop Initial Process Maps | 3. Prioritize Improvement Ideas | 3. Identify Root Causes | 3. Execute Project Plans | 3. Conduct Training |
| 4. Walk the Process | | 4. Analyze and Validate Data | 4. Perform Quality Control | 4. Share Lessons Learned |
| 5. Update Process Maps & Narrative | | 5. Define Potential Solutions | 5. Eliminate Variances | 5. Define Next Steps |
| | | | | |
| | | | | |

## Scope Statement: Closing Thoughts

Many project managers begin defining their project without developing an execution strategy. This piecemeal approach often leads to redundancy, omissions, and stakeholder confusion. Think of scope planning using an automobile analogy:

1. Where do you want to go? When you take a trip, you determine the basic requirements you need. This is, in essence, the Requirements Feasibility and Prioritization Matrix.

2. Next, you determine the route you will take and match the requirements to the various places you will stop or visit. You develop a roadmap that ensures you satisfy all of your requirements, and you build it in a relatively chronological order so the sequence makes sense. This is the Scope Statement.

3. We now have one more task. We need to ensure our roadmap includes all the key details required to be successful. We do the same in project management. A critical stop in scope planning is an overview of arguably the most critical planning document you will produce, the Work Breakdown Structure (WBS). In addition, you need to understand the purpose and value of a secondary document essential to supporting a WBS, the WBS Dictionary.

## Developing a Comprehensive Scope Statement: Alex's 7 Qs

Defining scope and getting it right is critical. Before you finalize discussions on what scope really looks like, ensure that you can answer seven critical questions. In addition, how you will ensure these seven questions are addressed needs to be a part of your overall scope planning documentation. If you fail to address any of these questions, chances for project failure increase dramatically.

Alex developed these seven key questions that need to be asked and satisfied to ensure a project is ready to execute. Figure 3.9 provides an overview of Alex's 7 Qs.

**Figure 3.9 The 7 Qs**

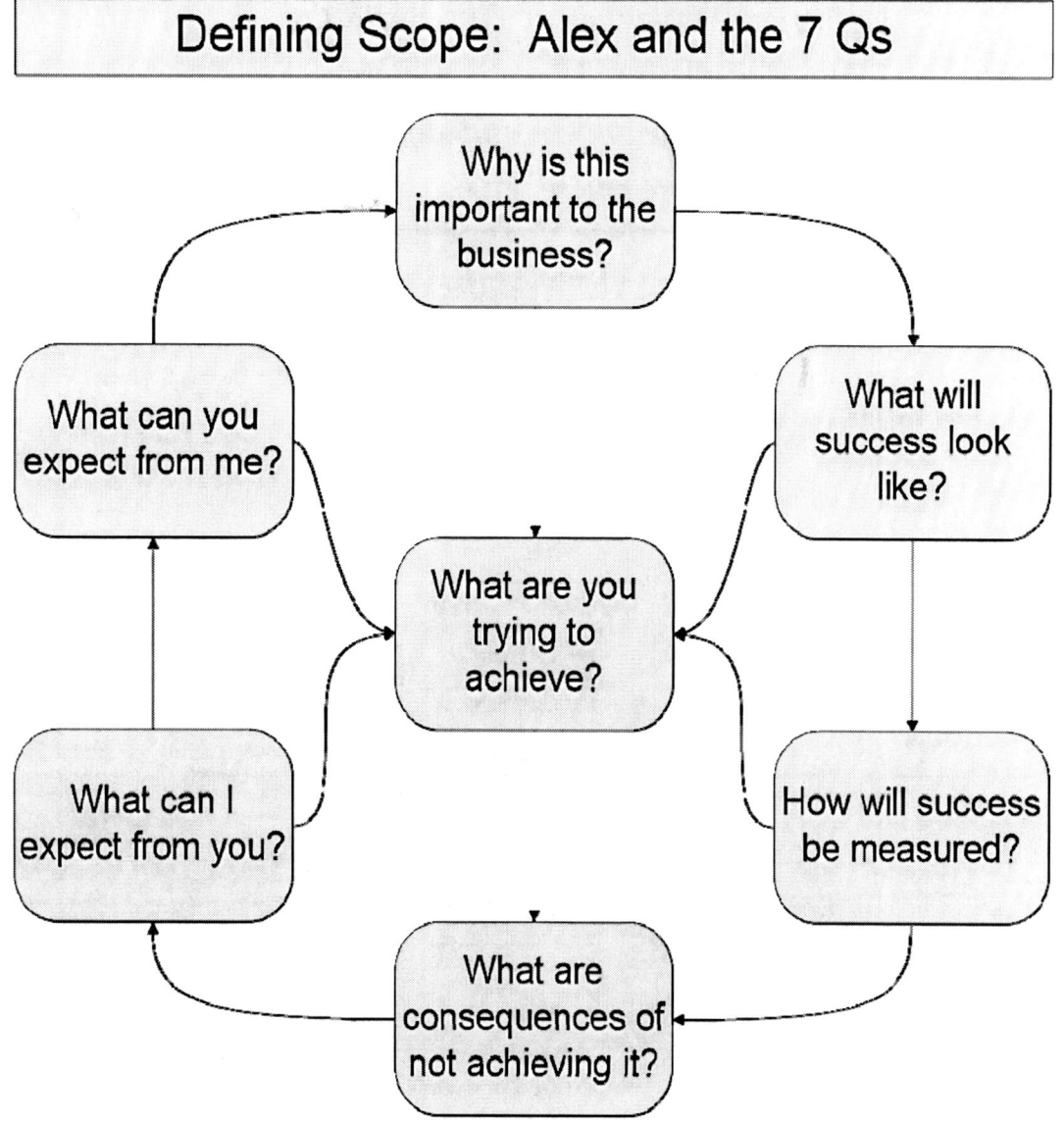

## The Work Breakdown Structure (WBS):  The Cornerstone of Project Planning

A WBS should be developed to support every project. The WBS summarizes all activities required to implement the Scope Statement in a logical manner that allows you to plan the project schedule, budget, communications requirements, risk factors, resource needs, and more.

Many project managers build a WBS that is too large and is not manageable. Our goal in this section is to show you how to build a simple WBS using the DMAIC Scope Statement example in Figure 3.10 that can be used to effectively manage scope and share key status on a single page with project stakeholders. We will address the details that are not included in the WBS in the WBS Dictionary.

> *Project Management Tip:  Build the WBS as a team. When complete, the WBS has the buy-in and support of the entire team.*

**Figure 3.10 Sample WBS Using DMAIC Approach**

Here is an example of a WBS using DMAIC. DMAIC is often used to define project activities to develop and improve processes.

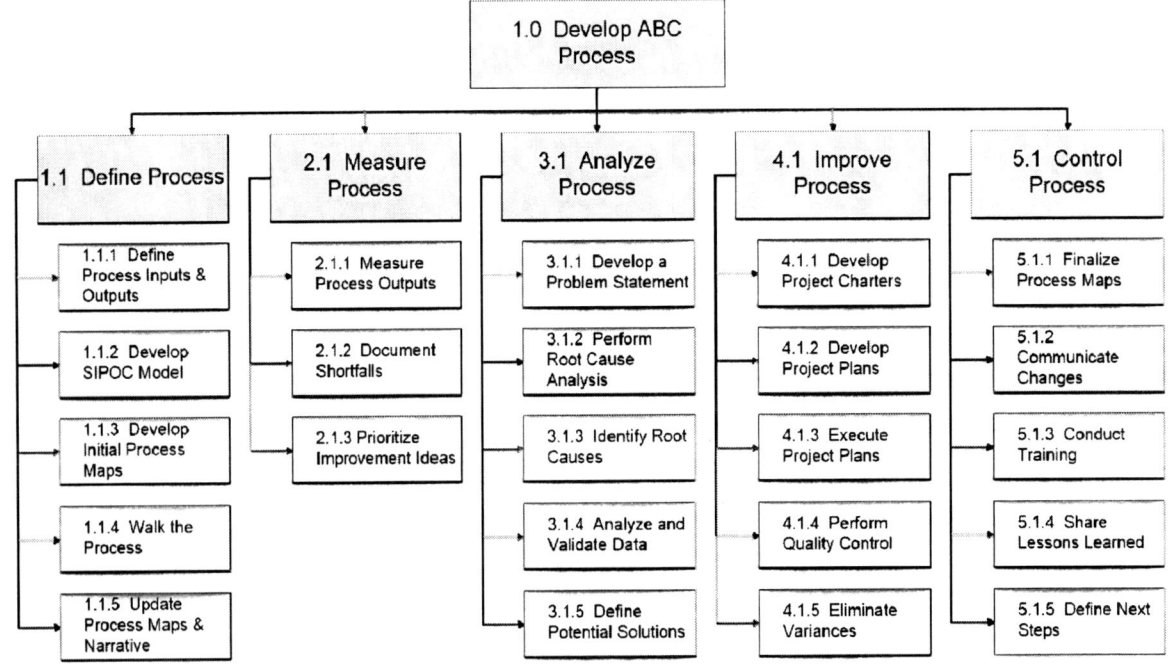

The WBS builds on the Scope Statement (See Figure 3.8) and defines all activities necessary to accomplish the project in relative order of accomplishment. You may have questioned activity 1.1.2 and asked "what is SIPOC?" SIPOC is a common process mapping method that directs you do define the process by identifying Suppliers, Inputs, Process activities, Outputs, and Customers. Here are some clarifications on the WBS.

- **WBS Hierarchy**: Build out the WBS from top to bottom. Each activity has a distinct identifier called a "Code of Account Identifier." The project level is Level 1 and designated as activity 1.0. The phase level that you defined in the Scope Statement is Level 2. Note this example uses the DMAIC model. Each Level 2 activity is designated as a two-number identifier. Level 3 activities are designated by a three-number identifier. Some WBS models may use a different numbering system. If so, no problem. Ensure each activity has a unique number for reference.

- **Chronological Order**: Strive to build the WBS in a manner that shows how the various activities must be implemented. At Level 2, Activity 1.1 should occur before Activity 2.1. At Level 3, activity 1.1.1 should occur before activity 1.1.2.

- **Work Package**: The lowest level of a WBS is referred to as a work package. Each work package needs to be assignable. Since this is a project management book, let me share a definition for you. The process of breaking the WBS down from Level 1 to Level 3 or lower is called decomposition.

- **KISS**: This acronym spells out "Keep It Short and Sweet." When possible, try to group like tasks within a single activity. For example, Work Package 1.1.1 in our example states "Define Process Inputs and Outputs." This is actually a five- or six-task process to complete this work package. The fewer work packages you have, the greater the utility of the WBS as it becomes a planning tool. We will show how to document the multiple tasks in this activity when we present the WBS Dictionary.

- **Action-Result**: Note that each activity (Levels 1 and 2) and work package (Level 3) is annotated using action and result verbiage. Remember the "SMARTWAY" method we introduced earlier in the chapter? Each activity and/or work package needs to pass the SMARTWAY test.

**Note:** Many project managers break out their WBS to levels well below Level 3. A best practice is for the project manager's WBS to be broken out to Level 3 and no further. Breaking out the WBS too far creates a document that may have too much information and may be difficult to manage. If you need to break out the WBS further, consider the creation of supporting WBS for more in-depth task management.

## WBS Variations

There are many variations of the WBS that can be used by a project manager to their advantage. Figure 3.11 shows some very simplified WBS variations for you to consider. Again, the fewer activities on the WBS, the more impactful the status when used.

**Figure 3.11 WBS Variations**

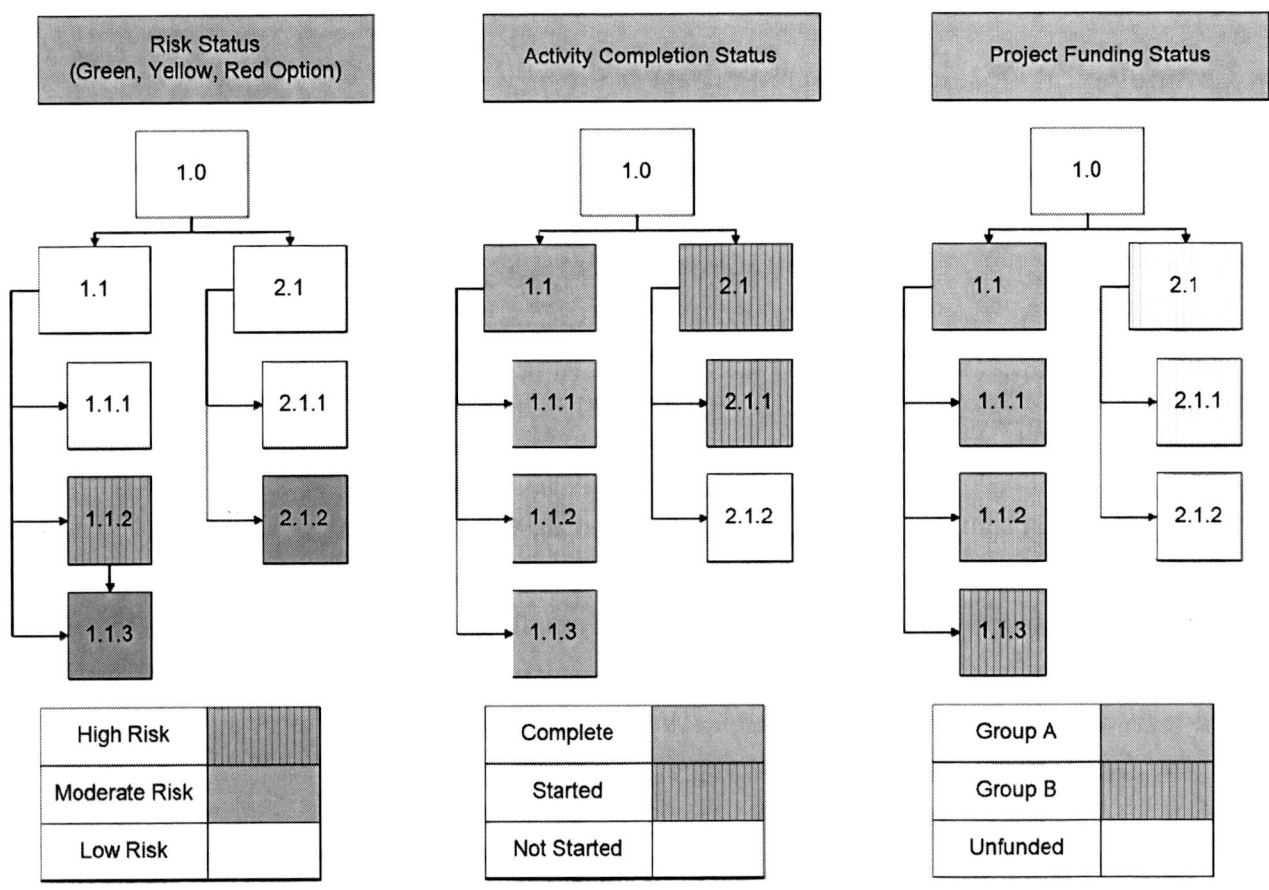

- **Risk Status:** Use the WBS as a means to show the risk of each project work package. A popular means of sharing risk status when you are able to use color media is to classify risk as high (red), moderate (yellow), or low (green).

- **Completion Status:** Use the WBS as a simple means to show completed work packages, work packages started, and work packages not started. Management often asks for completion percentages, which are sometimes not easy to provide. Many firms use the 50/50 method of reporting completion. (A project management best practice when actual percentages of completion are not practical to calculate) It is easy. Using the example in Figure 3.10 above:

  a. Three work packages are complete (1.1.1, 1.1.2, and 1.1.3). Each completed work package receives 100 points. Using our example, the score is $3 \times 100 = 300$.

  b. One work package is started (2.1.1). Give this work package a score of $1 \times 50 = 50$.

  c. One work package is not started (2.1.2). Give this work package a score of $0 \times 1 = 0$.

  d. There are five work packages worth a total of $5 \times 100 = 500$ points. The total based on a, b, and c above is 350 points. Divide 350 by 500 (350/500), and your percent complete is 70%.

- **Project Funding Status:** Use the WBS as a great way to show project funding status. You will often have multiple funding sources for a project that you need to share. In addition, it is important to show funding gaps and their impact.

## The Work Breakdown Structure (WBS) Dictionary

We have stressed keeping the WBS simple. The counter argument to this is the fact that a simple WBS does not define the activities that need to occur at the level of detail needed to be successful. This is a fair argument. Overcome this shortfall by using a Work Breakdown Structure (WBS) Dictionary. The WBS Dictionary allows you to describe the details of each work package without adding additional complexity to the WBS. It is also much easier to update and maintain than the actual WBS itself.

Figure 3.12 provides a WBS Dictionary format using the DMAIC WBS example in Figure 3.7. For simplicity, we have only shared the "Define" Phase. Remember, all templates are available at www.p17group.com.

**Note:** This actual template is best developed using Microsoft Word, Microsoft Excel, or a suitable equivalent. Visit our site—we're here for you!

## Figure 3.12 WBS Dictionary Example (DMAIC Process)

| WBS Identifier | Activity Attributes | References |
|---|---|---|
| | **WBS Dictionary Example** | |
| 1.1.1 | 1. Meet with customer—ensure key process outputs are defined specifically.<br>2. Inventory current inputs required to support outputs. Define sources. | • FY2016 Customer Satisfaction (CSAT) Report |
| 1.1.2 | 1. Map out initial process requirements.<br>2. Trace from Supplier-Inputs-Process Activities-Outputs-Customers.<br>3. Process maps MUST address all SIPOC criteria. | • Six Sigma memory Jogger II |
| 1.1.3 | 1. Map in Visio.<br>2. Use basic flowchart types.<br>3. Map using swim lanes. | • See swim lane examples for vendor management process on SharePoint |
| 1.1.4 | 1. Schedule one hour meet with process team and customer representative.<br>2. Walk through the process.<br>3. Document gaps, omissions, non-value add activities, and questions. | • Stakeholder Register and RACI designations |
| 1.1.5 | 1. Update initial process maps.<br>2. Ensure all issues discovered in 1.1.4 are addressed.<br>3. Assemble process measurement team. | • Stakeholder Register and RACI designations |
| | | |

The concept behind the WBS Dictionary is quite easy to grasp. Reference each work package by its Code of Account Identifier or number. Then describe the work package attributes. Many WBS Dictionaries provide actual links to references in the body of the document. To repeat a key point: add details in the WBS Dictionary and keep your actual WBS simple. The WBS and WBS Dictionary should be shared together.

## Special Topic: Multi-Phase Project Planning (Project Chunking)[8]

There are a number of sources that define the potential to use a technique called "Project Chunking." The *Project Management Body of Knowledge*, 5th Edition[9] refers to this practice as Multi-Phase Project Planning.

---
[8] Multiple Internet Sources: Search on "Project Chunking"

# Planning Scope: The Gift that Keeps on Giving

Figure 3.13 provides a brief overview of this methodology. After you review the figure, we'll dive a bit deeper into the subject.

**Figure 3.13 Multi-Phase Project Planning (Project Chunking) with PDCA Approach**

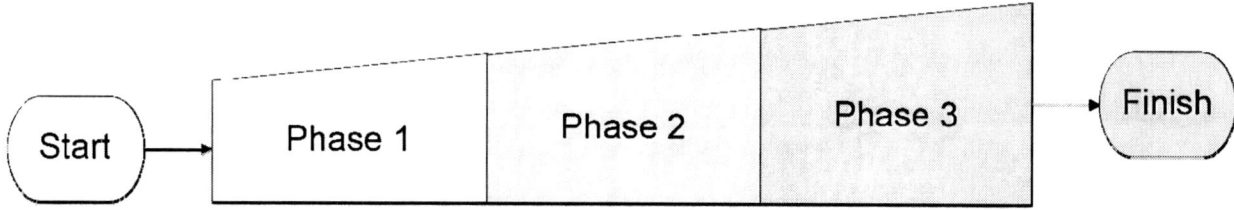

1. Break project into multiple Plan-Do-Check-Act phases
2. Review progress at the end of each phase
3. Make necessary changes at end of each phase to enable next phase

Project Chunking allows an iterative approach to project completion while maintaining traditional Waterfall methodology.

## Multi-Phase Project Planning (Project Chunking) Summary

Some projects may be highly complex, may require long durations to complete, or may have multiple deliverables with multiple dependencies. When this is the case, executing the project using a single PDCA cycle comes with a high risk. Multi-Phase Project Planning, or Project Chunking, allows the project manager to break out the complex project into smaller, more manageable phases. Rather than trying to complete the work as a single phase project, you break it into more reasonable chunks.

This technique allows for the completion of a traditional Waterfall project in iterations that make sense. It also avoids the need to implement an Adaptive Life Cycle project

---

[9] PMBOK, 5th Edition

management methodology such as Scrum. (**Note**: Agile project management has its place. However, the focus of this book is on traditional Waterfall. Stay tuned in the future, as Alex, Peter, and I have plans to publish an Agile project management book as well.)

A number of methods may be used to accomplish Project Chunking. Some projects may be broken out geographically. We will accomplish location one first. Then we will begin work on location 2. You may plan the project based on features. Accomplish the infrastructure first. Then build on the infrastructure until all features are logically completed. Dependencies and interfaces may drive a Project Chunking plan of attack. Another common method is to break out the project chunks by user groups. Here are some Project Chunking advantages:

- **Shorter Durations:** Breaking out a project into phases results in shorter durations between inspections and User Acceptance Testing (UAT). It allows the project manager to review progress on a product or service before final completion and make course corrections along the way as necessary.

- **Control Change:** Project Chunking allows you to fail faster and course correct quicker. You have an opportunity to validate where you are, and where you need to go next during each defined phase. If there are issues at the end of Phase One, the project manager can work with key stakeholders to determine what will be required to get back on track prior to initiation of Phase Two.

- **Avoid Surprises:** The longer the project duration, and the more complex the project, the greater the risk that the project will become a failed project statistic. Project Chunking allows you to include key stakeholders in the development process earlier and more often. It improves chances that at the end of the project, you can not only conform to requirements, but provide a product or service that is fit for use.

> *"Planning without action is futile, action without planning is fatal." — Cornelius Fitchner*

## Chapter 3 Summary

We covered a lot of ground in this chapter. We began our journey to effectively plan scope by carefully addressing the real requirements of the project. Determining what is in scope, and what is out of scope, is critical. We then turned our attention to defining the high level project requirements in a way that provided a roadmap for us to follow. We shared Alex's seven questions that must be answered before you are ready to move forward with further project planning.

We ended with a WBS, the cornerstone of planning that defines all activities needed for the project to be successful, and an overview of a WBS Dictionary, which is where detailed attributes for each activity or work package is shared.

Definition of scope begins with the Project Charter and is refined or "progressively elaborated" as the project progresses. We provide an anonymous quote below that shares in a humorous way what we want to avoid. We want to get the scope 100% correct.

We're not finished with Chapter 3. We will provide some additional "Food for Thought" questions after a word from Peter's Corner. He has some important words to share.

> *"I always complete my projec." — Anonymous*

## Peter's Corner: Chapter 3 Edition

*"Go Slow Now to Go Fast Later".*

Now is the time to identify, clearly elaborate, and agree on all requirements. Missed requirements, misunderstood requirements, anything around requirements – these are most often cited as root causes for why projects fail to be successful. *"But we have to move ahead – we have a deadline."* WRONG! They, your customer, may have a project finish date in mind – they may have told you the date – BUT until you have a realistic schedule, how can you agree to a date?

To move ahead without complete, mutually understood, and agreed upon requirements will result in conflict and disappointment. "Go Slow Now to Go Fast Later". Be tough – resist the pressure to move ahead.

People, teams create and deliver the project's product or service. Building the project team is an important task. If the project team is co-located, then bring them together to build the WBS. Team members will be much more invested in the project and to each other if they help create the WBS. In addition, team members will talk about issues, risks, dependencies, assumptions – things that are not part of the WBS yet are certainly part of the project.

**<u>Jot these thoughts down for later use</u>**

# Chapter 3 Food for Thought

1. Think of a project that you were involved in or knowledgeable of that didn't meet the desired scope. Based on what you learned in this chapter, what went wrong?

2. Based on your evaluation of the project that failed in question one, what would you have done differently?

3. A new project manager asks you to summarize the key objectives of defining scope. You have 30 seconds to respond. What will you share?

4. Think of a project you are involved in or may be considering. Create a list of all requirements and classify each as either functional or non-functional.

5. We use the PDCA model every day for both large and very small projects. Can you share an activity you formed where you used PDCA? (**Note**: You may not have thought of this action as a project. But if it provided something new and unique, it was ☺).

6. Creation of a WBS is great for planning projects? How can the WBS concept help you in other aspects of life?

7. Have you ever encountered a project that should have been accomplished using a "Project Chunking" methodology?

8. Peter's Deep Thought Challenges:

*Reflections*

True or False: Every project has a WBS. (Be prepared to defend your answer)

True or False: A good requirement tells us "What is needed, and why it is needed." (Be prepared to defend your answer)

# Chapter 4: Planning the Schedule: "I Want It Yesterday!"

It is stated that schedules are the number one source of conflict on a project[10]. Time and time again, management and customers want to create the perfect product or service in the minimal amount of time. Problem #5 shared in Chapter 1 addressed this situation. Ineffective estimates and unrealistic schedules are a major reason why projects fail.

In this chapter, we will introduce key concepts and methods you can use to develop and "sell" a schedule that will meet the needs of the project and allow management to make sound decisions. So fasten your seat belt—this chapter is about time.

## The Project Time Management Process

Our goal is to provide a simple, yet effective, process you can use to be successful. Project managers often "over engineer" schedules to the point where they create complex plans that are not understood and generally are not manageable. So, let's keep this simple. Here is a process that works.

1. **Review the Work Breakdown Structure**: Ensure each work package is measurable from both a time and cost standpoint. If not, redefine the work package.

2. **Determine Dependencies**: Which work packages can start simultaneously? Which work packages must wait to start until an earlier work package is completed.

3. **Estimate Work Packages**: Determine time required to complete each work package.

4. **Consider Leads and Lags**: Are there work packages with dependencies that can begin prior to completion of the first work package? Are there factors that may lead to delays after completing a work package that prevent you from immediately starting the next work package?

5. **Develop a Project Network Diagram:** Build a project network diagram that shows the end to end work flow from the first to the last work package.

---

[10] *PMP Exam Prep*, Rita Mulcahey, PMP

6. **Calculate the Critical Path:** How long will the project take? How does the schedule you developed compare to the original (time) objectives of the project?

7. **Balance the Schedule:** Match the final Schedule Baseline to the needs of the project. This is where your negotiating and influencing skills will come into play. **Note:** The Schedule Baseline is the final approved and accepted schedule for the project.

## Step 1: Review the Work Breakdown Structure (WBS)

The WBS is critical to completion of a project schedule that will satisfy the needs of the project. If you don't have a WBS, go back to Chapter 3 and develop one. Without a WBS, chances of developing a schedule that will unfold as planned are low at best. Before you begin project time management, ensure:

- Each work package is defined in a way that allows for estimation of time and cost.

- Each work package is assigned to a project team member with the expertise needed to determine realistic time estimates.

- Each work package adds value. Are there work packages that can be consolidated to reduce the complexity of the WBS? Are there any work packages that don't support one or more requirements? If so, eliminate it.

- WBS Dictionaries provide the work package attributes and definition required to determine reasonable time estimates.

## Step 2: Determine Dependencies

Some work packages can be started simultaneously. Others are dependent upon other work packages to begin. Figure 4.1 provides a visual that models this concept and introduces some key terminology.

## Figure 4.1 Project Dependencies

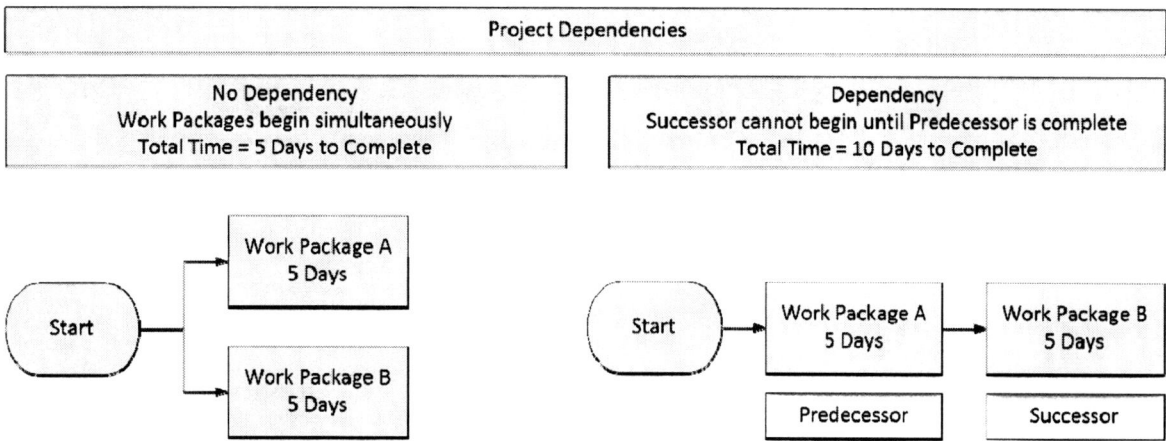

When dependencies exist, the terms "predecessor" and "successor" are often used to show dependency relationships. Simply explained, the "predecessor" is the first work package that needs to be accomplished. The "successor" work package follows the "predecessor." With that, it is now time to share three major categories of dependencies you must consider.

<u>Note:</u> You need to be aware of some of the less common dependency relationships.

- **Start to Start**: A successor activity cannot start until a predecessor activity has started. For example, you can't start a new document until you turn on your laptop.

- **Finish to Finish**: A successor activity cannot finish until the predecessor activity is finished. For example, you cannot finish your trip until you finish unpacking.

## Dependency Categories

- **External Dependencies:** External dependencies are generally driven by external factors such as policy, regulation, compliance, law, etc. An external dependency does not interfere with the work performed on the project. In most cases, the project can be accomplished whether the external dependency is adhered to or not. However, the external dependency cannot be ignored. Examples of external dependencies could include permits required to begin construction, licenses required by key personnel, safety requirements that must be met, etc.

- **Mandatory Dependencies:** Mandatory dependencies are integral to the project's deliverables development and cannot be broken. For example, you may dictate the need for a design before you can build a prototype. Without the design, the prototype can't be built. Another easy-to-understand mandatory dependency example is that you must have an engine in a car before you can start it. No matter how hard you try, you can't skip the engine installation step.

Note: The difference between external and mandatory dependencies can be confusing. We may argue that most external dependencies are indeed mandatory, and that is a fair argument. Remember that an external dependency does not impact the actual production of deliverables. I can still build a house without a permit. A mandatory dependency does impact the production of the deliverables. I can't build the house without building materials. I must acquire the materials before I build.

- **Discretionary Dependencies:** Discretionary dependencies can be broken. Discretionary dependencies are those included during schedule planning to reduce risk. For example, let's say you are paying top dollar to a construction crew to build a major section of a new facility. You inject a dependency that states all building materials must be on-site and inventoried before actual construction begins. A few weeks later, management dictates you accelerate the schedule. You elect to call in the construction crew and begin building prior to completing the building material inventory to save a few days. The good news? You may save a few days by eliminating the dependency *if* all building materials indeed arrived as planned. The bad news? You increased the risk of a work stoppage or delays if it turns out in the end that some of the needed materials did not indeed arrive as planned.

## Step 3: Estimate Work Packages,

Many project managers use a method called "One-Point" estimating. The concept is simple. You are asked how long a work package will take to complete and you give your best estimate—say, 10 days. The good news? One-point is easy. The bad news? One-point accuracy is estimated to be about 15%.[11]

Estimating schedules is difficult at best. Your estimating accuracy can be improved by using a form of Three-Point estimating. Three-Point estimating considers an optimistic, most likely, and pessimistic estimate when determining the final time or cost estimate. Two common Three-Point estimating methods are averaging and PERT. The averaging method is easy. Simply add up the optimistic, most likely, and pessimistic estimates and divide them by three.

The PERT acronym stands for Program Evaluation Review Technique. The premise behind PERT is simple. Statistical studies show that most time and cost estimates follow a normal distribution or bell curve. Our most likely estimate occurs within a small range about 4 out of every 6 times. Our best case or optimistic estimate occurs once in six times. Our worst case or pessimistic estimate occurs once in six times as well.

PERT (Program Evaluation and Review technique) uses the Three-Point method and provides a calculation to determine a revised estimate we can use to estimate work packages or an entire project. Figure 4.2 provides an example illustrating PERT.

### Figure 4.2 PERT Time Management Illustration

| PERT Time Management Illustration ||||
|---|---|---|---|
| Estimation Using PERT ||||
| Estimate | Amount | Multiplier | Sub-Total |
| Pessimistic | 36 | 1 | 36 |
| Most Likely | 21 | 4 | 84 |
| Optimistic | 10 | 1 | 10 |
| Total |  | 6 | 130 |
| PERT | Total/6 || 21.7 |

---

[11] *Project Management Body of Knowledge*, 5th Edition

- The pessimistic, most likely and optimistic estimates for a project are shown. We can assume these figures are based on real data available to the project manager.

- PERT states that the pessimistic estimate occurs 1 in 6 times. We weight the pessimistic estimate with a multiplier of one. The result: 16 days × 1 = 16.

- PERT states that the most likely estimate occurs 4 in 6 times. We weight the most likely estimate with a multiplier of 4. The result: 9 days × 4 = 36.

- PERT states that the optimistic estimate occurs 1 in 6 times. We weight the optimistic estimate with a multiplier of one. The result: 7 days × 1 = 7.

- To calculate the PERT, we add up all weighted estimates (59) and divide by 6. The calculation yields a result of 9.8 days. When using PERT, if the result is not a whole number, always round up. The result we use as our estimate is 10 days. **Note**: This would hold true had the estimate been 9.2. Still round up to 10 days.

- As we shared, some Three-Point models simply average the pessimistic, most likely, and optimistic values to calculate an estimate. This method is not as accurate as the PERT method. However, this is a more accurate method than simply using "One-Point" estimating as we explain below.

- Three-Point estimating is far more accurate than One-Point estimating. One-Point estimating uses the most likely entry without considering the optimistic and pessimistic values. A One-Point estimate generally has a 10 - 15% chance of being accurate. Consider using Three-Point estimating whenever possible.

PERT can be used in many ways. Figure 4.3 shows two common approaches. Some project managers use what we call a cumulative approach. They analyze each work package in the project, apply PERT analysis to each work package, and calculate a single estimate for the entire project. In the example shown, using the cumulative approach, we determine the best project estimate to be 21 days. Other project managers use what we refer to as an individual scenario approach. They establish an optimistic, most likely, and pessimistic estimate for the project. They extract the overall pessimistic, most likely, and optimistic estimates for the entire project, and then apply PERT to define the schedule estimate they will use for the Schedule Baseline.

## Figure 4.3 PERT Application

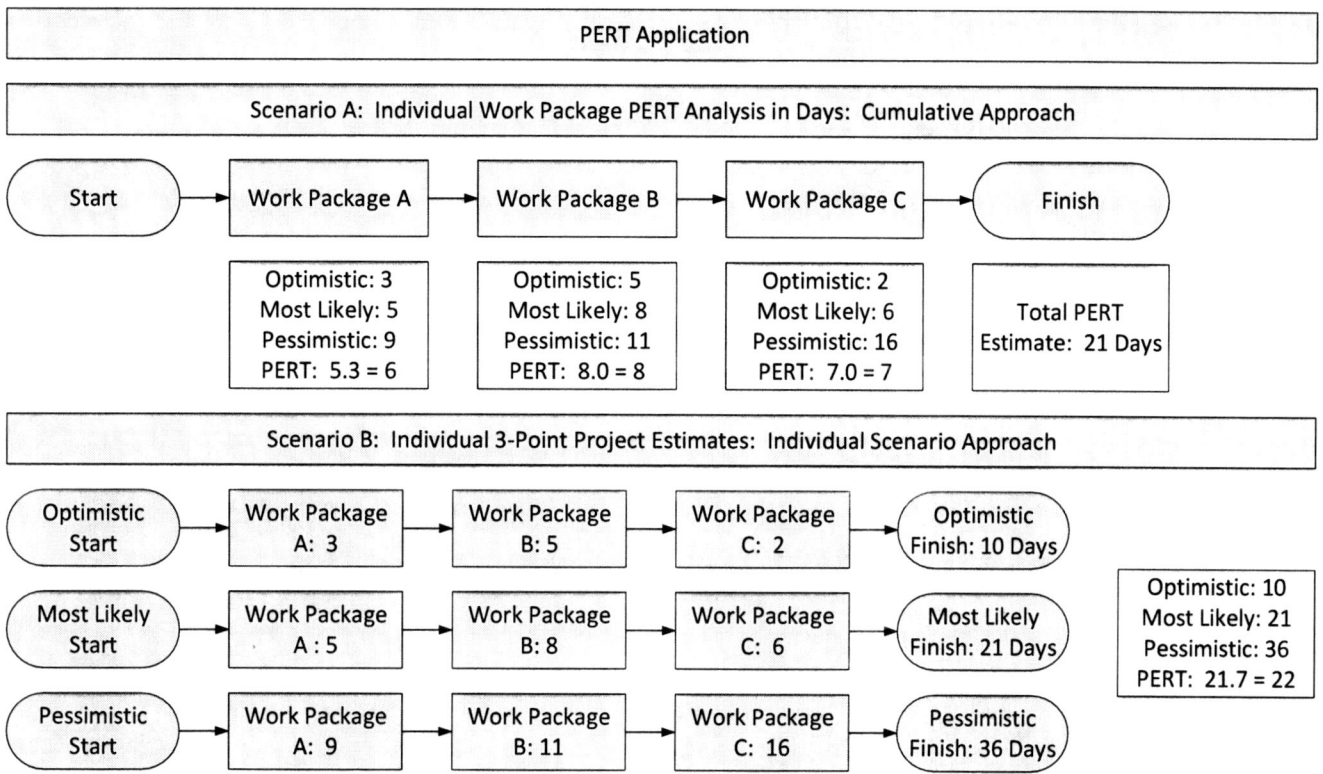

## Step 4: Consider Leads and Lags

Some work packages have special circumstances that need to be considered. Figure 4.4 shares two such circumstances where leads and lags may be used. As a quick explanation, a lead occurs when you can begin a successor activity prior to the completion of a predecessor activity. A lag occurs when you must delay the start of a successor activity despite the fact that the predecessor activity is complete. Many project managers refer to the delay as a "buffer."

**Note:** Buffers should only be used when there is a valid purpose for them. The delay must be based on a supportable purpose.

## Figure 4.4 Leads and Lags

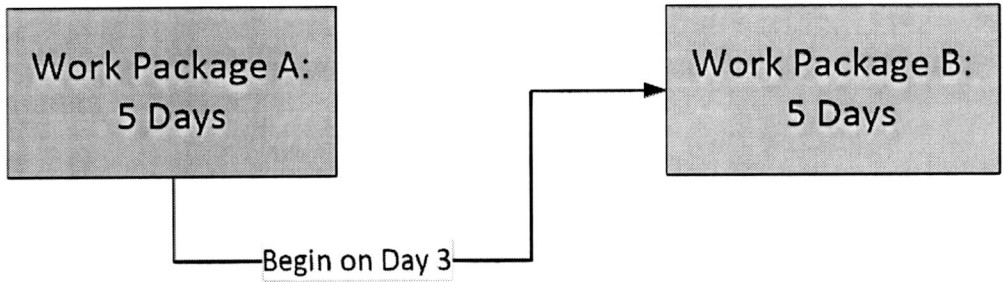

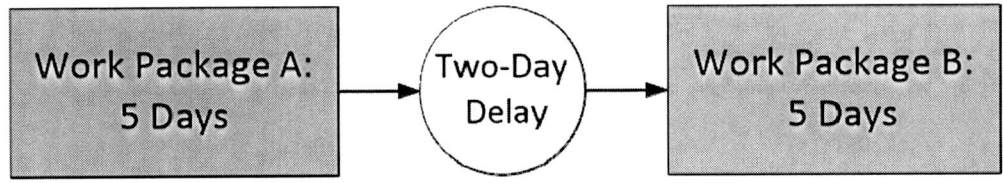

## Step 5: Develop a Project Network Diagram

We are now ready to complete the most important step in project time management, development of the Project Network Diagram. This step requires completion of Step 1, Review the WBS. In addition, it will consider steps 2 through 5 in this process and incorporate them into the final product. Figure 4.5 shows Project Network Diagram that supports the DMAIC WBS we shared in Chapter 3. Refer to Figure 3.9 for reference. We will use Figure 4.5 to complete our journey through steps 6 and 7 of the project time management process introduced in this chapter.

# Figure 4.5 Project Network Diagram Sample with DMAIC Approach

Note: Critical Path Work Packages are shaded in grey. Those Work Packages not on the Critical Path are not shaded.

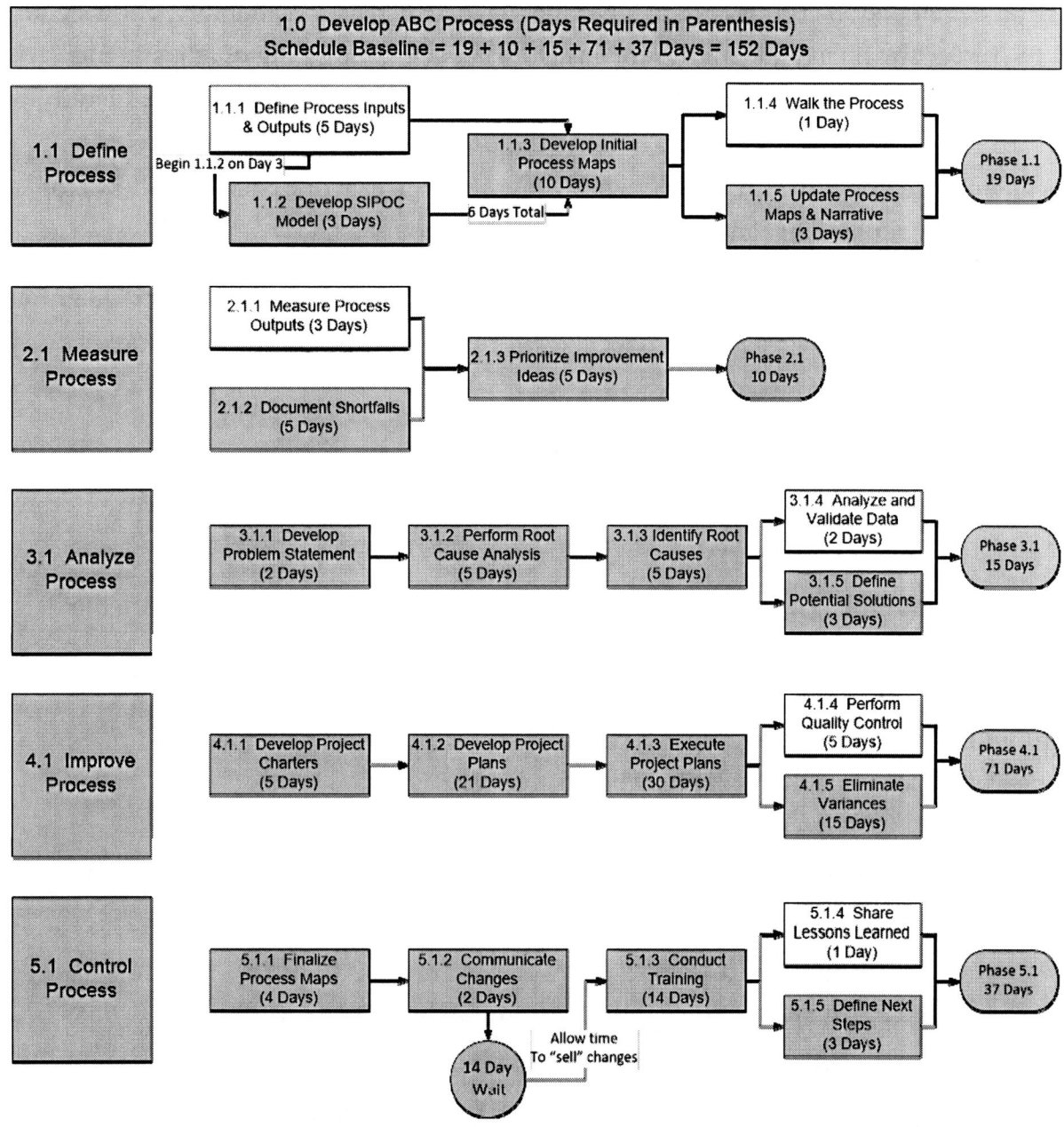

## Project Network Diagram: Clarifying Comments

When developing the Project Network Diagram, strive for organization and simplicity. From an organizational standpoint, break out the Project Network Diagram by phases as you did when you developed the Scope Statement. This practice increases readability, allows you to review the project by phase, and allows for easier analysis and targeting of adjustments when required. In Chapter 3, we stressed the fact that the fewer work packages you identify when developing a WBS, the easier it is to manage the project. This recommendation pays dividends when developing the Project Network Diagram. Fewer work packages allows for ease of understanding, planning, and analysis. Some final thoughts:

- **WBS Match:** The work packages in the WBS must match the Project Network Diagram. Do not add work packages in the Project Network Diagram not in the WBS and vice-versa.

- **Code of Account Identifiers:** Ensure that the Code of Account Identifiers used in the WBS is included in the Project Network Diagram for easy cross reference.

- **Define Leads and Lags:** Add comments when applying leads or lags to ensure the reviewer understands the details and purpose.

- **Apply PERT:** Refer back to Step 3. Use PERT as a means to ensure you don't present a "One-Point" schedule that will likely be unsuccessful.

> *Project Management Tip: Use the WBS Dictionary to add detail. Use the WBS and Project Network Diagram as a means to share the project's scope and schedule without overloading the reviewer with too much information.*

## Step 6: Calculate the Critical Path

The project's Critical Path is defined as the path of the longest duration. Most projects have multiple paths. In essence, the project's Critical Path answers the question, "How long will this project take to complete?" Be aware that some projects may have multiple Critical Paths. When this occurs, risk increases.

As you review Figure 4.5, note the work packages shaded in grey. These work packages are on the Critical Path. The Schedule Baseline for our sample project is 152 days. If the time estimate for any work package shaded in grey is changed, the Schedule Baseline *will* change.

A few work packages are not shaded in grey. These work packages are not on the Critical Path. These work packages have Float. This means you can adjust the time required to complete the work package without changing the Critical Path. For example, you discover that the "Perform Quality Control" work package 4.1.4 will actually take 7 days, as compared to the 5-day estimate you believed was accurate when the Project Network Diagram was finalized. This will not be an issue. As a matter of fact, you can spend up to 15 days on work package 4.1.4 before the schedule changes.

**Note:** Sometimes work packages that are scheduled to be accomplished simultaneously are unrelated. When this is the case, you can "Crash." For example, you may determine that work package 5.1.4, "Conduct and Share Lessons Learned," can be accomplished at any time during the 3-day period to complete work package 5.1.5, "Define Next Steps." If this is the case, you can Float the resources needed to accomplish 5.1.4 to any time over that 3-day period and use those resources to perhaps augment the resources working on work package 5.1.5 if it appears that completion of this Critical Path work package may experience delays.

## Step 7: Balance the Schedule

Always design your initial Project Network Diagram to meet the total scope needs of the project. THEN compare your schedule to the customer's desired project finish date and begin the hard work of negotiating and influencing, and thoughtfully revising the schedule to achieve a schedule that everyone agrees with.

There a few ways you can balance a schedule. If schedule is your number one priority, and the planned schedule does not meet the needs of the project, here are some actions you may need to take. **Note**: Fast Tracking and Crashing are referred to as "Compression Techniques."

- **Fast Tracking:** Fast Tracking is the art and science of eliminating discretionary dependencies and starting work packages simultaneously. The good news? When it works, you can sustain or accelerate a schedule. The bad news? The risk you initially hoped to mitigate through the assignment of the dependency is no longer mitigated. This may result in actually extending the project schedule beyond the original plan.

- **Crashing:** Crashing is using resources from a work package with Float and applying them to work packages on Critical Path. Crashing is also a double-edged sword. When Crashing works, you can sustain or accelerate a schedule. However, there is a cost. Whenever you stop activities on a work package and move resources, additional time is required for transition from the current work package, orientation with the new team, ramp up to become productive, and time to shut down and return to the prior work package. In all likelihood, additional resources will be required and additional costs will be incurred.

- **Negotiate:** As we stated earlier in the book, accelerating a schedule is not free. You may have to negotiate reductions in scope, and/or request additional resources.

## Chapter 4 Summary

We have now completed two key chapters on scope and time, and provided you a simple and effective way to plan and manage both scope and schedule. To develop an effective schedule, build on your WBS and follow the seven-step process we shared. Many project managers rely on sophisticated applications to help them plan and manage the project schedule. These applications are great, but normally require you to develop a certain level of expertise to use them effectively. In addition, there is a learning curve for stakeholders to understand the sophisticated reports these applications provide.

To be honest, most of you do not need that level of expertise to effectively develop and manage a project schedule. Keep it simple and be effective. Before we talk about building the budget in Chapter 5, let's make a quick stop at Peter's Corner and then share some "Food for Thought."

> *Key Quote:*
>
> *"Having a copy of MS Project makes you a project manager to the same extent that having a copy of MS Word makes you an author."*
>
> *Frank Parth (Former PMI Board Member)*

## Peter's Corner: Chapter 4 Edition

One of the biggest mistakes is to commit to a project finish date without developing a realistic project schedule. *"We don't have time to develop a real project schedule"*, or *"We don't know the full project scope so we will schedule as much as we can"*. Imagine the risk of committing to a date and not knowing how to get there, or exactly what you need to deliver.

Project teams delude themselves into thinking that they will figure it out, or a miracle will save them. When is the last time you witnessed a miracle?

The project team, and the project manager in particular, must be bold, tough and courageous. They must again, *"Go Slow Now to Go Fast Later"* – do the planning, the scheduling necessary to reduce schedule risk, the uncertainty in the schedule to an acceptable level. And, regardless of the level of risk in the schedule, the project manager must communicate the risk to the customer, the Sponsor and other key stakeholders external to the core project team. These stakeholders must know and understand that there is schedule risk, and that the project team will do its best to manage this risk so that the project meets it time commitments.

In later chapters we will cover risk, how to communicate risk, and manage stakeholder expectations. More on these subjects then!

## Chapter 4 Food for Thought

1. There are many reasons why projects fail to achieve their schedule objectives. Can you name three reasons that you feel are the primary causes of this situation? Once you define the problems, can you think of solutions to overcome the three causes you selected?

2. Think about the job you do every day. Can you define an external, mandatory, and discretionary dependency that must be considered to successfully perform your job?

3. Select an activity you must perform in the near future. Brainstorm the tasks associated with this activity, and develop an optimistic, most likely, and pessimistic time estimate. Justify your rationale for each assessment. Once you finalize your estimates, apply PERT to determine the time required to complete this task.

4. Define up to seven work packages required to make a peanut butter sandwich. Assess dependencies, and develop a Project Network Diagram. Use minutes as your unit of time to calculate your Critical Path.

5. Your manager gave you a project and said you had three weeks to complete it, no questions asked. What is your strategy?

6. Peter's Deep Thought Challenges:

*Reflections*

You and your project team developed a project schedule. You have Fast Tracked and Crashed the schedule and can only meet the date that your customer and Sponsor are demanding if your Optimistic (Best Case) schedule becomes a reality (recall PERT).

How will you approach and plan for the negotiation with them? If you "lose" the negotiation and agree to their date, then how will you set expectations, and will you and your team devote more effort than usual to risk management?

# Chapter 5: Planning the Budget: Spend a Little to Make a Lot

We now turn our attention to Problem #6. A key reason for project failure is "Poor Budget Planning." Our goal in this chapter is to share a few financial basics that will allow you to put together a simple and effective project budget to support your objectives.

A solid project budget needs to include a time-phased roadmap of funds needed to satisfy the resource requirements of the project. We begin the conversation by sharing types of resources you need to capture:

- **Personnel:** Summarize the cost of personnel needed to support the project. Some personnel may be external. When this is the case, there is almost always an associated cost. Some resources may be internal. When this is the case, you may or may not be responsible for the funding.

- **Equipment:** Equipment is categorized as any asset you will use over a long-period of time. New machines to allow you to increase manufacturing capacity, an additional server to improve your network, etc. are examples. Equipment assets are generally depreciated over time.

- **Supplies:** Supplies are consumables that are generally used up quickly. Items such as office supplies, facility necessities etc. are included.

- **Materials:** Materials are used in the manufacturing process. For example, a CD would be considered as materials for a firm that produces software applications.

## CAPEX and OPEX Funding/Cost Categories

Some businesses break out cost categories based on the type of asset being purchased. Two common cost categories you may encounter are Capital Expenses (CAPEX) and Operational Expenses (OPEX). The distinction between these two categories is defined below:

- **CAPEX:** CAPEX funds are used to purchase buildings, equipment, or other assets with a long life. In most cases, assets purchased with CAPEX funds are subject to depreciation. In general. CAPEX funds are used to *attain* new capabilities. This of course could impact your project budget.

- **OPEX:** OPEX funds are generally used to support the operational costs of running a product, business, or system. In general, we can say OPEX funds are used to *sustain* the business. They are generally included in the annual operating budget. You may need to budget OPEX funds to support your project.

## Project Cost Categories

There are many different types of costs you need to effectively capture in a project budget. Figure 5.1 outlines costs by category, and provides a brief overview of each.

### Figure 5.1 Cost Categories

| Cost Category | Cost Type | Cost Defined |
|---|---|---|
| Direct | Fixed | • Any initial set-up costs<br>• Includes long-term asset purchases subject to depreciation, such as buildings, equipment, etc.<br>• Always included in budget as "must pay" |
| Direct | Variable | • All costs associated with production<br>• Includes supplies, materials, etc.<br>• Always included in the budget as "must pay" |
| Feasibility | Sunk | • Costs associated with feasibility studies or Research and Development<br>• Cost of doing business; never included in project budget |
| Indirect | Multiple | • Costs incurred by a project that do not require expenditure of funds<br>• Examples include internal labor, utilities, etc. paid by other sources<br>• May or may not reference in project budget |
| Contingency | Contingency Reserves | • Estimated costs to address known risks<br>• Rule of thumb: 10% of all direct costs |
| Contingency | Management Reserves | • Estimated costs to address unknown risks<br>• Allocation varies based on the number of unknown variables |

Let's summarize the cost categories discussed above. Direct costs must always be included in your project budget. These are costs that require expenditure of funds. Feasibility, or sunk costs are never included in a project budget. They may impact project selection, but cannot be recouped. Indirect costs do not require payment. However, they are essential to capture if you need to show the total costs associated with a project.

Contingency costs are associated with risk. We will provide more in-depth information on identifying and quantifying the costs of risk in Chapter 9. As a prelude, however, contingency reserves support *known risks*. These are risks that have been identified. Some projects may have *unknown risks*. These are risks you suspect will impact the project in the future. However, it may be too early in the project to truly define these risks, or be aware of the extent of these risks, until the project progresses.

## Defining Budget Requirements

Defining budget requirements and estimating costs is the logical first step in the project budget development process. Figure 5.2 shares a sample budget template and project. We will use Figure 5.2 to share what you need to do to complete this step.

### Figure 5.2 Budget Template Sample

| Cost Factors | Estimated Direct Costs | Estimated Indirect Costs | Total Project Costs | Category (Direct/Indirect) | Quarter Needed/Comments |
|---|---|---|---|---|---|
| Personnel (Vendor) | $30,000 | $0 | $30,000 | Direct (200 hours x $150) | 2016 (Q1-Q4) |
| Personnel (Internal) | $0 | $108,000 | $108,000 | Indirect (900 hours x $120) | |
| Equipment | $25,000 | $0 | $25,000 | Direct | 2016 Q3 |
| Materials | $12,000 | $0 | $12,000 | Direct | $1000 per quarter |
| Supplies | $600 | $0 | $600 | Direct | $50 per quarter |
| Development/Construction | $35,000 | $0 | $35,000 | Direct | Room renovation 2018 Q3 |
| Travel | $6,000 | $0 | $6,000 | Direct | First 2 quarters 2016 |
| Training | $0 | $84,000 | $84,000 | Indirect (70 hours x $120) | 2016 Q4. Not part of budget |
| Support | $10,000 | $0 | $10,000 | Direct | 2018 Q4 |
| Licenses/Permits | $0 | $0 | $0 | N/A | |
| TOTAL | $118,600 | $192,000 | $310,600 | | |

| | | | |
|---|---|---|---|
| Contingency Reserves | 10% Cost Basis | $11,860 | |
| Management Reserves | 5% Cost Basis | $5,930 | |

## Sample Budget Template Clarifying Notes

Here is a brief overview of the Budget Template Sample highlights. Since we haven't shared this in a few pages, this Microsoft Excel template, along with all tools highlighted in this book, is available to you at www.p17group.com.

- **Direct Costs:** All direct costs are categorized, calculated, and summed. Remember, direct costs are those that must be paid. You need real funds in your project budget to accommodate these budgetary needs.

- **Indirect Costs:** All indirect costs should be categorized, calculated, and summed as well. Remember that indirect costs are "real" costs incurred by a project. However, they are not paid for from the project budget.

- **Total Project Costs:** Total project costs are the sum of all direct costs plus indirect costs.

- **Categorization and Comments:** There may be a need to insert some clarifying notes to better explain the logic behind a budget entry. For example, let stakeholders know that training as depicted in the example above is being paid for by external sources and does not need to be included as a direct cost.

- **Contingency Reserves:** Remember that Contingency Reserves are budget funds set aside to address identified risks. There are many ways to quantify the dollar impact of a risk. However, many project managers use a simple 10% rule of thumb. Multiply direct costs times 10% to request Contingency Reserves.

- **Management Reserves:** These reserves may or may not be needed depending upon the clarity and complexity of the project. Recall that Management Reserves are funds set aside to address risks that are currently unknown and have not yet been identified. There is no rule of thumb for calculating Management Reserves. In the example shown above, let's say there is a 5% unknown factor. That being the case, earmark 5% times the direct costs to establish a Management Reserves baseline.

## Estimating Project Costs

When developing cost estimates, try to be as precise as you can. A common tool used to identify and capture more definitive costs is referred to as a Resource Breakdown Structure. Figure 5.3 shares an easy to use Resource Breakdown Structure template you may wish to use for your project.

### Figure 5.3 Resource Breakdown Structure Template

| WBS Code of Account Identifier | Personnel (Direct) | Equipment (Direct) | Materials (Direct) | Supplies (Direct) | Total Direct Costs | Indirect Costs | Contingency Costs | Clarifying Notes |
|---|---|---|---|---|---|---|---|---|
|  |  |  |  |  |  |  |  |  |
|  |  |  |  |  |  |  |  |  |
|  |  |  |  |  |  |  |  |  |
|  |  |  |  |  |  |  |  |  |
|  |  |  |  |  |  |  |  |  |
|  |  |  |  |  |  |  |  |  |
|  |  |  |  |  |  |  |  |  |
| TOTAL |  |  |  |  |  |  |  |  |

Note: Consider using PERT methodology as it pertains to cost estimations (Refer to Chapter 4). Some project managers develop three budget estimates--Optimistic, Most Likely, and Pessimistic.

## Resource Breakdown Structure Highlights

- **WBS Code of Account Identifier:** Review your WBS. List each work package by Code of Account Identifier. This will ensure your cost estimate considers all activities required to complete the project.

    o As a project management note, this method of estimating costs at the work package level and aggregating total costs is known as "Bottom Up" estimating. Bottom up estimating provides you with, in most cases, the most accurate and valid estimate.

    o Bottom up estimating is particularly effective when there are many unknowns, or if requirements are a bit ambiguous. This method forces you to dig into the details to determine the most logical and effective cost estimate.

- **Estimate Costs by Category:** Estimate costs by category. For example, identify and enter cost estimates for supplies required to complete the project. This allows you to better explain exactly where the budget funds will be applied and allows for easier analysis and support. Here is a great chance to introduce you to a second cost estimation method called "Parametric Estimating." This is easy. If you know the quantity of units you require, and the cost of each, simply multiply the units times the cost to derive your cost estimate. For example, you need 20 widgets valued at $20 each. Your cost estimate is 20 × $20 = $400.

- **Consider PERT:** As in scheduling, there may be risk factors that drive an optimistic, most likely, or pessimistic estimate. If this is the case, refer back to our previous discussion of PERT in Chapter 4. It works well for both cost and schedule estimation.

## Depreciation

Equipment and assets lose value as you use them. When you buy a new car and drive it off the lot, it loses value immediately. In business, you are able to claim lost value of assets you purchase. The value lost on an annual basis can be claimed as depreciation. This concept can be important when estimating project costs. Understanding depreciation can reduce overall costs. Here is a quick illustration to show how depreciation can work in your favor and potentially reduce project costs. See Figure 5.4.

### Figure 5.4 Calculating Value of Depreciation

| Calculating Value of Depreciation | | | |
|---|---|---|---|
| | Scenario 1 | Scenario 2 | Cash Value = Depreciation Value × Tax Rate |
| Value of Project | $100,000 | $100,000 | |
| Depreciation | ($10,000) | $0 | |
| Revised Valuation | $90,000 | $100,000 | |
| Taxes at 30% | ($27,000) | ($30,000) | $10,000 ×30% = $3,000 |
| Cash Value of Depreciation | $3,000 | | |

In this scenario, you are managing a project that will increase revenue by $100,000. To support the project, you purchased equipment assets that you can depreciate at a rate of $10,000 annually. Why care?

You can add $3000 to your benefits, which reduces your costs. Here's how it works. Let's look at Scenario 1.

- Revenue will increase by $100,000
- You can depreciate $10,000
- Subtract $100,000 - $10,000 = $90,000. This is the revised valuation of the project
- Your corporate tax rate is 30%
- You will pay taxes on 30% × $90,000 = $27,000

Now let's contrast Scenario 1 to Scenario 2, where there is no depreciation to claim.

- Revenue will increase by $100,000
- You can depreciate $0
- Your corporate tax rate is 30%
- You will pay taxes on 30% × $100,000 = $30,000

Note the difference. With depreciation, you pay $27,000 in taxes. Without depreciation, you pay $30,000. The difference is $3,000 in your favor. Reduce costs by $3,000 and your project financials improve.

## Project Funding Requirements

We are now ready to finalize this chapter with a discussion on project funding requirements. Here is a given: firms very rarely give you all the funds you require up-front on day one. As a project manager, you need to provide the Project Sponsor with a timeline of when you require project funds. Figure 5.5 provides an overview of how to lay out project funding requirements.

## Figure 5.5 Project Funding Requirements

| Direct Budget Requirements | 2016 Q1 | 2016 Q2 | 2016 Q3 | 2016 Q4 | 2017 Q1 | 2017 Q2 | 2017 Q3 | 2017 Q4 | 2018 Q1 | 2018 Q2 | 2018 Q3 | 2018 Q4 | TOTAL |
|---|---|---|---|---|---|---|---|---|---|---|---|---|---|
| Personnel (Vendor) | $7,500 | $7,500 | $7,500 | $7,500 | | | | | | | | | $30,000 |
| Personnel (Direct-Internal) | | | | | | | | | | | | | $0 |
| Equipment | | | $25,000 | | | | | | | | | | $25,000 |
| Materials | $1,000 | $1,000 | $1,000 | $1,000 | $1,000 | $1,000 | $1,000 | $1,000 | $1,000 | $1,000 | $1,000 | $1,000 | $12,000 |
| Supplies | $50 | $50 | $50 | $50 | $50 | $50 | $50 | $50 | $50 | $50 | $50 | $50 | $600 |
| Development/Construction | | | | | | | | | | | $35,000 | | $35,000 |
| Travel | $3,000 | $3,000 | | | | | | | | | | | $6,000 |
| Training | | | | | | | | | | | | $10,000 | $10,000 |
| Support | | | | | | | | | | | | | $0 |
| Licenses/Permits | | | | | | | | | | | | | $0 |
| TOTAL | $11,550 | $11,550 | $33,550 | $8,550 | $1,050 | $1,050 | $1,050 | $1,050 | $1,050 | $1,050 | $36,050 | $11,050 | $118,600 |

This budget requirements spreadsheet is relatively self-explanatory and is used in conjunction with the sample budget template shared in Figure 5.2. Some keys to remember:

- Total funds required *must* match the estimated total for direct costs on the budget template.

- Show your total funding requirements over the life of the project. In this example, we have a three-year project where funds are released on a quarterly basis.

- Note that this spreadsheet is updated as the project evolves. Project funding needs will change as the project progresses. This tool allows you to baseline, and subsequently track, planned versus actual expenditures to determine the project budget status.

## Chapter 5 Summary

We have completed three key chapters and now have an understanding of the project's scope, schedule, and budget needs. During this chapter, we introduced you to types and categories of costs. We shared a simple and effective template to capture and aggregate project costs and provided shared a Resource Breakdown Structure that allows you to drill down to the work package level. We also provided a brief overview of how depreciation potentially impacts a project. We completed our journey by sharing a way to show project funding requirements to ensure you have funds for your project when needed.

We now turn our attention to a critical subject in project management, managing change. Before we continue our journey through Chapter 6 however, let's take a moment to absorb Peter's thoughts on project cost management. After we hear from Peter, we'll provide you with another edition of "Food for Thought."

## Peter's Corner:  Chapter 5 Edition

Planning the project budget is similar to planning the project schedule – we must address uncertainty. Recall PERT – the optimistic, the most likely, and the pessimistic estimates. Like the schedule, the budget follows a bell curve. As you go to the right on the curve towards Pessimistic, you are moving into Contingency and especially Management Reserves – reality is deviating from the most likely scenario and we need additional funds to cover risks we identified but cannot fully mitigate, and to cover risks that were not known, but found us.

If Contingency and Management Reserves are not part of your organization's normal practice, then you should try your hardest to negotiate for these. If you do not succeed to acquire one or the other or both, then by definition, there is more budget risk than otherwise. Be sure to communicate this to your customer, Sponsor and other key stakeholders.

## Chapter 5 Food for Thought

1. There are many reasons why projects fail to achieve their budget objectives. Can you name three reasons you feel are the primary causes of this situation? Once you define the problems, can you think of solutions to overcome the three causes you selected?

2. You want to remodel your kitchen. Can you develop a list of direct and indirect costs? What are the total project costs?

3. Your project team thinks analyzing and documenting indirect costs is a waste of time? Do you agree with them? If so why? Do you disagree? If so, why?

4. Think back to your kitchen remodeling project? What are some risks that could lead to additional costs?

5. Peter's Deep Thought Challenges:

*Reflections*

Think of a project that went over budget – not because scope changed but for other reasons (you may reflect back to question #1 above). What could you have done differently to prevent this negative outcome, or to reduce the overrun? What will you do differently going forward?

Most of us are quick to point fingers at others, at the "stupid" or broken process, or whatever. We fail to look inside ourselves and discover how we may be a part of the problem – and a part of the solution. Look inside, take some ownership.

# Chapter 6: Managing Change: Change Is Inevitable

There is a saying that project managers live by. We shared it back in Chapter 1 and it is worth repeating, "Manage change or it will manage you." Problem #7 we need to explore, and hopefully overcome, is "Ineffective Change Management and Control." According to PMI, the primary goal of the project manager is to "influence factors that lead to change."[12] You can do this by following this simple advice. First, ensure you develop a change management process to support your project. After you develop the process, communicate the process, and ensure transparency. Second, follow, and to the best of your ability, enforce the process.

Managing change—the journey begins! This chapter will introduce a number of key concepts you need to know to be successful as a project manager. Here is a brief overview of this chapter's highlights.

- **Project Management Change Process:** We will share a proven five-step process for managing project change.

- **The Change Timeline:** How do you introduce and "sell" a change? We will highlight a process you need to know when introducing changes to your project.

- **The Change Request Form:** We will share a project change request form Peter, Alex and I have used throughout the years that tracks to an easy to apply Project Change Log. This form has stood the test of time.

- **The Project Change Log:** We conclude by going back to the science of project management. We will share a simple Project Change Log you may wish to adapt that is—our catchphrase—"simple and effective".

## Effective Project Change Management: A Proven Process

As a project manager, change requests are inevitable. Stakeholders change, missions and visions change, and priorities change. There is a proven four-step approach to managing change that is tried and true. Let's walk through this process using Figure 6.1 as a guide.

---

[12] *Project Management Body of Knowledge*, 5th Edition

Figure 6.1 Project Change Management Process

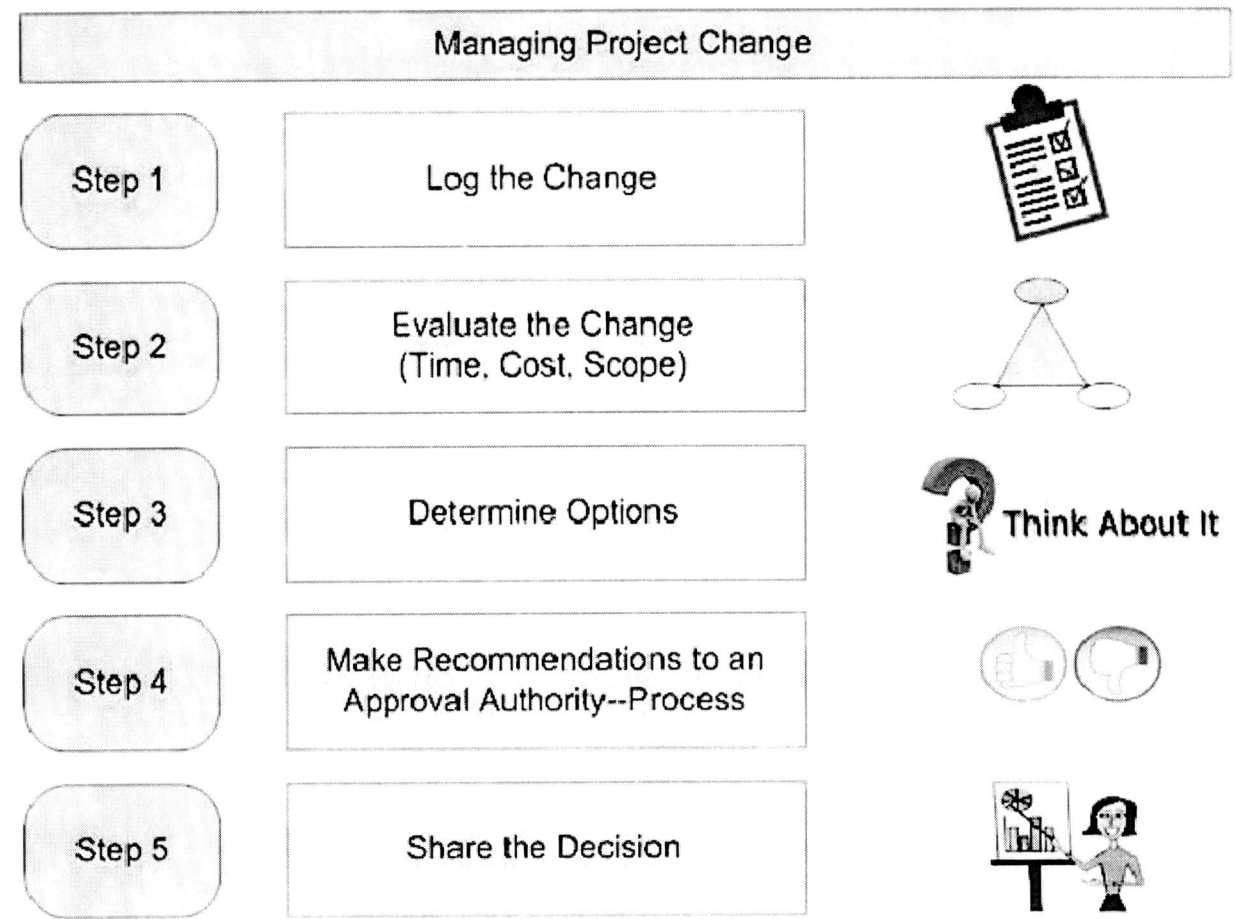

Let's talk a bit more about this important process. Here are some clarifying details on each step.

1. **Step 1:** The project manager needs to establish a standard change log that is available for all stakeholders to review at any time. Ensure all change requests received are logged in in a timely manner and given a unique designator (We will discuss this more in depth later in the chapter.)

> *Project Management Tip: Log changes when received. Let the submitter know you received the change.*

2. **Step 2:** Many project managers have a tendency to look at a change request and jump to immediate conclusions regarding its merit. Our advice in Step 2 is to slow down. Analyze the change and determine how implementation of the change would impact the approved scope, schedule, and budget. Here's the good news—if the change does not impact any of these three areas, then the project manager has authority to approve or disapprove the change. If the change will impact the triple constraints, then the Project Sponsor must approve or disapprove the change.

3. **Step 3: Determine Options:** Review the change request from a positive standpoint. Ask the project team key questions. What would it take to implement this change? Is there any way to implement this change and minimize the impact on the triple constraints? What are our options?

4. **Step 4: Make Recommendations to the Approval Authority and Process the Change:** It is now time to make a decision. In the project team's opinion, is this a positive or negative change? Use the data you compiled during steps 2 and 3 to support your recommendation. Before we move to Step 5, I want to take a moment to clarify and differentiate between the types of changes you will likely receive.

   a. **Preventative Changes:** There will be lots of requests to update the project plan, revise a process, etc. As long as these changes do not impact the triple constraints, the project manager should approve them and move on. Use discretion in terms of logging them or not.

   b. **Corrective Changes:** There may be times when a project team member proposes a change needed to get scope back on track. Or a change may identify a defect that needs repair. This type of change does not need to be logged, and may be addressed and approved internally by the project manager.

   c. **Stakeholder Changes:** Any stakeholder can request a change. As we shared earlier, stakeholders are anyone interested or impacted by the project. These are the changes that MUST be processed using the five-step process we are now sharing.

5. **Share the Decision:** Many project managers process project change requests in a vacuum. They receive the change, evaluate it, gain approval, and move forward. Sometimes this works. However, often times, the change is resisted, leads to discontent, and may result in previously supportive or leading stakeholders becoming resistant. Project managers need to be aware of the "change timeline." This is our next important subject in this chapter.

## The Change Timeline

Changes to a project baseline are not always accepted by all stakeholders. The project manager must also be ready to become a change manager as well. Figure 6.2 provides a change timeline[13] that shows the stages a stakeholder needs to move through before acceptance of change becomes a reality. We'll provide the picture, and follow it up with a few words of explanation.

**Figure 6.2 Change Timeline**

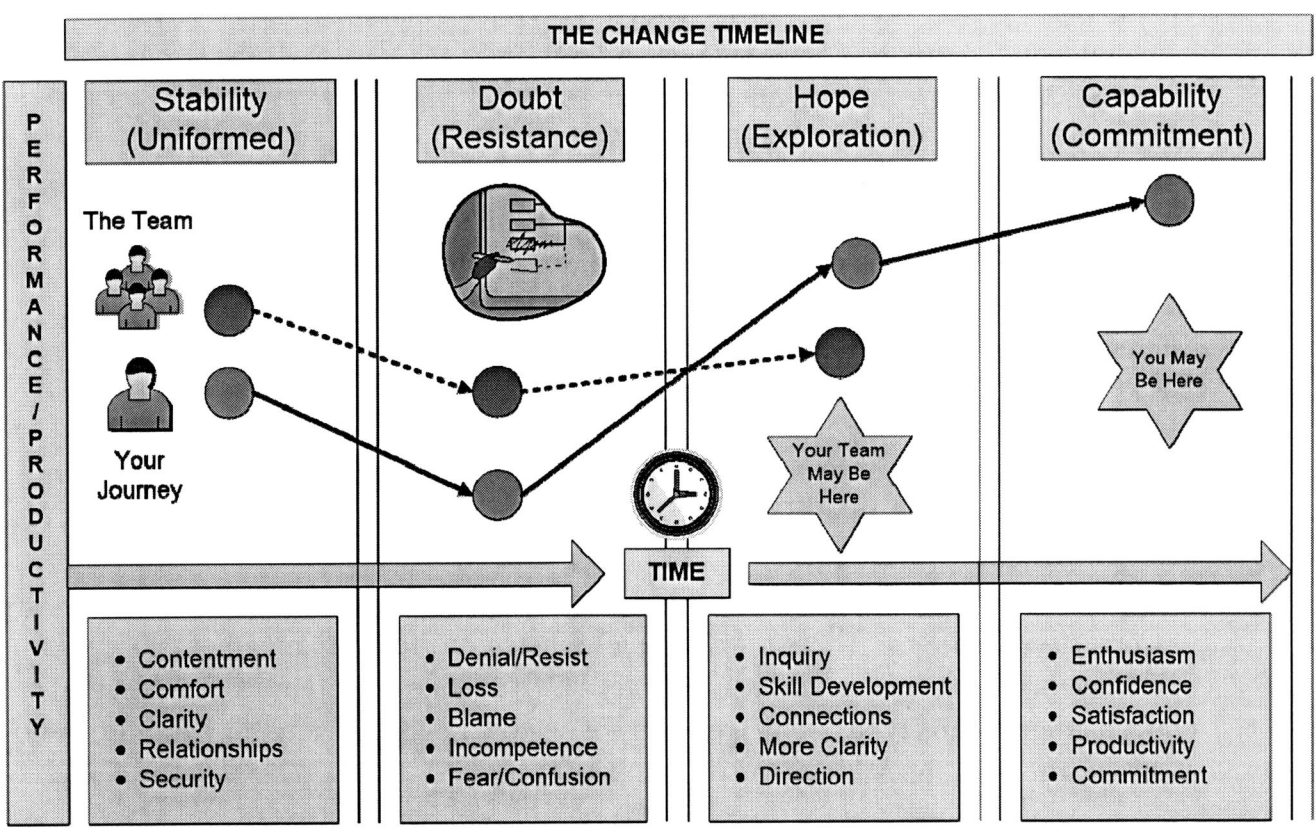

Let's walk through this model. You are a project manager and worked long and hard to develop a scope, schedule, and budget baseline that served the needs of the project. You shared this plan with the stakeholders and gained their acceptance. Your stakeholders are in the *"Stability"* Phase. Productivity is reasonable as stakeholders assume they understand what the project will produce, when it will be produced, and the price tag for the deliverables.

---

[13] Cynthia Holmberg, Microsoft Corporation, 2011

A project change is introduced and the rumors begin to fly. Many stakeholders will enter the *"Doubt"* Phase of the change timeline. Information about the change may be lacking, impact on the project may be unknown, and resistance may result. So how do you counter this?

First, use and enhance the interpersonal skills you possess to the maximum extent. Effective change management requires communications, negotiation, influencing, and motivational skills. Secondly, follow the change management process we introduced. It can help. Let's review our five-step process we just shared.

- Step 1 in the process is to log the change. Ensure all change requests are transparent to all. There may be questions, and that is ok. Respond quickly and positively.

- Step 2 discussed the need to evaluate the change. Do not perform this evaluation in a vacuum. Touch base with key stakeholders most impacted by the potential change and solicit their feedback. Try to iron out the issues behind the scenes.

- Step 3 is to determine options. There are many ways to effectively move from A to Z. Again, solicit input from those most impacted by the change. They may be able to share a win-win solution that is good for the project, and good for them.

- Step 4 is processing the change. Don't wait to take this step. The more complex or controversial the change, the more productivity will be impacted until a decision is made. The longer you wait, the deeper the stakeholders will resist and cement themselves in the *"Doubt"* Phase.

- Step 5 is to share the decision. Earlier, Peter shared an acronym called WII-FM. Try to show how the change will result in a positive impact in the long run when the stakeholders ask "What's in it for me?"

Phase 3 of the change timeline is the *"Hope"* or Exploration Phase. This is where you need to become a salesperson. Acknowledge others' fear of change. At the same time, show the value of the change if implemented. Be able to show stakeholders that in the end, the project will go from "Good to Great"[14] if the change is implemented.

---

[14] *Good to Great*, James Collins

Your last goal is to ease the stakeholders into phase 4, the *"Capability"* Phase. Update all key project documentation. Communicate and socialize the change in the most positive way you can. Laud those who support the change and applaud those who lead it. Periodically, let people know that the benefits that were promised in the change are being realized. Work to sustain the gain.

<u>Note:</u> All stakeholders do not progress through the change timeline at the same time. If you review Figure 6.2, you may have noticed that in this example the project manager is in the *"Capability"* Phase. However, the team is still in the *"Hope"* Phase. As a project manager, you need to understand that a "one size fits all" change methodology will not be 100% successful. You need to realize that all stakeholders are different and will accept change at their own pace. Your ultimate goal in the end is to move all stakeholders to the *"Capability"* Phase if possible.

## The Project Change Request Form

Peter, Alex and I have emphasized that effective project management is both an art and a science. We have shared a little science by introducing a step by step project change management process. We added some art with the change timeline. Our next stop is introduction of a change request form that accomplishes two goals. First, it provides an effective means for stakeholders to submit changes. Secondly, it forces stakeholders to answer key questions essential to evaluate and analyze the change.

The Project Change Request Form should be included as part of your overall Project Management Plan. Normally, your Integrated Change Control process is part of your Communications management Plan. Chapter 8 will share highlights of this critical document. Your Integrated Change Control process should include change management policy and procedures, a standard Change Request Form, and a Project Change Log. We'll review the form in Figure 6.3 in a moment. But first, here are a few tips to remember to ensure success.

- **Education:** Ensure all key stakeholders are aware of the policies and procedures you develop to process change requests. This includes knowledge of the standard change form, and where they can access the project change log to review the status of their submissions.

- **Enforcement:** Do not accept any change requests that are not submitted using the standard change form. As you will see, the form is designed to address all the key questions you and your team will need to know. You need this information.

- **Collaboration:** There may be times when you want to walk through the form with a key stakeholder. Help them complete the form and provide guidance. The time you spend assisting the stakeholder upfront will be time saved later in the process.

> *Project Management Tip: Poor change management almost guarantees "Scope Creep."*

### Figure 6.3 Sample Project Change Request Form

| Project Change Request Form | | | |
|---|---|---|---|
| **Project:** | *(Completed by Requestor)* | **Change ID:** | *(Completed by PM)* |
| **Date Requested:** | *(Completed by Requestor)* | **Requested By:** | *(Completed by Requestor)* |
| **PM:** | *(Completed by Requestor)* | **Requestor Email:** | *(Completed by Requestor)* |
| **Decision:** | *(Completed by PM)* **Accepted, Accepted with Modifications, Rejected, Deferred, Further Analysis Required** | **Decision Date:** | *(Completed by PM)* |

**Proposed Change:** Detailed description. Focus on business needs, requirements; solution is secondary.

*(Completed by Requestor)*

**Reason for Change:** Focus on benefits that will accrue after the change is made. Describe why this change was not addressed earlier in the project. Indicate who or what is driving this change.

|  |
|---|
| *(Completed by Requestor)* |

**Impact Analysis:** Consider impact to work products, quality, schedule, scope, budget, people, resources, other projects. List cost/benefit/Return On Investment (ROI). Consider impacts to all groups and stakeholders. List assumptions, dependencies, and risks. Define approval levels.

*(Completed by PM/team)*

**Implementation Options:** Consider options to implement this change. What strategies are recommended? How will implementation impact current scope, budget, and schedule milestones?

*(Completed by PM/team)*

## Project Change Request Form

**Decision:** Accept As-Is, Accept with Modifications, Defer, Reject, Further Analysis Required

| Decider (s) Name: | Date | Comments/Modifications |
|---|---|---|
|  |  |  |
|  |  |  |
|  |  |  |
|  |  |  |

**Decision Notes:** Reasons for Decision. Decision follow-up actions necessary.

*(Completed by PM/team)*

| | |
|---|---|
| **Close-Out Checklist (As Applicable):** | |
| | Change logged in Project Change Log (all changes, regardless of decision, must be recorded) and posted on project site |
| | Scope documentation and other key project documentation updated |
| | Design document, test plan, test cases, training notes, etc. updated |
| | Schedule and budget updated |
| | Status Report updated |
| | Change communicated to stakeholders |

## Project Change Request Form: The Essentials

The Project Change Request Form we developed addresses essential information you need to know to effectively evaluate a change. Here is a quick overview of some of the form's highlights.

- **Basic Information:** The beginning of the form requests basic information to differentiate this change from other requests. The requestor may ask for your assistance here. It is always a nice touch to provide the requestor with the change designator or number you will use to process the change. It provides the requestor with a sense of assurance that the change is important and will be addressed.

- **Proposed Change:** Many stakeholders will try to provide a solution rather than requesting additional functionality, reliability, etc. Discourage solutions, and strive for a detailed overview of exactly what the stakeholder needs or wants. Strive for clarity, and avoid ambiguity. This section is not complete until everyone who reviews the change has a similar interpretation of exactly what the desired change is.

- **Reason for Change:** Peter and I almost felt evil when we developed the instructions for this section. Obviously, the value proposition for the change and who is driving the change is critical information you need to know. Our favorite question by far, however, is *"Describe why this change was not addressed earlier in the project."* This question does discourage many non-value changes from coming your way.

- **Impact Analysis:** This section is critical. What will this change do to the current project? Some changes may be minimal. However, others may change the project objectives to the point where massive re-planning is required. Some changes are so extensive that they require going back to square one and essentially starting over.

- **Implementation Options:** The ultimate goal of a project manager is to integrate value added changes into the project with minimal change to the original stated objectives of the project. We have shared a number of methods with you throughout this book to include Fast Tracking, Crashing, modifying scope, requesting additional resources, or extending the schedule. Remember that you need to let stakeholders know that nothing is free. The majority of changes require some type of trade-off to accomplish. You need to clearly define those trade-offs.

- **The Decision:** We provided a basic overview of the decisions you need to reach. They include: Accept As-Is, Accept with Modifications, Defer, Reject, Further Analysis Required. Try to reach your decision as quickly as practical. In addition, ensure you are able to support your decision. Some reject or defer decisions may very well frustrate stakeholders. You need to able to justify why you said no or wait. Even accepted changes require support. Remember the "Change Timeline." One stakeholder group may be delighted with the change. However, another stakeholder group may look upon the change as a poor idea and push back.

**Note:** A common decision making methodology often used to review project change requests is called the "OARP" method. Stay tuned in Chapter 11. We share this methodology, and we think you'll find it useful.

## Project Change Log

Our final topic in Chapter 6 discusses the need to develop a standard Change Log that is available for all stakeholders to review. Peter and I developed a "simple and efficient" change log that correlates with the Change Request Form we just shared. Let's review a sample Project Change Request Log. This is a simple Microsoft Excel spreadsheet that is available to you—as we've shared before ☺--at www.p17group.com. With that, let's walk through the Project Change Request Log example shared in Figure 6.4.

- Note that we condensed the columns in this example so you can see each section clearly in the book. The actual spreadsheet provides ample space to annotate the information required to complete the form.

### Figure 6.4 Project Change Request Log Example

| Project Change Request Log | | | | | | | | |
|---|---|---|---|---|---|---|---|---|
| Change # | Requestor | Date Submitted | Proposed Change | Reason for Change | Impact Analysis | Implementation Options | Status | Decision |
| | | | | | | | | |
| | | | | | | | | |
| | | | | | | | | |
| | | | | | | | | |
| | | | | | | | | |
| | | | | | | | | |

The Project Change Request Log complements the Project Change Request Form we featured earlier. Information requested on the Project Change Request form is reflected in the Project Change Log. Here are a few thoughts on the Project Change Request Log:

- **Change Number:** Each requested change should be assigned a unique change number. Let the submitter know the tracking number as soon as possible when a change is received.

- **Change Log Access:** Ensure the Requestor has access to the change log. Let them know they can check the status of their request at any time.

- **Status:** Ensure you update the status of changes regularly. Doing so will save you many requests from Requestors for status updates.

- **History/Archives:** Maintain an active and inactive log. Stakeholders should be able to review changes that were previously approved, along with those rejected or deferred. Sharing history will often preclude duplicate requests, and likely eliminate requests for changes previously not approved.

**Note:** You may want to establish a Change Control Board (CCB), or some type of Project Steering Committee to review and manage project change requests. A CCB works best when the project is high priority, there are many stakeholders involved, and/or the potential for stakeholder frustration and push-back is high.

These bodies serve a valuable purpose of taking the "bad-guy" decision making off the back of the project manager. The CCB should be managed by the project manager, chaired by the Project Sponsor, and consist of key stakeholders most impacted by the project. Collectively, the CCB can look upon each change in a holistic sense, determine which changes make sense and which do not, and take the pressure off the project manager who may not be in the best decision to determine whether the change has merit.

> *Alex's Push-Back Tip: You may want to satisfy a stakeholder who presents a change that cannot be approved by letting them know you see the merit of the idea and are willing to advocate for the change in the next version or project. This normally allows you to maintain the commitment of the potentially disgruntled stakeholder.*

## Chapter 6 Summary

Ineffective change management and control are huge reasons why many projects fail. Process all changes as soon as received and follow the process we shared. You'll find it works. Understand the change timeline. People need time to digest change, and not everyone progresses through the change timeline at the same speed.

Develop a standard Change Request Form and use it. Educate stakeholders on your change management process and stick with it. Process changes when received, maintain current status, and communicate with requestors. If you adapt the information shared in this chapter, we are confident you will succeed in "influencing factors that lead to change."

It's now time for another edition of Peter's Corner. Once Peter shares his thoughts, we'll challenge you once again with some food for thought.

> *"The P in PM is as much about 'people management' as it is about 'project management'."*
>
> *-- Cornelius Fichtner*

## Peter's Corner: Chapter 6 Edition

Before, and certainly by Baseline, the project's key stakeholders should not only be aware of the change management process – they need to understand it, and agree to use and abide by it. This way you can hold them accountable to using it later--rather than trying to "sell" it to them in the heat of battle-- when emotions are flying around the pressure to accept changes.

When presenting a proposed change to the deciding person or group, I like to think of it as "teeing up options for decision making". Give the deciding person or group a *concise and crisp* presentation of the options, facilitate to a decision, then promptly implement the decision. But a word of warning . . .

Perhaps the proposed change would provide great benefits – but these can wait – for the next project. "Guard the Baseline" when appropriate. Usually you want to finish the current committed scope – finish the project – and have more time for other current projects. Consider this: you are struggling to meet the project's committed finish date. A change request comes in that would add scope AND extend the project finish date. Get the change accepted, and your team's struggle to meet the finish date is gone. Not so fast: what will happen to all the other projects that you and other team members were going to devote more time to or start when this project is finished? Did you include this in your thinking and impact analysis for the change request? Think through the potential consequences of each requested change.

When approaching the end of a project, and if the team is struggling to 'make the date' – what if a change request comes in? There comes a time when any distraction will cause the team to miss the date. Tell the requestor that even to evaluate (not implement) the request will cause the project finish date to slip. Put this burden on them, and see what they want to do. Which leads to another important point . . .

Evaluating change requests not only takes the project manager's time, but also team member's time. This time is rarely if ever included as part of the resourcing and schedule – these are built without regard for this time and effort. You might say that these are in Contingency and/or Management Reserve (what if you do not have these?). People remember the Baseline Schedule date, the Baseline Budget. These get stuck in their heads and even with approved changes you have to expend effort managing and resetting expectations. It is better to build what you can (in this case time and effort to evaluate change requests) into the Baseline plans than to ask for more at a later date.

## Chapter 6 Food for Thought

1. Recall a change request that impacted a project you were working on either on your job or in your personal life. Describe the process you used to evaluate and determine if the change was valid. How did the process work? What went well and what could have been done better?

2. Describe a personal experience where you or someone you know was impacted by a change? How did the change timeline impact the final result of the change?

3. A stakeholder asks you to accept a major change proposal. After reading this chapter, how will you respond to the stakeholder?

4. An associate asks you to describe the number one thing to remember when managing project change? What will you tell them?

5. Peter's Deep Thought Challenges:

*Reflections*

Change is all around us. Change is happening faster. The longer the project's duration, the greater the probability that the project's deliverables will not be what is needed. Put another way, the longer the project's duration, the more likely that the frequency of change requests will increase as the project progresses.

The worst case is that the project's deliverable is obsolete when made available – "dead on arrival." One way to mitigate this risk (or eventuality) is to design the project or "chunk" the project in pieces. How can we design the project so that we provide deliverables (for use) along the way, AND create "choice points" where we can make course corrections as we finalize plans for the next [major] deliverable? Benko and McFarlan[15] call this "Project Chunking". I highly recommend that you read the chapter in their book that explains this. (We will touch upon this more in Chapter 11.)

For now, however, reflect on a project (past, present, or future). How can this project be re-imagined so that it provides deliverables, value/benefits, along the way?

---

[15] *Connecting the Dots: Aligning Projects*, Benko and McFarland

# Chapter 7: Project Human Resource Management: The People Make the Difference

Andrew Carnegie[16] was a Scottish immigrant who became a wealthy entrepreneur during the United States' industrial revolution. Andrew built his wealth in the steel industry, and is known to have many prolific quotes. One that pertains to the importance of project resource management states, "You can give me all the resources, money, and equipment for my factories. But if I don't have passionate employees, then my factories will eventually turn to dust."

Carnegie's quote holds true for your project team. You can have the greatest project idea and plan in the world. But if the right people are not motivated, then the likelihood of project failure is high. This chapter will address the need to manage and care for the project team. Problem #8 in Chapter 1 stated that "Lack of Resource Planning" is a major issue. Let's address that problem in this chapter.

## Introduction to Project Resource Management

There are a number of critical success factors that a project manager needs to consider to interface with key stakeholders and effectively address project human resource management considerations. Here is a quick list of must-do tasks.

1. **Functional (Resource) Managers:** In many organizations, you may not have control of the human resources you need to effectively plan and implement the project. When this is the case, you need to negotiate effectively with the individuals who are responsible for acquiring the project team members you need. We refer to these managers as "Functional Managers." In some firms, they are referred to as "Resource Managers." Oftentimes, Functional Managers are not excited about allocating the personnel you need for success of your project. And this resistance is understandable. Before we leave this subject, we want to provide a few tips to help you be successful.

    a. **The "When" Factor:** Do not ask for personnel until you can definitively show when you will need them. You need to have an onboarding and release plan. Asking a

---

[16] Andrew Carnegie, 1835 - 1919

Functional Manager to release personnel for the entire duration of a project is a hard sell at best!

b. **The "Why" Factor:** Try to share the value proposition for the project. Having an approved Project Charter with adequate level of sponsorship is a huge plus. If possible, try to show the Functional Manager how the project will support his or her organization. WII-FM works!

c. **The "Who" Factor:** Try to avoid requesting specific people unless this is absolutely essential. Define the roles and skill sets required and allow the Functional Manager to define the best fit. Negotiate as required if the assigned personnel do not meet your needs.

d. **The "How" Factor:** Share how the personnel you require will be used on the project. You need to make the case that the need for an individual possessing a particular skill set is necessary to project success. If possible, show the Functional Manager how the project work the individual will accomplish will aid him/her in the future at their primary job.

e. **The "Help" Factor:** Functional Managers generally need to document performance for the personnel they manage. Offer to provide input for the individual(s) who will support your project to the Functional Manager that he/she can use when it is time to complete a performance appraisal.

2. **Core or Project Management Team:** These are the project team members who will assist the project manager in completing many critical planning documents and assisting in the execution of the project. Here are some key considerations to consider:

a. **Expertise:** Select personnel that possess the expertise required to plan and manage the project. There is a saying I derived that states, "Know what you know, know what you don't know, and surround yourself with people who know what you don't know."

b. **Training:** There may be no one available who possesses the skill sets you require for your project. If that is the case, you may need to consider adding training activities (and budget) to the project.

c. **Availability:** Asking Functional Managers to provide project management team members is a challenge. You may want to work out a resource sharing plan with the Functional Manager. For example, the project management team member is available to you 50% of the time.

3. **Extended Team:** These are the project team members who provide specific work and support. These individuals generally work part-time and not continuously on the project. Key considerations for extended team members include:

    a. **Develop a WBS and Schedule:** You can use the project WBS to share the "what" and project schedule to share the "when" information that Functional Managers and prospective extended team members themselves need to know.

    b. **Share the Change:** Project scope and schedules may change as a project progresses. Keep Functional Managers apprised of changes that may impact the timing or duration of when their personnel are needed.

## Building the Team: The Tuckman Model and Situational Leadership Merge

Managing a project team is more than just assigning individuals to work packages. Bruce Tuckman[17] developed a very popular and useful four-stage team development model that is widely used by project managers. Paul Hersey and Ken Blanchard[18] worked together in the 1970s to develop a second model called the Situational Leadership Model based on the theory there is no "one best" leadership style.

Peter, Alex and I have merged these models to show how a project manager needs to develop a team based on the particular team development stage the team is in. Figure 7.1 shares this merged model for your review. Let's review the model, then discuss what it means to you.

---

[17] Bruce Tuckman, Tuckman's Team Development Model, 1965
[18] Situational Leadership Model, Hersey and Blanchard

# Figure 7.1 Tuckman Team Building Model and Situational Leadership

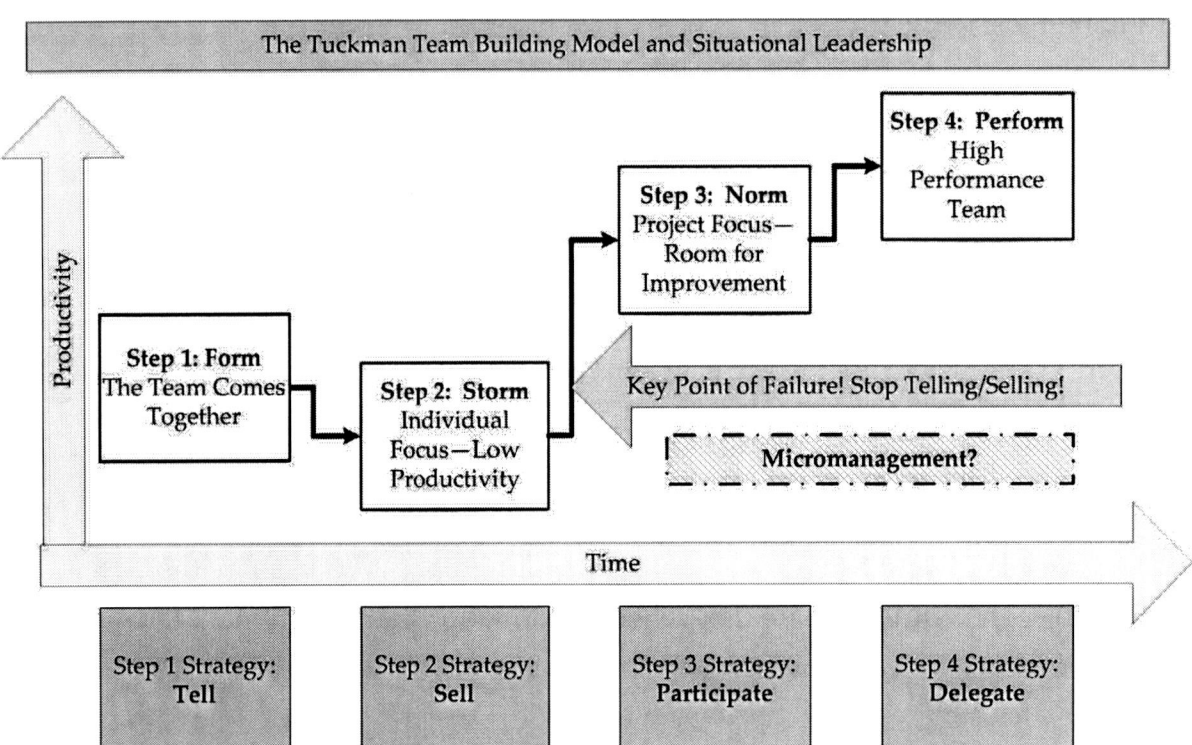

Now let's take a closer look at this model and share the story it tells. As you review the model, the Tuckman stages are labeled as Form, Storm, Norm, and Perform. The Tuckman model shows that productivity is relatively low during the Form stage, and lessens during the Storm stage. As a project manager, your goal is to get the team through the Form and Storm stages as quickly as possible to the Norm and Perform stages where productivity of the team is highest.

## Step 1: Form

During the Form stage the project team is coming together. The best strategy to employ to get people through the Form stage is to "Tell." In the Form stage, people have a need for task related information. You need to address the following questions:

- What is the project? Share the "What" details (Project Charter).
- Why should I care? Share the "Why" details (Business Case and/or Project Charter).
- Where do I fit? Share the roles and responsibilities of each project team member.

## Step 2: Storm

During the Storm stage productivity declines. Project team members begin focusing on what their personal involvement in the project means to them. They analyze the positives and negatives. Oftentimes, confidence is reduced and motivation is lacking. The best strategy to get people through the Storm stage is to "Sell." Here is where you reiterate key task information, and begin to build a relationship with the team member. Consider following these recommendations:

- Have a conversation with each team member. Try to determine if any of the "what and why" information you shared in the Form stage requires clarification or more context.

- Address the WII-FM questions. Let the team member know that they are needed and valued. Reassure and build relationships.

- Alex is a strong believer that celebrating successes as you progress in a project, no matter how small, is a great way to lift the team and keep them in the game. Alex's advice is spot on. Very often, people wait until the end of the project to say thank you. This is the wrong approach. You need to celebrate success along the way and avoid the "big-bang" theory of appreciation at the end. So the bottom line here, a thank you goes a long way in lifting people out of the storm.

## Step 3: Norm

During the Norm stage productivity increases. Project team members begin focusing on the work of the project. Trust is growing, teamwork is improving, and work is being accomplished. There is still room for improvement, but you are well on your way to success. The best strategy to employ during the Norm stage is to "Participate." Provide task related "what, why, and how" guidance only when needed. Concentrate on nurturing relationships you began to build during the Storm stage. Some tips for success:

- Provide support as needed. Let the team member know you are accessible.
- Reassure the team and maintain relationships. Applaud their successes.
- Address issues when they occur.
- **STOP** Selling and Telling

Review Figure 7.1 one more time. A key to moving the project team from the Storm to the Norm stage is to STOP selling and telling. I'm sure you have heard of the term micromanagement. Our model provides a compelling visual. Some project managers are constantly sharing their what, why, and how thoughts. This sharing is critical during the Form and Storm stages. However, the majority of project team members are most productive when they feel empowered to autonomously perform the work assigned to them.

As a project manager, you need to distance yourself and trust your team to do the work they were assigned. It is tempting to step in and try to convince the member to do things your way. However, there are many ways to complete an activity successfully. Empower the team member to take ownership, and your reward will be increased productivity, a more motivated workforce, and increased credibility as a leader. One final caveat—in the Norm phase you are best served to "Participate". This includes getting involved if something is going wrong. Sometimes it is difficult to determine when to step in. When in doubt, err on the side of the project team member. Peter, Alex and I have shared on so many occasions that project management is both an art and a science. You have just had some of the art shared with you in this section.

**Step 4: Perform**

During the Perform stage productivity is the highest. The project team is focused, confident, motivated, and excited to achieve results. The preferred strategy in this stage is to "Delegate". Stay out of the team's way, get involved only when necessary, and reap the benefits of a high performing team. Your primary job when the team is in the perform stage is to sustain the gain. Our tips are simple:

1. Address issues only when required.
2. Allow the team to be first point of conflict management and let them self-correct.
3. Keep your finger on the pulse.

<u>Note:</u> It takes time and energy to move a team from the Form to the Perform stage. In addition, it is difficult to keep the team there. It doesn't take much for the team, or an

individual team member to revert back to the Storm. In addition, different people often advance through the Tuckman Model at their own pace. You may have some members in Norm and Perform. However, there may still be a few members in the Storm. Project changes, personnel changes, insufficient communication, and failure to address issues are all reasons teams revert back to the Storm. Our third tip we shared to maintain the Perform stage is worth repeating: *keep your finger on the pulse.*

## The Staffing Management Plan

It is now time to revert back to the science. One of the key tools we highly recommend is a Staffing Management Plan. Figure 7.2 shows a condensed version of a Staffing Management Plan and RACI template. This simple spreadsheet allows you to define the required human resources based on where and when each work package occurs in the WBS and schedule.

### Figure 7.2 Staffing Management Plan and RACI Template

| Staffing Management Plan and RACI Template ||||||||||
|---|---|---|---|---|---|---|---|---|---|
| Code of Account Identifier | Role | Organization | On-Board | Release | Costs | R | A | C | I | Comments |
| 1.1.1 | | | | | | | | | | |
| 1.1.2 | | | | | | | | | | |
| 1.1.3 | | | | | | | | | | |
| 2.1.1 | | | | | | | | | | |
| 2.1.2 | | | | | | | | | | |
| 2.1.3 | | | | | | | | | | |

A Staffing Management Plan allows you to define the personnel you need when you need them. It is a great tool to use when working with Functional Managers to explain the specifics of who you need on your project team and when you need them.

- **Code of Account Identifier:** Account for every work package in your WBS. Determine project team requirements by work package.

- **Role:** Define roles needed to accomplish each work package. It is best to avoid by-name requests unless absolutely critical. It is best to share the need for a job type such as developer, tester, etc. Once a name is identified, you may want to document the name in the comments section of the plan.

- **Organization:** Some projects require human resources from multiple organizations or groups. When this is the case, define the applicable organization. For smaller projects, this entry may not be a requirement.

- **On-Board:** Define the approximate start date for the work package. Share the schedule with the Functional Manager, and later with the prospective project team member once designated. Let everyone know that you will inform them if any schedule changes occur that impact the original plan.

- **Release:** This is the date you expect the work package to be completed. Once again, let everyone know that you will inform them if any schedule changes occur.

- **Costs:** Assign any costs as applicable for the human resources you will need. In many cases, you will not be charged for the use of internal personnel. However, this possibility exists. If the personnel you need are from external sources, they will not be free. You need to calculate the cost for these resources and ensure they are covered in the project budget.

- **RACI:** We defined RACI criteria in Chapter 2. It is worth a quick review. Assign each team member a role. Those who are Accountable and Responsible will have a higher level of involvement than those who are Consulted or Informed.

| RACI Terms Defined | | |
|---|---|---|
| | R | Responsible for doing work on the project |
| | A | Accountable for outcomes |
| | C | Consult as Subject Matter Expert |
| | I | Inform as the project progresses |

- **Comments:** Share any clarifying comments applicable to ensure everyone has the level of understanding they need to support the staffing needs of the project.

<u>Notes:</u> Here are a few additional considerations regarding the Staffing Management Plan.

1. This plan will change as the project evolves. Update the plan as required, and share changes with all impacted stakeholders.

2. Consider requesting resources by phase if the project duration is long. As the saying goes, ""The best laid plans of mice and men often go awry."[19] Try to gain hard commitments for the personnel you need when the project kicks off. Share the long-term schedule, but don't worry about locking in actual personnel until the project nears that phase.

3. Remember that Functional Managers have a job to do. Sharing their resources can be difficult. Build a relationship with the Functional Managers and work with them to find a win-win solution. You may have the authority to reach out for the human resources you need. This is the science of project management. However, people skills are still needed. This is the art piece.

4. Some project managers like to develop a Responsibilities Assignment Matrix (RAM) for each work package. The RAM supplements the RACI, and drills down on actual responsibility, execution, and approval requirements. Figure 7.3 provides an example of a RAM to support Work Package 1.1.3 we used to share the WBS format in Chapter 3 (See Figure 3.7). The RAM normally is added to the WBS Dictionary that supports the work package.

---

[19] *Of Mice and Men*, John Steinbeck

**Figure 7.3 Responsibility Assignment Matrix (RAM) Example**

| Responsibility Assignment Matrix (RAM) Work Package: 1.1.3 Develop Initial Process Maps | | | | | |
|---|---|---|---|---|---|
| Activity/Group | PM | Customer | Dev Team | Test Team | Vendor |
| Define Outputs | E | C | | | |
| Define Suppliers | E | | C | | |
| Develop Initial Maps | A | | C | | E |
| Validate Process | C | C | C | E | C |
| Finalize Initial Maps | A | C | | C | E |
| | | | | | |

| Legend |
|---|
| A: Approval Required |
| E: Execute |
| C: Consult With |

*Alex's Project Management Tip: Create and post an organizational chart for the team and post it on the wall. This action will provide a great visual to supplement your RACI and/or RAM, and also serve as a means of reminding stakeholders that they play an vital role in the success of the project.*

## Project Human Resource Management: Final Thoughts

Effectively managing the project team is one of the most challenging aspects of project management. Here are some final tips to help you succeed in this area.

- **Issues Management:** Issues are defined in many ways. One definition is a risk that has occurred. These types of issues need to be documented and addressed. We will share much more in Chapter 9 on this subject. A second type of issue, however, impacts the individual team members. These issues are defined as questions or problems impacting team members that may prevent the project from progressing successfully. These are issues you don't advertise, but must give the highest priority.

    o Use MBWAT. This acronym stands for "Management by Walking and Talking." Meet with all project team members on a periodic basis. Ask them how they are doing. Build that relationship of mutaul trust, respect, and empathy.

    o There may be times when a project team member is not able to satisfy the needs of the project. When this occurs, try to help the individual succeed to the greatest extent you can. Provide training, find others who can assist, and give the individual every chance to stay with the project. If all fails, however, you may need to ask the Functional Manager for a replacement project team member. When this occurs, try to minimize to the greatest extent possible the number of people who are aware of the situation.

    o If you read the *Project Management Body of Knowledge*, 5th Edition, it discusses the need for "Issue Logs" to help manage the project team. There are two Issue Logs you need to develop. The first is the one you share. These are risks that have occurred and are now classified as issues. The second is the one you don't share. These logs are used to track personnel issues and not meant for wide distribution. When issues occur, address them immediately.

- **Satisfy the Needs of the Project Team Member:** Always remember that the people working on your project are human beings. While you may not be able to accommodate all their wishes, there are certain things you should strive for.

- o Put the "square peg in the square hole." Whenever possible and practical, try to assign people to work that motivates them. We share an Emergenetics model in Chapter 10 that shows how different people have different motivations and work preferences. Models such as Emergenetics and others are very helpful in allowing us to place team members in jobs where they are best suited when the project allows for it.

- o Allow team members to grow their skill set. Many people are motivated by learning new things. Where possible, allow the team members to practice and expand their skills. We talked earlier about David McClelland's Three Needs Theory. People are motivated by achievement, and when they feel empowered to share new ideas and grow.

- o Celebrate successes. Every project has its good days and bad days. Whenever possible, celebrate successes. Provide kudos when they are warranted. Use the two most powerful words you possess as a project manager: "thank you."

- o Don't be afraid to have fun. Another quote that is so true is, "All work and no play makes Jack a dull boy."[20] Try to find times when you can enjoy the company of the people on your project team. Simple things such as celebrating a birthday, doing some non-work activities, etc. go a long way in building a team.

## Managing the "Virtual Team"

Managing a virtual team increases the human resource management level of complexity. There are a number of major challenges you will face. The most common challenges include:

- **Culture:** People from different cultures have values, religious beliefs, work ethics, etc. that may not match yours. There is another old saying, "When in Rome, do as the Romans."[21] This is true for managing cultural differences as well.

---

[20] James Howell Proverbs, 1659
[21] Ambrose

- For starters, learn as much as you can about the culture of your virtual team members BEFORE you begin communicating and planning.

- Second, try to adapt to the cultural norms of the team whenever possible. If not possible, let them know why.

- **Technology:** Technology challenges are many. As the project manager, you are accountable to ensure all stakeholders get the right information in the right amounts at the right time. Here are three key tips:

    - First, ensure the technology you want to use is available. If it is not, change media or provide it.

    - Second, ensure the technology is suitable for all. Do not require team members to use systems that they are not familiar with until they can be trained.

    - Finally, consider sensitivity and confidentiality. Determine the security requirements of your project before you deploy the communications plan.

- **Time Zones and Distance:** Time zones limit availability of team members. For example, most New York team members will begin work three hours before Seattle team members arrive. In addition, the New York team members will depart three hours before the Seattle members. If working hours are 9:00 am to 5:00 pm, you effectively have a 5-hour window between 12:00 pm and 5:00 pm EST where the New York and Seattle team members are available during normal work hours. Distance is also a challenge. Trying to arrange times for face-to-face meets is difficult at best. And the technological choices are limited.

    - It is important to try to leverage technologies such as Skype, Lync, ClearSlide, etc. to ensure the maximum amount of face-to-face and voice recognition time. The Tuckman Model is very difficult to negotiate through other media such as email.

    - In addition, try to share the pain. Periodically require BOTH the Seattle and New York teams to participate in meetings, calls, etc. during their off hours if necessary.

If possible, (dependent on funding, priority of project, number of virtual members, etc.) try to plan at least one event where everyone can meet physically in the same place.

- **Scheduling Factors:** There are a number of additional factors you must consider based on geographical factors. In many countries, holidays fall on different days of the year. For example, there are many holidays celebrated in India that are not celebrated in North America and vice versa. In addition, illness may play a factor as well. Influenza, viruses, etc. often localize in a given part of the world. The more virtual team members you have, the greater potential there is for your project to be impacted. Some tips:

  o Try to develop a calendar that clearly shows all holidays, non-working time, etc. so the project team can plan accordingly.

  o Add time buffers when possible for potential illness issues, especially during prime illness months in winter.

## The Team Charter[22]

The best teams are those that thoughtfully and thoroughly discuss and agree on goals and norms early in a project. A Team Charter is a set of expectations with which everyone on the team agrees. You can also think of a Team Charter as an operating agreement on which everyone has signed off. Not every team needs a Team Charter. It is important to note that a Team Charter does *not* replace a Project Charter. However, if you believe a Team Charter will add value, there are six key areas to address. Figure 7.4 outlines these six areas.

### Figure 7.4 Team Charter Format

| Team Charter Category | Expectations |
|---|---|
| Meeting Norms | Expectations include when, where, and how often to meet. What is expected of members with regard to attendance, timeliness, and preparation? In general, how should meetings be conducted (will there always be an agenda? Is there an appointed meeting leader or project manager?) |

---

[22] Adapted from Washington University

| | |
|---|---|
| **Working Norms** | Expectations involve standards, deadlines, how equally effort and work should be distributed, and how work will be reviewed. Expectations also include how to ensure adequate listening and support and how differences of opinion or decision gridlock will be handled |
| **Leadership Norms** | Expectations include whether a team leader is needed, if leadership is rotated, distribution of leadership and responsibilities (e.g., project manager, facilitator, etc.), and how to keep the leader from doing all the work (or not doing enough of the real work) |
| **Communications Norms** | Expectations center on when communication should take place, who is responsible for ensuring effective communication occurs, what the main mediums of communication should be (phone, email, ClearSlide, etc.), and how to discuss feelings about the team or its members. Coordinate this with the Project Communications Plan |

| Team Charter Category Continued | Expectations |
|---|---|
| **Consideration Norms** | Expectations center on being considerate of members' comfort with things such as, swearing, humor, etc., and the ability to change norms if members are uncomfortable with what is going on in the team |
| **Continuous Improvement Norms** | Expectations revolve around the protocol (e.g. frequency of discussion, problem identification procedures) for addressing group performance issues. Examples of issues include the following: Are team goals being met? Why or why not? Are individuals able to meet their own individual goals within the context of the team? What works and what doesn't work about team structure? How effectively do we make decisions and resolve conflict? |

> *Project Management Tip: Team Charters do not need to be part of the formal Project Management Plan. They are generally developed and approved internally by the team. You may want to generate a Team Charter that includes management norms and seek their approval of the document and expectations included within.*

## Chapter 7 Summary

This was a relatively short chapter. However, it is a very important one. Managing human resources, in particular the project team, requires all the skills a project manager has in his or her tool box. We shared the Tuckman Model for developing a team. Remember that a one size fits all leadership style will only yield partial results. As a project manager, you need to determine the needs of your team, and manage appropriately.

We shared a "simple and effective" Staffing Management Plan that you can use to share which human resources you need, when you need them, and what the roles and responsibilities entail. This is great planning document that will change as the project evolves. Share this with key stakeholders, Functional Managers, and collaborate with them to ensure you have the right people on the bus at the right time. We shared a few of the challenges of managing virtual teams. We will revisit this topic in chapters that follow. We also introduced a new tool for your toolbox—The Team Charter.

Chapter 8 is an exciting chapter that discusses your number one challenge as a project manager; communicating effectively. But before we begin, we can't leave this chapter without a trip to Peter's Corner to gain his insight. And finally, a little food for thought that we'd like you to consider when reflecting on the critical aspects of project human resource management.

> *Project Management Tip:*
> *Take care of your team, and*
> *they will take care of you.*

## Peter's Corner:  Chapter 7 Edition

People build and deliver deliverables, not processes and tools.  People are not robots.  People have emotions, feelings, and egos.

Why I am reminding you of these things?  Because most project managers live in their heads, not in their hearts.  Because most project managers are not aware of team members' feelings and attitudes.  They may not even be aware of their own feelings and attitudes – they and their team members are unaware robots trudging through the project as best they can.  What a miserable situation!  So much lost opportunity and unrealized potential.

To avoid the foregoing situation, Dan, Alex and I have brought Emotional Intelligence (EQ) into all the projects and project teams we coach.  Briefly, EQ is about becoming self-aware and socially awar, and being able to manage one's own self as well as relationships with others, such as a project team.  It is about aligning your intentions with your behaviors and actions.  It is also about sensing others and using these cues to move the agenda and relationship where you (and the project) want it to go.

EQ is very powerful, and a detailed tutorial is beyond the scope of this book.  We recommend that you pick up Emotional Intelligence 2.0 by Jean Greaves and Travis Bradberry[23].  Read it and use it.  It will have a huge positive impact on your ability to develop relationships and influence people to do what the project needs from them.  It will also help you to move the project team more quickly to the Perform stage.  The Emotional Intelligence Model is provided for your reference in Figure 7.5.  We do, however, want to share this model with you at an introductory level.

One more thought – the conversations that aren't being had are critical. The most obvious example of this is the "elephant in the room" that no one is brave enough to talk about.  Your job is to assure that the elephant is revealed and discussed.  This is easy compared to sensing and teasing out the subtle "background conversations" that go on in everyone's minds.  Some of these are important to the project and the health of the project team.  Your job is to sense these and bring them out.  EQ will help you to do this – but you will need more – you will need to be VERY AWARE, and be willing and able to act on what you sense.  Good luck!  The journey will be well worth it in both your project and your life.

---

[23] *Emotional Intelligence 2.0*, Bradberry and Greaves

The EQ model contains four areas that every project manager needs to attempt to master. To share Alex's thoughts, "Project managers are responsible for the environment—building trust, encouraging healthy conflict, ensuring commitment, holding people responsible, and getting results." [24] These five areas are highlighted in Patrick Lencioni's *Five Dysfunctions of a Team* as key success factors.

To improve your ability in the four EQ skills, you need to understand each skill and what it looks like in action.

## Figure 7.5 Emotional Intelligence (EQ) Model

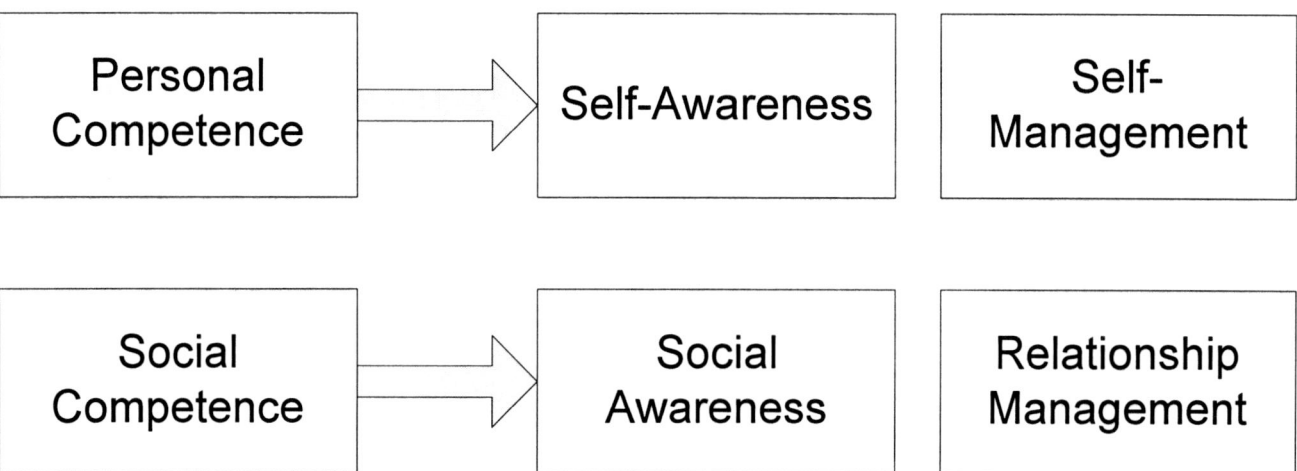

These are the four skills that comprise EQ. Personal Competence skills are more about you. Social Competence skills are more about how you interact with other people.

- **Self-Awareness** is an understanding of you. What drives you, what frustrates you, and how do you react in certain situations?

- **Self-Management** builds on self-awareness. Once you know yourself, how can you control your actions and reactions in a manner that best serves you?

- **Social Awareness** is dependent upon achieving Personal Competence. Once you are able to manage yourself, you are better able to view the world around you without blinders.

---

[24] *Five Dysfunctions of a Team*, Lencioni

- **Relationship Management** is the ultimate goal of the EQ model. All three skills we discussed allow you to better build and maintain those relationships that are critical to your success as a project manager, and in life.

To reiterate, buy the book and learn as much as you can. We've only touched the surface of a very deep and fruitful concept. Successful project managers generally possess high degrees of EQ. See an important definition from Alex below.[25]

> *Alex's Word of the Day: Equanimity*
>
> *Great project managers practice equanimity. This is the art of maintaining mental calmness, composure, and evenness of temper, especially in difficult situations.*

---

[25] Oxford University Press

## Chapter 7 Food for Thought

1. Review the Tuckman model. Can you think of a time when a team you were a part of was in the "Storm" phase? Describe the actions of the people during that time.

2. Refer back to question 1. What measures were taken to move the team from "Storm" to "Norm?" What worked? What didn't work? In retrospect, can you think of anything that could have been done differently?

3. Describe a leader you would classify as a "Micromanager." How did he/she manage? How did other workers react to his/her "Micromanager" tendencies?

4. Now describe a leader who was effective? What made this leader effective? How did workers react to his/her leadership methods?

5. A project manager shared that they think development of a Staffing Management Plan is a waste of time? Do you agree with their assessment? Why? Do you disagree with their assessment? Why?

6. What are some challenges you experienced managing virtual teams? How did you address these challenges? What worked and what didn't?

7. How do you maintain your equanimity?

8. Peter's Deep Thought Challenges:

*Reflections*

A Functional Manager will not provide a key human resource when needed by the project. What options would you consider to resolve this issue, and under what circumstances? (Hint: Think about the Project Manager's Triangle, or the Project Charter, or WII-FM, or ..., be creative and think of scenarios and possibilities.)

**Note:** A great project manager must possess many skills, including critical and strategic thinking, collaboration, negotiation, influencing, and several more. Take an inventory of your soft skills and continue to hone these skills. We can never be too good at anything.

# Chapter 8: Project Communications: The 90% Rule

We now turn our attention to the "glue that holds the project together." Effective communications is arguably the most challenging aspect of a project manager's job. Problem #9, as shared in Chapter 1, stated that "Poor Communications Management and Team Dynamics" are major causes of project failure. We address these causes in this chapter. PMI [26] states that most project managers spend 90% of their time on communications related activities. For most this is a very sobering statement--ignore or deny it at your peril.

Figure 8.1 provides a common Communications Model. It illustrates the communications challenges a project manager faces every day.

## Figure 8.1 Communications Model

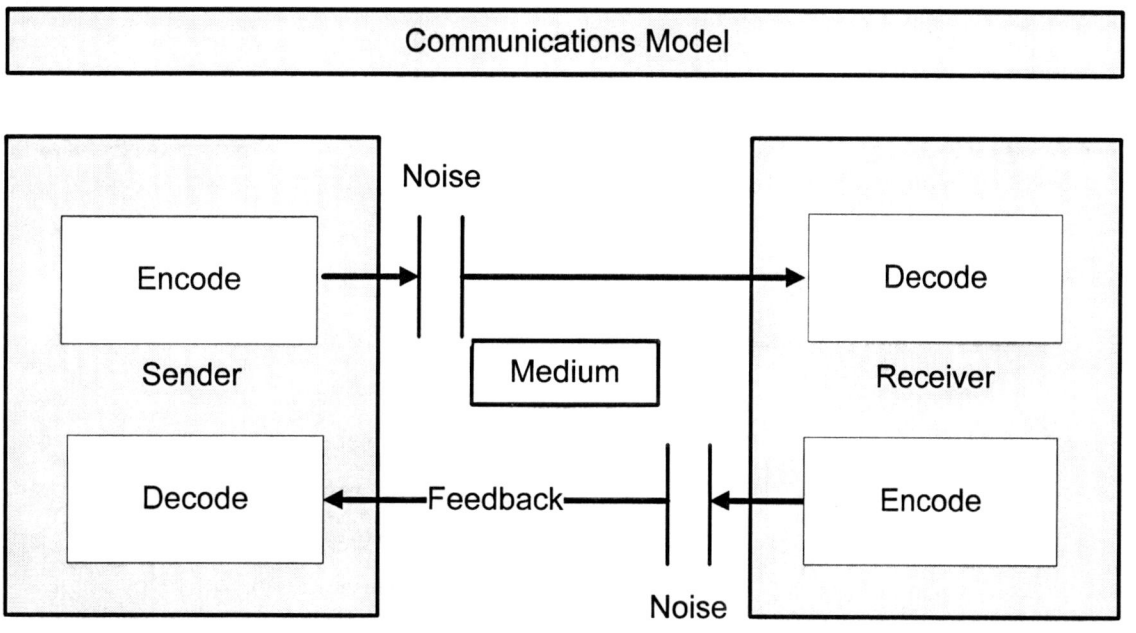

---

[26] *Project Management Body of Knowledge ®*, Fifth Edition

Let's take a moment to review the many challenges this model poses that the project manager needs to consider. Effective communications is one aspect of project management you really want to get right.

1. **Sender Encode:** As a project manager, you need to encode your communications in a manner that will be understood by the receiver. You need to determine the audience for your communications. Next, you should analyze the receiver's level of knowledge. Finally, determine how to best present your message in a way that will be understand. Many project managers encode communications in a manner that works for them, but may not resonate with the receiver. Empathy is in play here. Put yourself in the shoes of the receiver and ask yourself, *What would work for them?*

2. **Medium:** The medium is "how" you will communicate. In some models, it is referred to as the "communications channel." Many project managers are dependent upon email as their primary medium. And the good news? Sometimes it works. But the bad news? Sometimes it doesn't. Get to know your key stakeholders and try to determine the medium that works best for them. Some stakeholders may not be receptive to email but have no issues using chat technology. Others may prefer periodic face-to-face visits. Someone; often attributed to Ben Franklin, Albert Einstein, or Mark Twain—who knows -- defined insanity as, "doing the same thing over and over again and expecting a different result." You may think this quote is overused, but it applies here. If you send two or three emails and get no response, does it really make sense to send a fourth?

3. **Receiver Decode:** We send the communication to the receiver. Should we assume they will stop what they are doing immediately to read and respond? Likely not. If your message is that important, follow through with the receiver to ensure the message sent was the message received. A good rule of thumb is to use a medium that differs from the original medium you used. For example, if you reached out by email, engage the stakeholder by telephone to ensure they received the communications, that they understand it, and that they are willing to respond. Don't assume that they "got it."

4. **Receiver Encode:** Let the receiver of the message know if and when a reply is required. Oftentimes, it is best to spell out the response expectations in the email, letter, memo, etc. up front. Try to be reasonable when establishing reply deadlines. In most cases, the receiver has other things to do.

5. **Sender Decode and Feedback**: Feedback may sometimes state disagreement with your goals and objectives. Try not to take negative feedback personally. All feedback is a gift. Review the response. Did the receiver address your issue or question? Is the response satisfactory? If there is disagreement, or the receiver missed the point in their reply, set up a follow-up meeting. When this is the case, face-to-face is the richest form of communications and highly recommended. If distance or schedules are an issue, use a medium such as Skype or ClearSlide—or whatever works for you that results in synchronous (real-time) communication.

6. **Noise:** The communications model with the five above components is challenging enough. However, we are about to increase the complexity of effective communications. Noise factors, sometimes referred to as "communications blockers" are additional realities that can limit the effectiveness of your communications. Typical noise factors include distance, culture, language, time zones, timing, attitude, and more. Think about these noise factors as potential risks that can impact your communications negatively. Before you attempt to communicate, mitigate any potential noise factors.

## Why Plan for Communications: The Grapevine Effect

I can assume (I know that is dangerous☺) that most of you are aware of the "Grapevine." Children sometimes play a "Grapevine" game called "Telephone." I am continually amazed by the number of project managers who look upon communications as a waste of time. There are hundreds of trite little sayings in project management and here's one more to add to the list. "You can manage communications or communications will manage you." Trite? Probably. True? Definitely!

Figure 8.2 provides a visual of the Grapevine. Hopefully, we can inspire you to put some time and effort into your communications planning after we share this visual.

# Figure 8.2 Grapevine Visual

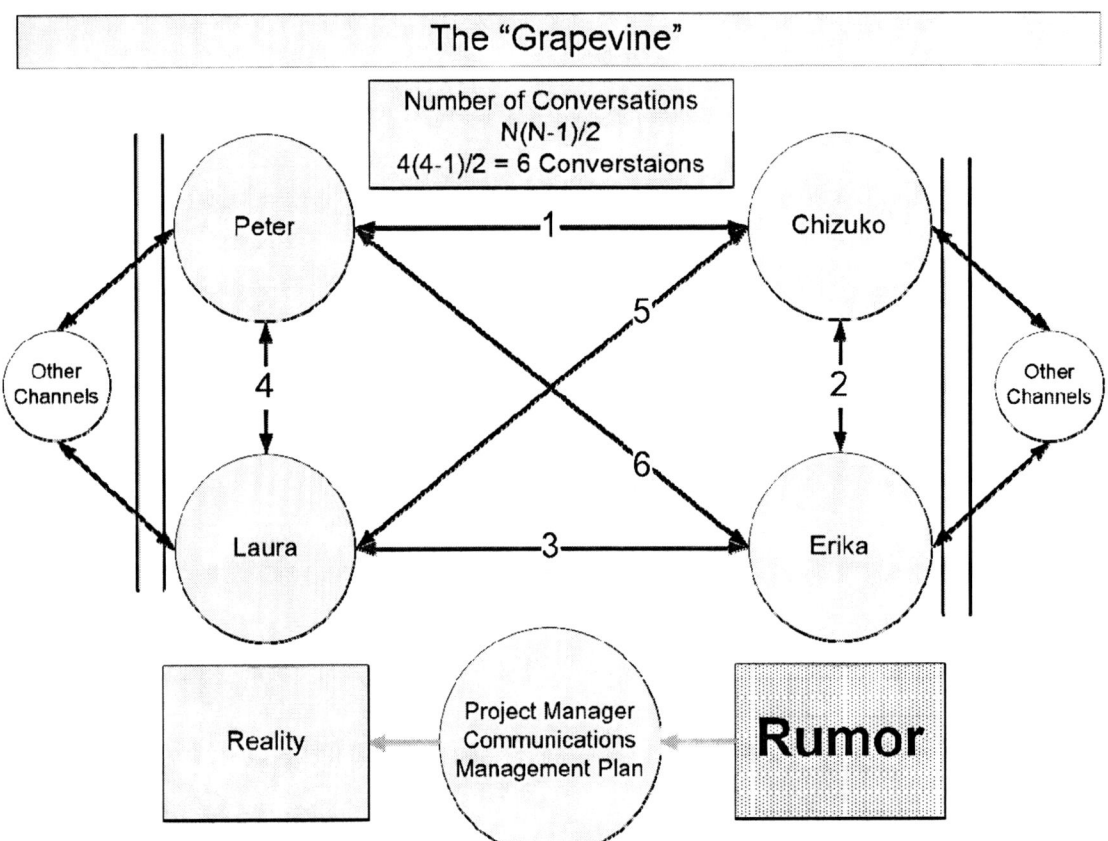

Welcome to the Grapevine. In this scenario, we have a small project team comprised of four individuals. Peter, Laura, Chizuko, and Erika discuss the project internally on a daily basis. In addition, each of these four project team members discusses their project and other topics with others in external communications channels as well.

As a project manager, you need to ensure that the project team has accurate information. The Communications Management Plan, and execution of the plan, ensures that your project team understands the reality of the project. Without a solid Communications Management Plan, there is no assurance that the project team will understand the reality of the project. If the reality of the project is not shared by the project manager, then the project team will create its own version of reality, oftentimes through the creation of rumors. Here is a worthy quote from Peter. "In the absence of information, people will always fill in the gaps and create their own version of reality. People have a strong preference for black or white (certainty or clarity) as opposed to grey (uncertainty or ambiguity)".

You may have noted we shared a simple algebraic equation in our expression of the Grapevine. There are four people on our imaginary project team. The potential exists for six rumors within the group assuming that each project team member talks with all other team members. We can explain the math:

- The number of team members = 4
- Multiply 4 times 3 (the number of team members minus 1). This is $(4 - 1) = 4 \times 3 = 12$
- Divide this result by two. $12/2 = 6$.

This is a mathematical way to determine the number of rumors you may have to kill if you choose not to use a Communications Management Plan.

Imagine you have a project team with 10 people. Applying the math: $10(10 - 1)/2 = 45$ potential rumors. Ouch! Imagine the time and effort to squelch 45 rumors. Let's revisit our trite little saying we shared earlier, ""You can manage communications or communications will manage you."

**Note:** If you wish to pursue project management certification through PMI, you will want to know how to calculate the number of conversations a project team may have. These conversations are referred to as "Communications Channels" by PMI.

## The Communications Management Plan

We are now ready to share a very critical project management tool and technique, the Communications Management Plan. First, we will share a template that Peter, Alex and I developed many years ago that is "simple and effective." We'll then share key communications activities and appendices we highly encourage be part of the plan. We'll close this chapter with an extension of the Communications Management Plan that you as the project manager may use to recognize communications challenges and address strategies to overcome them.

Figure 8.3 provides a template of a standard Communications Management Plan. This is a document that can easily be created using a word processing or spreadsheet software application. As yet another reminder, this template is available to you at www.p17group.com.

## Figure 8.3 Communications Management Plan Template

| Communications Management Plan for Project: (List Project Name) | | | | | |
|---|---|---|---|---|---|
| Communications Item (What) | Owner (Who-Sender) | Audience (Who-Receiver) | Timing (When) | Medium (How) | Purpose (Why) |
|  |  |  |  |  |  |
|  |  |  |  |  |  |
|  |  |  |  |  |  |
|  |  |  |  |  |  |
|  |  |  |  |  |  |
|  |  |  |  |  |  |
|  |  |  |  |  |  |
| Version: | | | Date: | | |

Creation of a Communications Management Plan is not difficult and the contents of the plan are relatively straight forward. Here is a quick overview.

- **Project:** Each project should have a distinct project plan. While many projects are alike, each project has some unique property that distinguishes it from others. There may be times when you want to develop a Communications Management Plan for a program. Good news—this template works quite well for a program as well. Just change the header on the top of the plan.

- **Communications Item:** (The "What" Factor) Apply "KISS" here: Keep It Short and Sweet. Use common and relevant designators to describe the specific communications you plan to implement. Terms such as status report, sponsor one-on-one, etc. work well here.

- **Owner:** (A "Who" Factor) Define who is responsible for managing the communications item. For a small project, this will likely be the project manager. For a large project, however, you may have the luxury of having a project management team. If this is the case, assign a project management team member who may be best suited to manage the particular communications item.

- **Audience:** (A second "Who" factor) It's time to break a common paradigm. Every project stakeholder DOES NOT need to receive every project communication. This part of the plan is critical. Try to determine who truly needs to receive the information you are providing. We shared the official definition of a stakeholder is anyone who is either "interested or impacted" by the project. If the communications you are performing does not satisfy either of this criteria—don't share it. An old adage in effective communications is—"send the right information to the right people at the right time". Determine who the "right" people are. Use the RACI presented previously in Chapter 2 to help you determine who should get what communications.

- **Timing:** (The "When" Factor) Many project managers use the "random" method of communications. They send out information when the timing is right for them. As a clarifier before we begin, there will be times when you have to share unplanned communications. However, the majority of communications activities should be planned and scheduled. Use the timing section to create a "Rhythm of the Project." Establish set times for key communications activities that stakeholders can plan for and come to rely on. For example, you may schedule the Change Control Board every second Thursday at 1:00 PM. Or perhaps, you may send out the weekly project status report every Friday afternoon. The project manager needs to establish expectations and be consistent. Stakeholders will appreciate this consistency, and in all likelihood, their engagement in the project will be sustained or improve.

- **Medium:** (The "How" Factor) We discussed project manager overuse of email as a primary medium earlier. Sometimes, email works great. However, you need to consider other mediums when planning communications. Try to plan for the most practical method to obtain the best results. For problem-solving sessions, face-to-face is optimal. There are times to have meetings, and times not to have them. (More on this later in the book.) There may be times when you need a voice medium to discuss complex issues. Choose the medium that best suits your specific communications goals.

- **Purpose:** (The "Why" Factor) We mentioned earlier that you should only communicate with the people who need it. Unfortunately, there are some project stakeholders who need to be communicated with who may not see the need for the communications. A project manager needs to be a sales professional at times. You need to convince stakeholders that certain communications are important and provide a value proposition. Explain why the stakeholder should care. Remember WII-FM.

- **Version and Date:** The communications required to keep a project moving in the right direction will change as the progress progresses. It is important to update the Communications Management Plan as the communications needs of the project change, and share these changes with the affected stakeholders. Keep the plan updated, let stakeholders know what the current plan version is, and communicate these updates.

## Communications Management Plan: Key Success Factors

The effective development and implementation of the Communications Management Plan is critical. Numerous articles have been written that point to ineffective communications as a key reason why projects fail. Here are a few key success factors to remember as you develop and execute the Communications Management Plan.

- **Plan Development:** Develop the plan as a team. Let project team members know ahead of time if you need them to own parts of the plan. Don't catch them by surprise.

- **Pre-Coordination:** Have the "Meeting before the Meeting." Let stakeholders know what the expectations are for them. If possible, try to determine the timing and media that is most convenient for them if you have that choice. In addition, the time to "sell" the plan is before you officially submit it to the project's stakeholders. This holds true for updates as well. If you change something, pre-coordinate the change before you finalize the new version. Don't assume buy-in and commitment.

- **Sharing:** Ensure the finalized plan is available for all stakeholders to review on a 24/7 basis. Let stakeholders know where the plan resides, and ensure they have the appropriate permissions (if applicable) to review it.

- **Check In:** Periodically check in with key stakeholders to ensure the plan is working for them. Stakeholder situations change—be willing to flex with those changes. Ensure that you are providing the right amount of information to the right people at the right time.

- **Maintain the Plan:** This is worth repeating. Keep the plan up to date. When versions change, immediately let all affected stakeholders know of the changes.

## What to Communicate

There are many communications activities that are critical to a project success. The extent of your activities will be determined by multiple factors to include criticality of the project, virtual team members, size of the organization, etc. Figure 8.4 provides a long list of potential communications activities that may or may not be pertinent to your project. We also share best practices in terms of mediums and frequency.

### Figure 8.4 Potential Project Communications Activities

| Communications Activity | Recommended Frequency | Recommended Medium | Clarifying Comments |
|---|---|---|---|
| Change Control Board (CCB) | Every Two Weeks | Face to Face, Skype, ClearSlide, etc. | Meet with Sponsor and leadership team to discuss proposed changes that will impact the approved project baseline |
| Customer/User Acceptance | End of Phase | Face to Face, Skype, ClearSlide, etc. | Meet periodically with the customer to share progress as you complete key project phases. Use this meet to gain acceptance and/or course correct |
| Incentives | End of Phase | Face to Face, Skype, ClearSlide, etc. | Find a time to say "thank you." Recognize those stakeholders who contributed to success. May accomplish this in conjunction with team building |

| Communications Activity | Recommended Frequency | Recommended Medium | Clarifying Comments |
|---|---|---|---|
| Lessons Learned | End of Phase | Face to Face, Skype, ClearSlide, etc. | Share and document what went well, what can be improved, and ideas to improve. Capture these ideas for improved performance on current and future projects |
| Portfolio/Program Support | Monthly | Face to Face, Skype, ClearSlide, etc. | Provide status of your project as it impacts the Portfolio and Program. Determine if any Portfolio or Program changes occurred that may impact your project |
| Sponsor One-on-One | Weekly | Face to Face | Discuss key project issues, changes, escalations, etc. May elect an every other week cadence if applicable. If face-to-face is not feasible, choose a media where voice and visual is possible |
| Status Reporting | Weekly | Email | Determine process and timing for status reporting. Includes time, cost, scope, and risk status. More on this subject in Chapter 11 |
| Status Meeting | Weekly | Face to Face, Skype, ClearSlide, etc. | Meet with key stakeholders to define project status. May shift to an every other week schedule if applicable |
| Team Building | Monthly | Face to Face, Skype, ClearSlide, etc. | Find non-work activities to bring the team together. Remember the Tuckman Model? Team building is not a frivolous activity |
| Vendor Meeting | As Required | Face to Face, Skype, ClearSlide, etc. | Establish a rhythm to meet with vendors assigned to the project to discuss status, issues, etc. |

## Project Communications Plan Appendices

Here are some additional appendices you may need to consider including in your Communications Management Plan as applicable.

- **Change Management Process**: Recall Chapter 6. Your end to end change management process to include the Project Change Log, standard Change Request Form, and clarifying instructions should be housed in the Communications Management Plan.

- **Glossary of Terms**: Every project is unique. Include any specific terminology, definitions, acronyms, etc. that will be commonly used in project communications. A very common status reporting methodology is the green, yellow, red or "traffic light" reporting system. We discuss this more in Chapter 11. Definitions of these status indicators should be included.

- **Escalation Management:** You may wish to provide a method to effectively escalate issues. In a large project with multiple stakeholders, an established hierarchy may very well eliminate confusion.

- **Constraints:** Some plans feature an overview of constraints—those factors that limit what you may or may not do. Applicable standards, regulations, boundaries etc. that impact the project must be shared.

## Overcoming Communications Issues: The Communications Management Plan "Plus"

Not everyone will be on board and support the needs of the project's communications. There are many reasons for this situation. Our final section provides an extension of the Communications Management Plan you can use to identify existing or potential communication challenges and develop strategies to overcome them.

### Figure 8.5 Communications Management Plan Plus

This revised version of the standard Communications Management Plan includes two new columns. We will share the what and why behind these two columns after we share the plan template.

...gement Made Simple and Effective

| Communications Item | Owner | Audience | Timing | Medium | Purpose | Challenge | Strategy |
|---|---|---|---|---|---|---|---|
| | | | | | | | |
| | | | | | | | |
| | | | | | | | |
| | | | | | | | |

Communications Management Plan Plus

The Communications Management Plan Plus is a simple extension of the standard plan we shared earlier. There are two additional columns added. Use this plan for you and your team to determine what is working, what is not working, and determine strategies to overcome what is not working. Here are a few additional thoughts:

- **Distribution:** Do not share this "Plus" version of the Communications Management Plan with stakeholders. This is a tool you and your team use internally to identify and address communications risks and issues.

- **As Required:** Not all communications items will have challenges to overcome. When that is the case, there is no need for an entry.

- **Addressing the Challenge—Step One:** The first step the owner should take if a challenge develops is to try to meet face-to-face with the stakeholder presenting the challenge. The majority of challenges are often quite simple to resolve. They may occur based on lack of understanding, timing that is not convenient, or a medium that doesn't address the communications need. A simple tweak often eliminates the majority of challenges. (Recall our Communications Model and "Grapevine" at the beginning of this chapter.)

- **Escalations:** There may be times when a stakeholder simply cannot or refuses to support the communications need of the plan. When this is the case, you may need to escalate the issue to a Functional Manager or a Sponsor for resolution. Before you escalate, you may want to ask the unsupportive stakeholder for their thoughts on resolving the issue. Work with them to resolve the issue, and let them know that you may have to escalate the issue before you do so. There is an old adage I learned from a crusty Sergeant many years ago: "Praise in public, punish in private." Handle non-supporters professionally. There may be a legitimate reason why they cannot support the project - don't "burn your bridges".

- **Incentives:** One final thought. A project manager has a number of power sources they can use to address challenges and issues. Reward power is at the top of the list in terms of effectiveness and value. Thank the stakeholders who are supporting the project as often as possible for their inputs. This will go a long way in setting a positive example for all stakeholders, and possibly sway some of the non-supporters to comply.

## Chapter 8 Summary

We covered a lot of ground in this chapter. The Communications Model highlights the challenges of effective communications and expresses how easily the project's stakeholders may create their own versions of the realities of the project. If the project manager does not consistently share the reality of what is happening on the project, rumors will develop and impact the project negatively. The key to success is simple—develop a Communications Management Plan and use it.

Update the plan to reflect the realities of the project as it progresses. Don't assume everything will work as planned and documented. Proactively look for challenges, and develop win-win strategies to overcome them. Communications is 90% of your job—you've got to get this right.

In our previous chapter we discussed a few of the many challenges in managing virtual teams. The Communications Management Plan is a key tool to ensure you keep everyone moving in the right direction. Despite your best efforts, there will be times when all stakeholders do not comply with the project planning. When that occurs, you need to take action sooner than later.

We will now move our focus in Chapter 9 to project risk management. Peter has some thoughts to share; we have some food for thought for you to ponder, and then it's time for risk.

# Peter's Corner: Chapter 8 Edition

Communications is 90% of project management. There, we said it again. This is *huge*! So let's explore a few more ways to significantly improve project communications.

Each of us has beliefs and mental models. We have been conditioned over the years to think, behave, act, and *listen* in certain predictable ways. This is unfortunate when it comes to communications. Why? Because our beliefs, mental models, and conditioning cause us to be poor listeners.

Let's take an example. There is a key stakeholder on your project who is a "naysayer" – she is not only unsupportive, she is going around bad-mouthing your project. Huge damage! You are angry. But you are a non-confrontational type. So you ignore this naysayer. Bad decision! One naysayer can do more damage than seven supporters.

So you rally your courage, come up with all the reasons you are right, and then go to battle. You engage the naysayer, the battle roars on with each fighting bravely from their hardened positions. It ends in a stalemate. Each of you leaves even more hardened in their positions, anticipating Round 2.

You reflect on what went wrong in Round 1. You develop a new approach for Round 2. You want this to be the final Round as this is exhausting and you have many other project activities you must do.

In Round 2 you totally surprise the naysayer. You ask open-ended questions and LISTEN DEEPLY. This means that you *temporarily suspend your beliefs, mental modes, and conditioning*, as well as everything you hold to be true about the project. Be *totally present* – look the naysayer in the eye (face-to-face is ideal); mute your "background conversations"; and easiest of all, lose your smartphone, computer, and all other distractions. I am willing to bet that the naysayer will share a perspective or fact – something you were unaware of or chose to ignore, deny, or discount. What they share is "gold" for you and your project. When you agree that they are "right", they are very likely to be more open to your perspectives and facts. Work them towards a shared reality or the "truth". This may take time – another meeting or two. But it is worth it. Remember, it takes seven or more supporters to balance the negativity of one naysayer.[27] For an excellent presentation of how to incrementally change a person's beliefs or position, see *The Theory That Would Not Die: How*

---

[27] *The Theory That Would Not Die: How Bayes' Rule Cracked the Enigma Code, Hunted Down Russian Submarines, and Emerged Triumphant From Two Centuries of Controversy*, Sharon Bertsch McGrayne (New Haven, CT: Yale University Press, 2012.

*Bayes' Rule Cracked the Enigma Code, Hunted Down Russian Submarines, and Emerged Triumphant From Two Centuries of Controversy.*

We actually covered two key concepts above: Deep Listening and Incrementally Changing One's Beliefs and Position. Think about it – rarely will you have overwhelming evidence that you are right and they are wrong. You will have to chip away (and they will also) until you achieve a shared reality.

One more thought. Recall the Communications Management Plan Plus, with Challenges and Strategies (and Owners). As part of the recurring project team meeting, I show the team's Communications Management Plan Plus. I ask owners to color the items they own Green, Yellow, or Red. We discuss the items colored Red first. The owner presents what it will take to go Green. The rest of us provide help – ideas – as needed. Sometimes the communications challenge derives from one key stakeholder or stakeholder group, and we must figure out how to get this stakeholder (group) to go Green. This is where the concepts above come in handy.

As Dan said above, communications is 90% of project management. Make sure your project communications are well planned, and excellent. Dan also said that one key reason for project failure is a stakeholder(s) who is not on board – unsupportive or worse, a naysayer. Ignore these at your peril.

## Chapter 8 Food for Thought

1. Review the communications model. Can you provide a positive example when it worked for you? What went well? Can you provide a negative example when the model broke down? What went wrong?

2. Can you recall a project you were involved in where rumors developed and caused problems? What problems resulted? What was done, if anything, to eliminate the rumor?

3. Review Figure 8.4. Choose a communications activity where you believe you may encounter a challenge? What is the challenge, and how will you overcome it?

4. A project team member feels that creation of a Communications Management Plan is a waste of time and energy? Do you agree with this assessment? If so, what are your reasons? Do you disagree? If so, what will you share with the team member to change their mind?

5. PMI® states that 90% of a project manager's time is spent on communications related activities? Do you agree with PMI? Support your opinion.

6. Peter's Deep Thought Challenges:

*Reflections*

Recall a time where you and another person had a heated argument over something—perhaps politics, religion, the best way to do something, etc. Some of the "best" arguments are with your significant other ☺.

    A. How did the argument end?

    B. Did either's person's beliefs or positions change, or begin to change (soften) during or by the end of the argument?

- If so, what caused this change or softening?

- What role did you have in causing this change (in your beliefs/position and/or the others' belief/position)?

- What will you do differently next time to have a better outcome? (e.g., change your and/or their belief/position faster; create less anger, negative emotion, etc. during the conversation; end with a stronger relationship, more respect for each other, and increased ability to listen and move to a shared reality)

Okay, we are well into this book. *So I can give you a Deep Reflection.*

Earlier, we introduced EQ. We said that one part of EQ is self-awareness. This means that we are aware of our self – our thoughts, our behavior, our words, our body language – and the impact these have on others.

Here is the Deep Reflection: Have you ever stepped outside yourself, and observed yourself? As if another person was observing you? Some experts refer to this as the "I" observing the "me." Sort of spooky yet very powerful. Next time you are in a heated argument, step outside the "me" and be the "I". Watch the "me" – is the "me" being and doing what it should in order to move the argument towards a shared reality? If not, how does the "me" need to change what it is being and/or doing?

*Being* a great communicator is really challenging. It takes awareness, alertness, and tremendous sensing – being totally open and present. Good luck on your journey. It will have huge payoffs.

# Chapter 9: Managing Risk: "Manage Risk, or It Will Manage You"

Project risk management is essential to project success. Risk management begins on day one of a project and doesn't end until the final closure and transition of the product or service that the project created. The high-level objective is to reduce the impact of threats and enhance the impact of opportunities. Problem #10 that leads to project failure is "Failure to Manage Risk and Poor Execution." Risks are reality. If you don't find and address risks, they will find you.

Project risk is defined as an *uncertain event* or condition that may have a positive or negative impact on project time, cost, or scope (quality). I am sure this statement goes against your traditional thoughts on risk. Most project managers understand risk as bad. However, some risks can be good.

Two categories of risk are important for project management. *Known risks* have been previously identified and analyzed. The project manager's objective is to manage known risks. *Unknown risks* have not been identified. A key objective of risk management is to identify unknown risks so they, too, can be part of the planning process and be managed. *Risk planning cannot be completed until all other planning is finalized. However, risk planning begins from Day 1 of the project.*

A consistent approach to risk should be developed. A solid risk management function can reduce project problems by as much as 90%[28]. In this chapter, we will introduce you to a Risk Management Plan that will guide the way for a solid risk management program. We will also introduce a number of tools and techniques that are useful for identifying and managing risks. We highlight a key tool you need to use called a Risk Register. Welcome to project risk management—the story begins! This is worth repeating: failure to manage risk as a *big* problem. Let's ensure we minimize the impact as much as possible on your project!

## PIER-C: A Risk Management Methodology

Effective project risk management requires a step-by step approach to be successful. The "PIER-C" model[29] defines a proven approach and will serve as our guide for this important chapter. Figure 9.1 shares the "PIER-C" model.

---

[28] Project Management Institute (PMI)
[29] *Passing the Risk Management Professional (PMI-RMP) Certification Exam the First Time*, Yeomans

### Figure 9.1 The PIER-C Approach

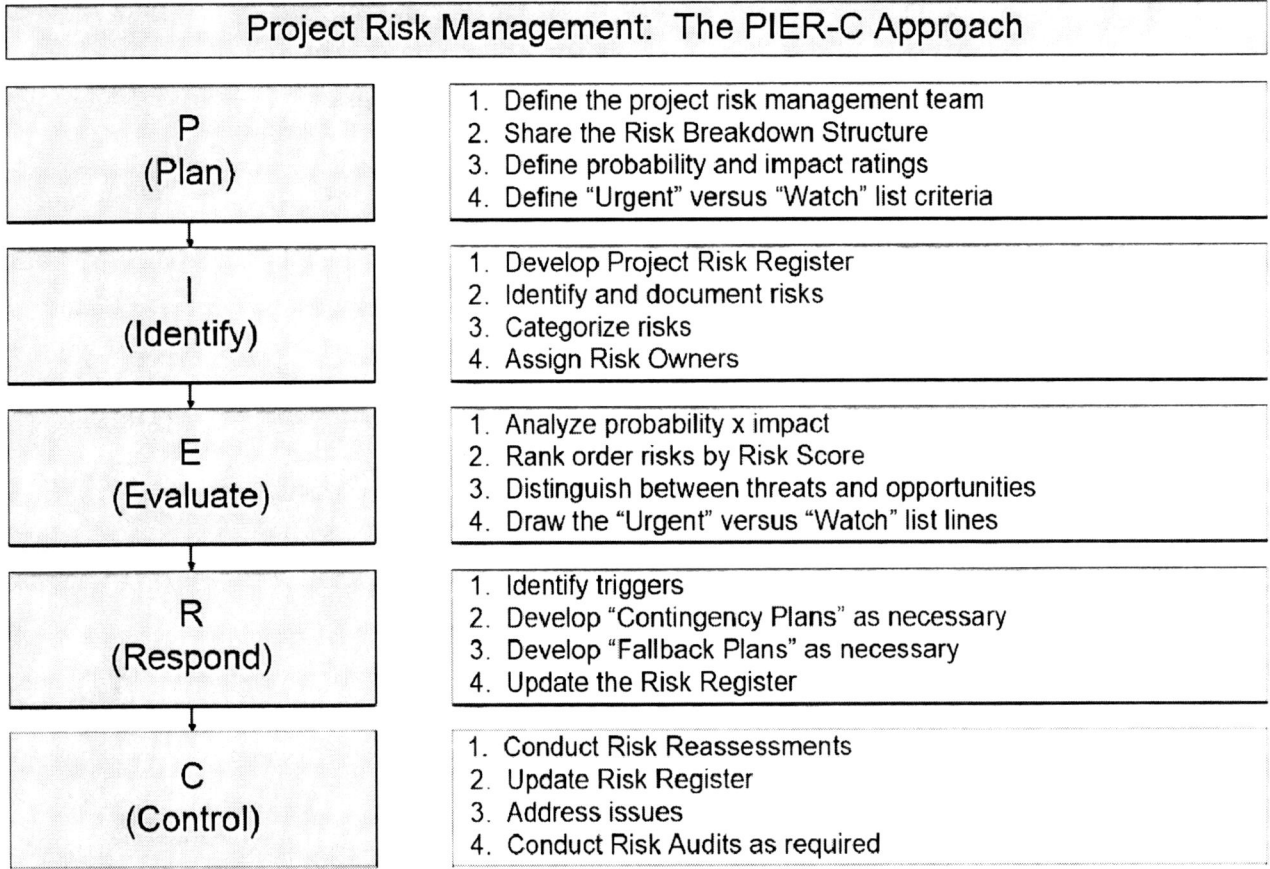

PIER-C walks you through a five-step approach. Follow the steps in order and you will ensure project risk is managed before it manages you. Here is a summary of the five steps:

- **Plan:** Remember PDCA from Chapter 2? A few planning activities need to be performed before you start identifying risks. You need to identify the risk management team.

    o Have you ever heard of a Risk Breakdown Structure (RBS)? If not, stand by. Peter and I have an example you can apply to the majority of your projects that eliminates inefficient risk identification meetings.

    o Not all risks are equal. We will guide you on establishing probability and impact ratings you can use to analyze and qualify all risks. In addition, we will share a "Probability Risk Matrix." Sounds complex, doesn't it? It's not. It's just a simple way to visualize the relative urgency of risks, as well as the risk profile of your project.

- **Identify:** The key to success during the identify phase is to establish a Risk Register. We have an example you can apply to any project that is tried and true. In addition:

  o There are many ways to identify risks. But here is the trick: risk can be both negative (threats) and positive (opportunities). We will share SWOT analysis as a means to use your RBS to find both types of risks. Threats can obviously impact a project negatively. However, opportunities are a way to counter threats and put your "triangle" back together again. We will also highlight the Delphi Technique as a way to identify risks when the stakeholders may not feel comfortable verbalizing them.

  o We will discuss categorization of risks. You may have multiple risks with low ratings in a single category. However, a large number of risks in a given category, regardless of their probability and impact ratings, are likely a red flag.

  o We will also discuss the concept of Risk Owners. These are individuals responsible for given risks. Believe it or not, the project manager sometimes doesn't need to do everything. And in some cases, they shouldn't be doing certain activities. Remember, "Know what you know, know what you don't know, and surround yourself with people who know what you don't know."

- **Evaluate:** As we just shared, all risks are not created equal. We will share tips on how to analyze probability × impact and come up with a risk score. We will also share how to distinguish opportunities from threats. Finally, we will share the concept of the "Urgent" versus "Watch" list.

- **Respond:** Not all risks require an in-depth response. In addition, you may choose from among seven response options to respond to a risk. Many managers, when faced with a potential risk, quickly share these two words: "Mitigate it!" Here's the good news: mitigate is a viable response to a risk. Here's the bad news: mitigate is one of seven potential responses and may not always be the most viable choice.

- o  Some risks may have an early warning system. For example, bad weather is a viable risk cause. The good news, in most cases, is that bad weather doesn't always catch us by surprise. We have time to react to the bad weather before it occurs. It is important to recognize and document "risk triggers." Something that occurs that warns us of a pending risk is a "trigger." More on that in a bit.

- o  Some risks require a single Contingency Plan only. This is Plan A. However, other risks may have a large impact and warrant a Plan B. We refer to the Plan B as a Fallback Plan. We will discuss this more in detail later as well.

- **Control:** Risk management begins on day one of a project and doesn't end until the final "i" has been dotted and "t" crossed. We will discuss Risk Reassessments, or how often you review risks and update your Risk Register. We will also talk about "issues" and "benefits" management, such as what do you do when a risk happens? We'll end with a discussion of Risk Audits, which is simply your review of a response to a risk that occurred.

## PIER-C Step 1: Plan

Planning is the first step in effective risk management. It sets the stage for all risk management activities that follow. It is a best practice to develop a "Risk Management Plan." This is a simple plan that provides guidance and information to the members of your risk management team. Figure 9.2 highlights a "simple and effective" Risk Management Plan format you should consider.

## Figure 9.2 Risk Management Plan Format

| Risk Management Plan for Project: | |
|---|---|
| Risk Management Team | |
| Definitions of Probability and Impact Ratings | |
| Probability and Impact Matrix | |
| Risk Reassessment Schedule | |
| Risk Contingency Reserves | |
| Clarification/ Comments | |

## Risk Management Plan Highlights

Each project is different. The amount of information you need to share to stakeholders regarding project risk management will vary based on project complexity, duration, scope, etc. Tailor a Risk Management Plan accordingly. Here are the potential entries:

- **Risk Management Team:** Define stakeholders or team members who will be tasked to manage the end-to-end project risk management function. You may even want to consider developing a RACI if it makes sense. For a small project there may be a single entry; the project manager. For larger and more complex projects, you may want to designate applicable key stakeholders and "Risk Owners." Here are the functions expected of a Risk Owner:

- o Risk Owners are assigned to specific risks. In essence, the Risk Owner manages each of their risks as a mini-project. They ensure the risk is defined, qualified, and determine appropriate primary and secondary risk responses.

- o Should a risk occur, the Risk Owner manages the response, documents results, and determines next steps. They also participate in Risk Reassessments, and lead Risk Audits. More on these activities later in the chapter.

- **Definitions of Probability and Impact Ratings:** Each risk must be evaluated using a Probability × Impact = Risk Score methodology. This process is referred to as "Qualitative Risk Analysis." *Do not* treat all risks in the same manner. Some risks have a small impact and probability, others have a large impact and probability.

    - o Using the probability × impact rating system allows you to differentiate risks, and focus on those needing the most attention. Include a rating system you will consistently apply in your Risk Management Plan.

    - o Figure 9.3 provides an example of a very common rating system using a five point scale for probability and impact. We include two rating systems, one for positive risks and one for negative risks.

# Figure 9.3 Probability and Impact Rating System Examples

## Scoring Positive Risks

| Evaluating Risks (Probability x Impact) ||
|---|---|
| **Qualifying Probability of Occurance** | **Qualifying Impact** |
| 5 — High Probability 81% – 100% | 5 — High Impact Near 100% Project Success |
| 4 — High to Moderate Probability 61% – 80% | 4 — High to Moderate Impact Near 75% Project Sucess |
| 3 — Moderate Probability 41% – 60% | 3 — Moderate Probability Near 50% Project Success |
| 2 — Moderate to Low Probability 21% – 40% | 2 — Moderate to Low Impact Near 25% Project Sucess |
| 1 — Low Probability 1% – 20% | 1 — Low Impact Near 0% Project Sucess |

**Project Success:**
Ability to successfully achieve or exceed one or multiple scope, time, and cost goals as established at Baseline

## Scoring Negative Risks

**Evaluating Risks (Probability x Impact)**

| Qualifying Probability of Occurance | | Qualifying Impact | |
|---|---|---|---|
| 5 | High Probability 81% – 100% | 5 | High Impact Near 100% Project Failure |
| 4 | High to Moderate Probability 61% – 80% | 4 | High to Moderate Impact Near 75% Project Failure |
| 3 | Moderate Probability 41% – 60% | 3 | Moderate Probability Near 50% Project Failure |
| 2 | Moderate to Low Probability 21% – 40% | 2 | Moderate to Low Impact Near 25% Project Failure |
| 1 | Low Probability 1% – 20% | 1 | Low Impact Near 0% Project Failure |

**Project Failure:** Failure to achieve one or multiple scope, time, and cost goals as established at Baseline

- **Probability and Impact Matrix:** A common practice in project risk management is creation of an "Urgent" risk list, and a "Watch" list. This practice allows you to differentiate risks based on the Probability × Impact = Risk Score you assign to the risk. As we mentioned, all risks are not equal. You need to focus on the highest rated threats and opportunities rather than treating all risks the same. In addition, you need to provide your risk management team with specific actions required based on the overall risk score for the risk. Figure 9.4 provides an example of a Probability and Impact Matrix you can include in your Risk Management Plan. This example is based on the 5 × 5 scoring model we introduced in Figure 9.3.

# Figure 9.4 Probability and Impact Matrix

- **Risk Reassessment Schedule:** Risk Management begins on Day 1 of the project and continues through project closure. If you recall, potential risks were documented in the Project Charter to help determine the feasibility of the project before moving to the planning phase. Risk Reassessment is the formal term used to define your team's periodic reviews of risk. For a normal project, we recommend you meet once a week to review risk status. For a smaller project, you may only need to meet every other week, or establish a cadence that makes sense for you.

    o Based on the scope of the project, you may need to designate a stand-alone risk status meeting. For a smaller project, you may include risk as part of your overall project status meet that includes reviews of scope, schedule, budget, etc.

    o Ensure your proposed Risk Reassessment schedule is referenced in your Communications Management Plan. When you review risk, you want to ensure you have the "right people on the bus" present and accounted for.

- **Risk Contingency Reserves:** We introduced the concept of reserves in Chapter 5. Your Risk Management Plan should provide guidance as follows:

- Are Contingency Reserves available for identified or known risks? If so, how much contingency reserve funding is available, and who will manage these funds?

- Are Management Reserves available for unknown risks? If so, how much management reserve funding is available, and who will manage these funds?

- If reserves are used, how will these be reported to ensure the project budget is updated?

- **Clarification/Comments:** Use this section to outline any comments you may have. If your organization uses an RBS, which we highly recommend, point to the RBS location or attach it to the plan.

  - An RBS is used during our next PIER-C step—Identify Risks. It allows the project manager to walk through a variety of common risk causes to determine which are applicable to the project, and provides an organized way to identify risks.

  - Figure 9.5 provides a sample RBS you can use to get started if your organization does not have a standard RBS. This example is a simple spreadsheet that you can adapt to your organization. It lists some of the most common risks that impact multiple project types.

**Note:** Risk can either be positive or negative. Negative risks, or threats, need to be identified and addressed. You want to stop them in some way. On the other hand, positive risks, or opportunities, need to be identified and encouraged to occur. Positive risks can help balance negative risks. More on this potential paradigm shift later.

## Figure 9.5 Risk Breakdown Structure (RBS) Sample

| Risk Breakdown Structure | | |
|---|---|---|
| Risk Category | Negative Cause | Positive Cause |
| Communications | Status "Green" Culture | Willingness to Code Status "Yellow" |
| | Multiple Communications Blockers | Few Communications Blockers |
| | Many Acronyms | Few Acronyms |
| | Email Dependency | Use of Multiple Mediums |
| | Poor Meeting Management | Strong Meeting Management |
| | Poorly Defined Communications Tools | Standard and Accepted Communications Tools |
| Cultural | Different Time Zones | Same Time Zone |
| | Various Work Schedules | Similar Work Schedules |
| | Various Value Systems | Similar Value Systems |
| | Language Variations | Few Language Variations |
| | Various Religious Beliefs and Practices | Similar Religious Beliefs and Practices |
| Financial/ Budget | Highly Constrained Budget | Few Budget Constraints |
| | Funding Source Questions | Funding Sources Defined |
| | Cost Overrun Potential | Limited Cost Overrun Potential |
| | Many Dependencies | Few Dependencies |
| | Multiple Assumptions | Few Assumptions |
| | Low Estimation Confidence Level | High Estimation Confidence Level |
| Legal/ Regulatory | Legal Constraints | Minimal or No Legal Constraints |
| | Regulatory Constraints | Minimal or No Regulatory Constraints |
| | Unknown Legal Factors | Known Legal Factors |
| | Unknown Regulatory Factors | Known Regulatory Factors |
| | Travel Restrictions | No Travel Restrictions |

| Risk Breakdown Structure |||
|---|---|---|
| Risk Category | Negative Cause | Positive Cause |
| Organizational | Stakeholder Disagreement | Stakeholder Agreement |
| | Sponsorship Undefined | Sponsorship Defined |
| | Multiple Competing Projects | Few Competing Projects |
| | Complex Organizational Structure | Simple Organizational Structure |
| | High Reorganization Potential | Low Reorganization Potential |
| | High Vendor Dependencies | Low Vendor Dependencies |
| | High Impact on Existing Processes | Low Impact on Existing Processes |
| Personnel | Low Skill Sets | High Skill Sets |
| | Low Interest/Commitment levels | High Interest/Commitment Levels |
| | Limited Capacity | Sufficient Capacity |
| | Limited Functional Manager Buy In | High Functional Manager Buy In |
| | Many Virtual Team Members | Few Virtual Team Members |
| | Various Work Schedules | Standard Work Schedule |
| Project/ Solution | Poor Linkage to Vision and Portfolio | Direct Linkage to Vision and Portfolio |
| | Requirements Definition Vague | Specific Requirements Definition |
| | Measurability Questions | Measures Concrete |
| | Limited Time to Plan | Adequate Time to Plan |
| | High Potential for Changes | Low Potential for Changes |
| | Long-Term Plan to Deliverable | Short-Term Plan to Deliverable |
| Schedule | Accelerated Schedule Pressure | Adequate Scheduling Flexibility |
| | Many Dependencies | Few Dependencies |
| | Multiple Assumptions | Few Assumptions |
| | Low Estimation Confidence Level | High Estimation Confidence Level |
| | High Potential for Schedule Changes | Low Potential for Schedule Changes |
| Technology | New Technology | Proven Technology |
| | Few Subject Matter Experts | Adequate Subject Matter Experts |
| | Architectural Conflicts | No Architectural Conflicts |
| | Multiple Interface Requirements | Stand Alone System |
| | Focus on Solutions | Focus on Functionality and Scenarios |

## PIER-C Step 2: Identify

Risk identification is a critical second step in the PIER-C process. During this step, identify and document as many risks as possible. Use the RBS we shared a few pages earlier to use a structured approach to identify risks. The highlights of the Identify step include:

- Creation of a Project Risk Register. A Risk Register is a document, normally a spreadsheet, which allows you to list risks you identify.

- List *both* negative and positive risks. Negative risks will find you, so find them first. Opportunities will pass you by unless you find them. While negative risks have potential to impact scope, extend schedules, and lead to cost overruns, positive risks may allow including more scope, compression of schedules, or experience cost benefits.

Let's begin the Identify risk discussion by introducing a critical tool, the Risk Register. Once we complete this discussion, we will share two great ways that leverage your RBS to effectively identify and document risk.

Figure 9.6 provides a sample Risk Register. The columns have been compressed for readability. This template and more are available (have we said this before??☺) at www.p17group.com. Note the project management tip below.

> *Project Management Tip: Identify positive risks first. In most cases, you will identify more opportunities than if you wait to identify opportunities after you identify threats.*

### Figure 9.6 Standard Risk Register Template

| # | Cause | Event | Impact | Risk Owner | Category | Probability | Impact | Risk Score | Trigger | Response |
|---|-------|-------|--------|------------|----------|-------------|--------|------------|---------|----------|
|   |       |       |        |            |          |             |        |            |         |          |
|   |       |       |        |            |          |             |        |            |         |          |
|   |       |       |        |            |          |             |        |            |         |          |
|   |       |       |        |            |          |             |        |            |         |          |

Standard Risk Register Template
Project: (List Project by Name)

Current as of: _____   Total Risk Score: _____

Sections Completed During "Identify" | Sections Completed During "Evaluate"

## Building the Risk Register

The Risk Register is normally developed as soon as the project planning begins. As you go through each planning process, risks are identified and added. For example, as you plan scope, risks will be identified. Add them to the Risk Register when you find them. The RBS we shared earlier is a great way to determine if risks are present as you develop the project plan. In terms of planning steps, the Risk Register is the last planning document you finalize before you recommend project approval, cancellation, delay, etc. to the Project Sponsor.

- **Risk Number:** Each risk should be assigned a unique designator so the risk may easily be referenced. Normally, project managers use a simple 01, 02, 03 etc. numbering system.

- **Risk Metalanguage:** The first three columns in the Risk Register reflect the best way to document a risk. Identify the cause first, determine potential events that may occur as a result of the cause, and document the impact to the project from the event. This methodology of Cause, Event, Impact, is referred to as "Risk Metalanguage." Figure 9.7 shows how Risk Metalanguage works.

## Figure 9.7 Risk Metalanguage

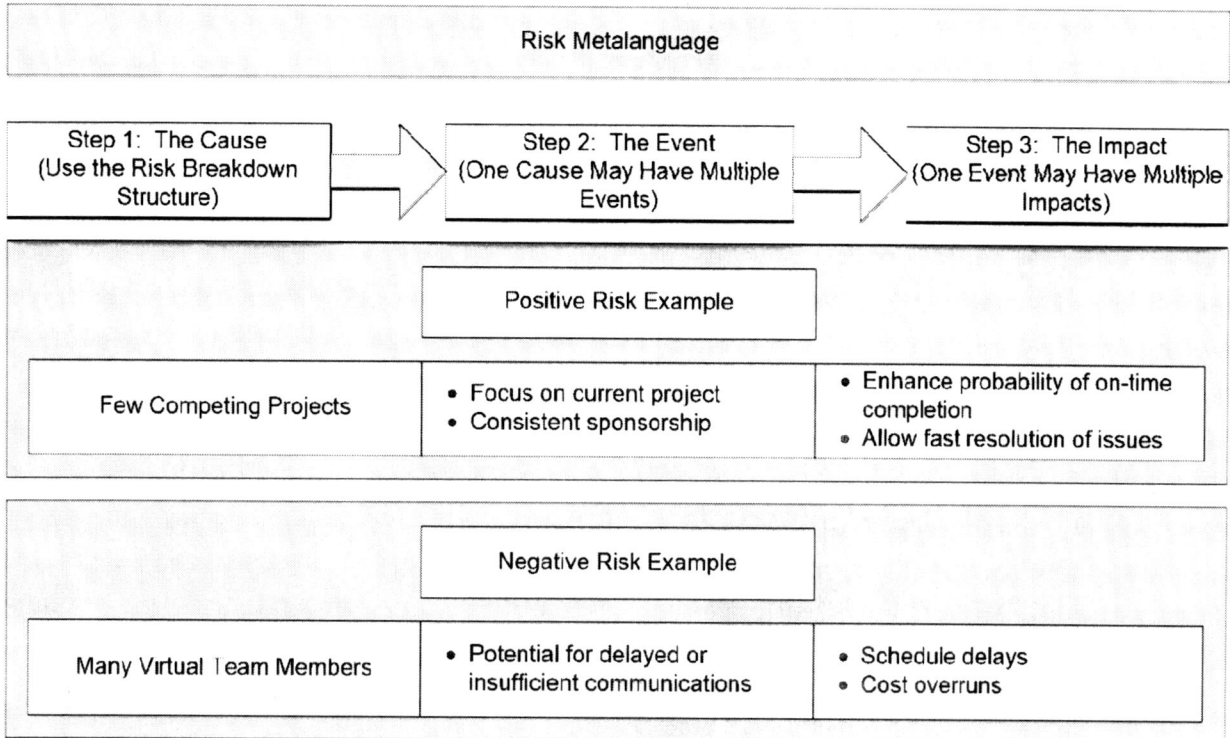

- **Risk Owner:** We discussed the role of the Risk Owner. As we shared, each risk should be assigned to a member of your team. By default, the Risk Owner becomes the project manager when no one is assigned. Annotate the Risk Owner on the Risk Register. And, more importantly, let them know they are the Risk Owner. Risk Owners need to be aware of their assignment, capable of managing the risk, and committed to doing so.

- **Category:** Categorizing risks is not just a best practice. It makes sense and adds value. You may have a number of low probability and low impact risks in a category. This is important to know. While each individual risk may not present high impact, the cumulative nature of these risks may. In most cases, when you have a large number of risks in a given category, there may be an underlying cause that is much more severe. As the old saying goes, "where there's smoke, there's fire." Use the categories in your RBS as your default.

We will stop here for a moment. A Risk Register is completed in steps or phases. During the Identify phase, complete the first part of the Risk Register. During the Identify phase, the goal is to identify as many risks, both positive and negative, as you can. Don't worry about qualifying the risks by probability and impact, identifying triggers, or determining responses—yet! Trying to analyze each risk from end-to-end will detract from the goal. To repeat: identify as many risks as you can and analyze them later.

Before we leave the Identify phase, we want to share two additional tools that are great ways to identify risks. The first tool we will preview is SWOT Analysis. The second is the Delphi Technique.

## Additional Risk Identification Tools

### SWOT Analysis

SWOT Analysis is a very popular method to use when brainstorming risks. SWOT is defined as Strengths, Weaknesses, Opportunities, and Threats analysis. Positive risk causes are viewed as potential strengths. Negative risk causes are viewed as potential weaknesses.

Try to determine the most applicable causes, both negative and positive. If you have an RBS, great! You can review the RBS and pick those causes that apply. If not, use the one we provided in the book. It will get you started. Then, try to determine threats that may stem from weaknesses and opportunities that may be realized from strengths. Figure 9.8 shows how SWOT Analysis works.

> *Project Management Tip: The Pareto Principle applies to risk management. Normally, 20% of all risks will have 80% of the impact. Find those 20%.*

## Figure 9.8 SWOT Analysis

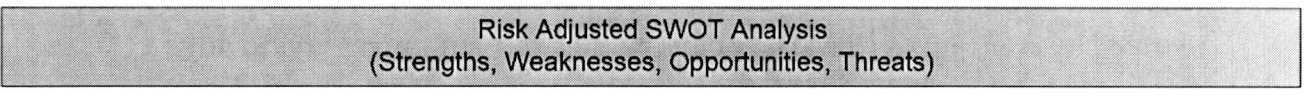
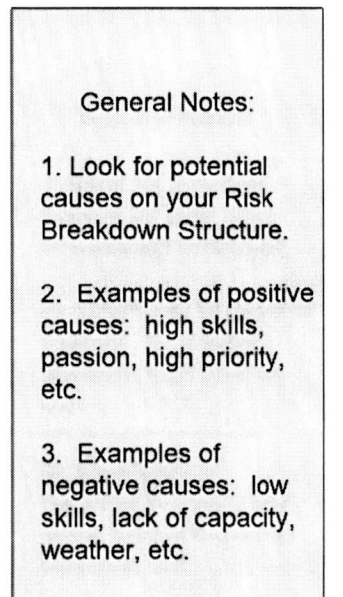
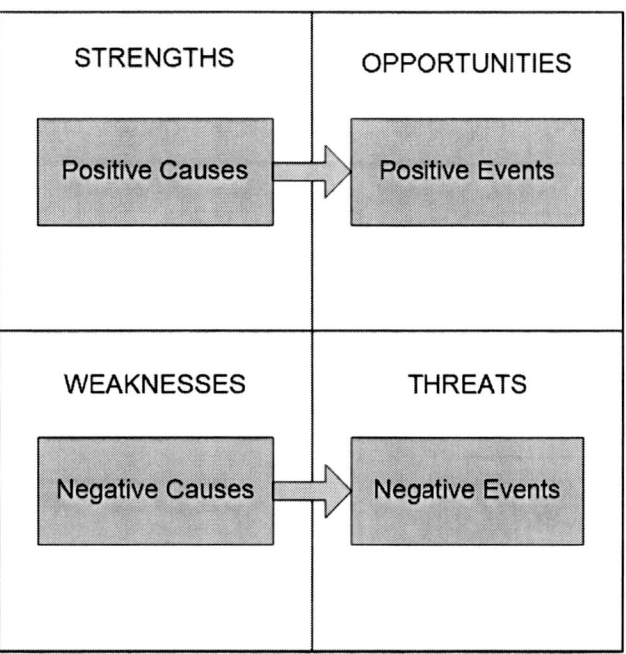

## Delphi Technique

There may be times when stakeholders are reluctant to verbalize the risks for a project. There are many reasons for this. Some cultures do not feel comfortable verbalizing the negative. In some cases, political factors may prevent stakeholders from being open. In other cases, stakeholders may be spread out so much in the virtual environment that having a single risk identification meeting is not practical.

The Delphi Technique is a way to solicit inputs from individual stakeholders using a variety of media. All inputs are anonymous. Here are a few scenarios to consider before we share a visual of the process.

- Collocated Environment: Ask all stakeholders to attend a meeting. Follow the process in Figure 9.9.

- Virtual Environment: Use surveys, interviews, email, etc. to attain the inputs you require. The key to success is creating trust that you will not disclose the responses you received by name unless the stakeholder requests or authorizes you to do so.

## Figure 9.9 Delphi Technique

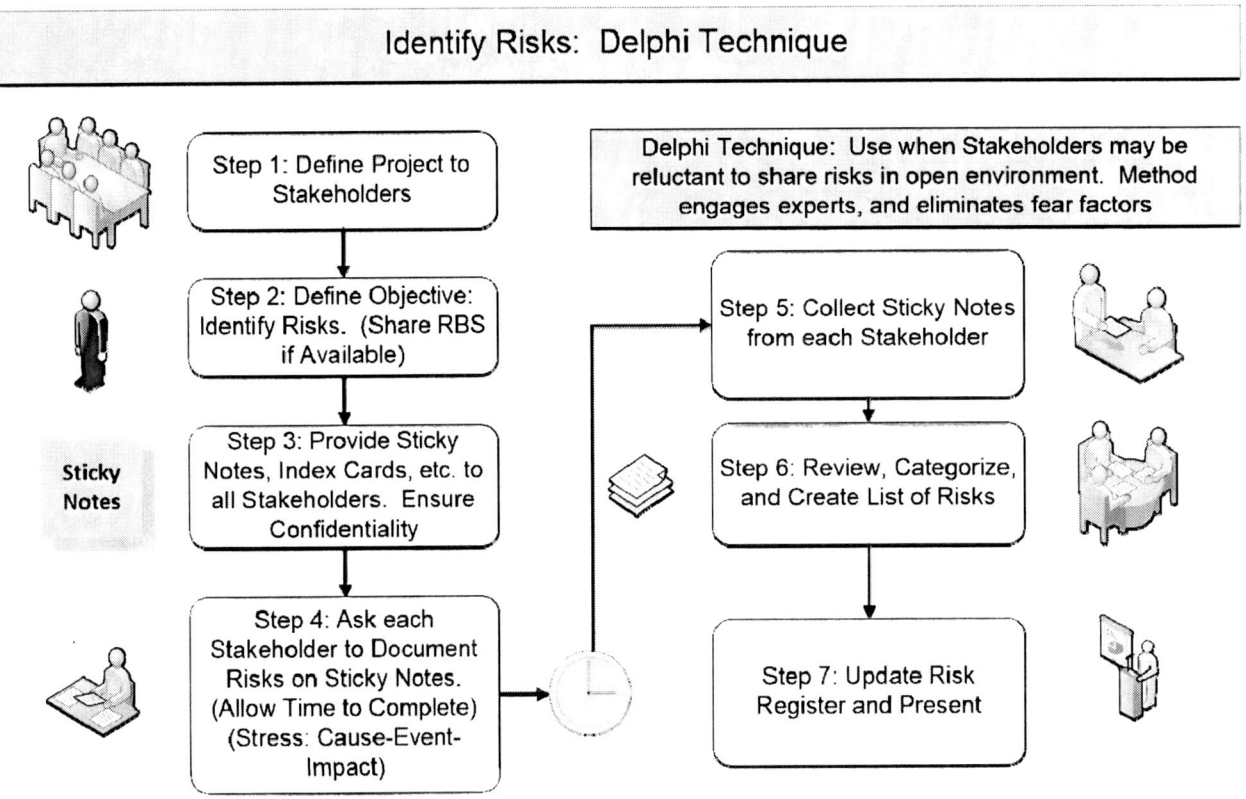

## PIER-C Step 3: Evaluate

You have been wonderfully patient☺. You *may* now begin the analysis or risk evaluation phase. There are many ways to qualitatively or quantitatively assess each risk. Quantitative analysis models such as Expected Monetary Analysis, Decision Trees, and statistical models etc. are occasionally required. However, 95% of all projects can be adequately evaluated using the qualitative analysis method of Probability × Impact = Risk Score. We will focus on the 95% in this section.

Determine Risk Owners if you haven't already done so. Remember, if no Risk Owners are assigned, the project manager takes the lead. Here is the step-by-step evaluation process. As you go through each step, update the Risk Register we shared earlier in the chapter.

1. **Assign or Validate Risk Owners to Each Risk.** Ensure the Risk Owner has the technical expertise necessary to manage the risk. Management incudes facilitating the evaluation of the risk, identifying risk triggers (more on this in a bit), and determining an initial response to the risk. Remember—we want threats *not* to happen. We want opportunities *to* happen.

2. **Assign Probability × Impact scores and calculate the Risk Score.** You can do this in many ways:

   - Risk Owner assigns probability and impact. Risk Score is shared with stakeholders for review and feedback.

   - Stakeholders review each risk and subjectively score probability × impact. You may elect to have stakeholders vocalize their scores, or use a form of Delphi Technique with sticky notes. In the event there are different opinions on probability or impact scores, allow a short discussion. In some cases, scoring variations are due to an unclear or incomplete understanding of the risk. In other cases, the probability and/or impact to one group may be different than to another group.

   - In the event that there are variations in scoring after discussion, assign the risk to an individual who believes the score is high. In addition, score the risk high based on the uncertainty of the risk. For example, Bob believes the impact of a risk is a 5 for his group. Pedro agrees with Bob from his perspective as well. Ivana on the other hand believes the impact is a 3. Score the risk as a 5. Ask either Bob or Pedro to act as Risk Owners. Their goal will be to try to reduce the risk score through their responses.

   - Some organizations calculate a Total Risk Score. They add up the total value of risks, and trend this number to determine if project risk is getting better or worse. One goal of good risk management is to reduce the overall Total Risk Score for negative risk by eliminating risks, or reducing the probability and/or impact through their responses. A second goal is to increase the overall Total Risk Score for positive risks. Note some project managers compare Total Risk Score by project to determine which projects should be approved, and which should not be approved.

3. **Search for Triggers:** Some risks simply happen. There is no way of predicting the occurrence until it becomes an issue. However, some risks provide an early warning. This early warning is referred to as a "Trigger." For example, in most cases, weather has a trigger. Let's look at this negative risk example: Cause: Snowstorm—Event: May close roads and impact employees coming to work—Impact: Key milestones may be missed. In most cases, (I know we are talking about weather forecasts☺) weather is predictable. If you learn Monday that a large snowstorm is predicted for Wednesday, you can implement your response early to do what is possible to reduce the impact of the risk you know will likely become an issue. When you identify a Trigger, annotate it on the Risk Register.

4. **Determine an Initial Response:** Complete the final section of the Risk Register. We will further develop responses for high scoring risks in the Response phase of PIER-C. In most cases, the Risk Owner drives the conversation to develop an initial response.

5. **Sort Risks by Risk Score:** Sort risks by Risk Score. The highest scoring risks are on top, the lowest scoring on the bottom.

6. **Designate risks as "Urgent" or "Watch" list.** Remember Pareto, 20% of the risks will generate 80% of the impact.

7. **Current as of Date:** Date the Risk Register. This document will change as the project evolves. It is important to ensure all stakeholders are using the most current edition. Use version control.

<u>**Evaluation Notes:**</u>

1. Use the probability and impact scoring system you developed during the Plan phase. Score each risk consistently using a single scoring system.

2. Use the Probability and Impact Matrix you developed during the Plan phase to determine which risks are on the urgent list, and which are on the watch list.

3. Break out your Risk Register in two sections. One section should show positive risks, and the other should show negative. As we noted, some organizations compare the Total Risk Score for negatives risks against the Total Risk Score for positive risks. This practice provides a means to determine which scenario is the greatest, opportunities and threats. In addition, knowing the Total Risk Score for positive risks provides an estimate of how you may be able to compensate for the impact of negative risks.

4. Update your RBS when new risk causes, positive or negative, are identified. An up to date RBS provides future project managers with a comprehensive list of risk causes that may impact their project and precludes the need to "reinvent the wheel."

## PIER-C Step 4: Respond

Developing responses for the highest impact risks is essential. In this section, we will share the types of responses you need to consider, and provide an overview of seven ways to respond to a risk. We begin our response journey with a quick look on how risk responses are generated. Let's turn our attention to Figure 9.10 for the rest of the story.

### Figure 9.10 Risk Response Generation Process

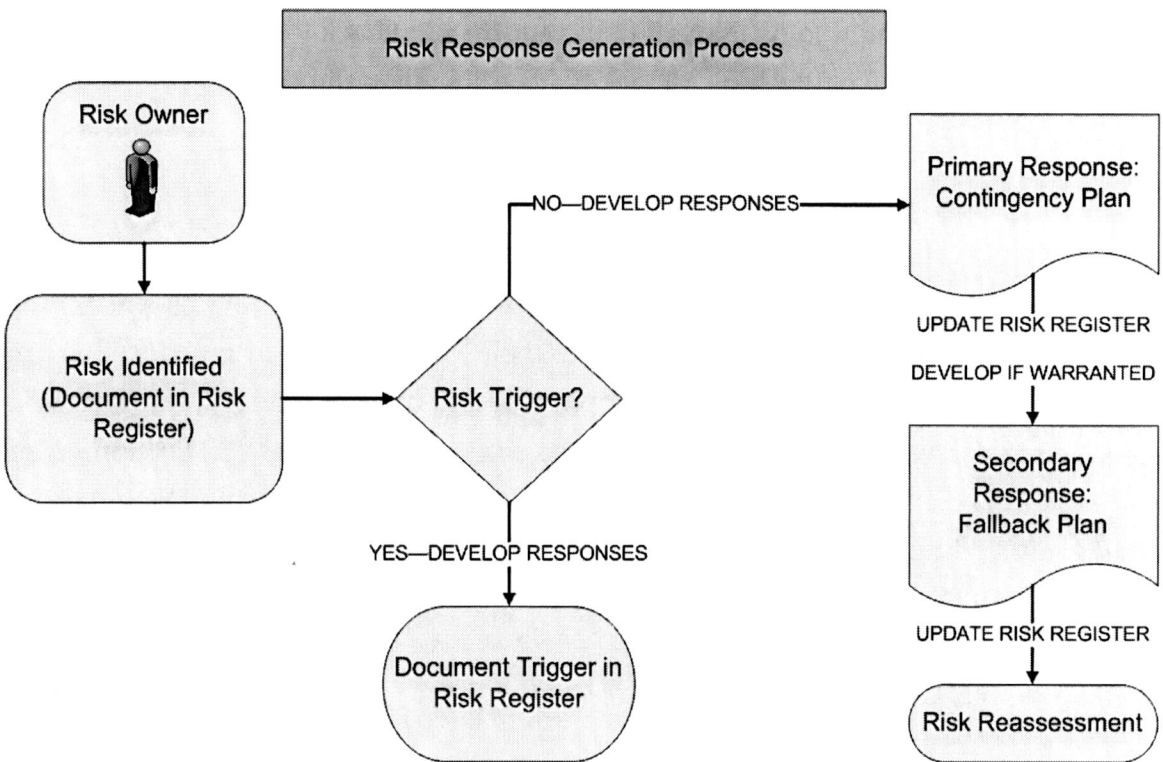

The Risk Owner is responsible for ensuring key risk information is included accurately in the Risk Register. The project manager, of course, oversees the process and is ultimately accountable. As we shared earlier, if there are no Risk Owners assigned, this job falls on the project manager. Here is a quick walk through the risk response generation process:

- **Triggers:** After the risk is identified, the search for triggers begins. If triggers are found, they are documented in the Risk Register. If no triggers are found, the process now turns its attention to generation of appropriate levels of risk response.

- **Develop Contingency Plan:** The primary response to a risk is referred to—after all, this is a project management book—as a Contingency Plan. In real terms, think of the Contingency Plan as your Plan A. Every risk on the Risk Register should have a Contingency Plan. The Contingency Plan will likely be very high level with minimum detail for risks on the "Watch" list. However, risks on the "Urgent" list need more detailed Contingency Plans. We shared earlier that all risks are not created equal. Spend time developing more detailed Contingency Plans when the Risk Score warrants it. Document your Contingency Plan when complete in the Risk Register.

- **Develop Fallback Plan:** There may be times when the probability and impact of a risk warrants a Plan B. We call this Plan B a Fallback Plan using current project management terminology. Not all risks require a Fallback Plan. This increases the level of work required, so develop Fallback Plans only when the situation warrants it. Fallback Plans also need to be included in the Risk Register.

<u>Note:</u> You want to keep your Risk Register simple and easy to read. Many risk responses may warrant more space than you have in the Risk Register column designated for responses. Many project managers add an additional tab to their Risk Register designed to share more in-depth processes. Link the response to the applicable risk by using the risk number we assigned to the risk when the risk was identified. PMI uses the term WBS Dictionary as we shared earlier. Let's think out of the box here. How about a Risk Register Dictionary? Things that make you go hmmm.

## Risk Response Strategies

We earlier stated many managers have fallen in love with the term "Mitigate." Sometimes these managers are correct: you *do* want to mitigate a risk. In many cases, however, these managers are wrong. Mitigate is one of seven potential risk responses you can generate. Figure 9.11 shares risk response terminology you should include in all responses. Admittedly, gaining acceptance for these seven response definitions may require some education of stakeholders on your part. However, understanding this response terminology allows you to share the essence of what your responses entail, and whether the risk is an opportunity or a threat, in a single word. That, my friend, is efficiency.

**Figure 9.11 Risk Response Strategies Defined**

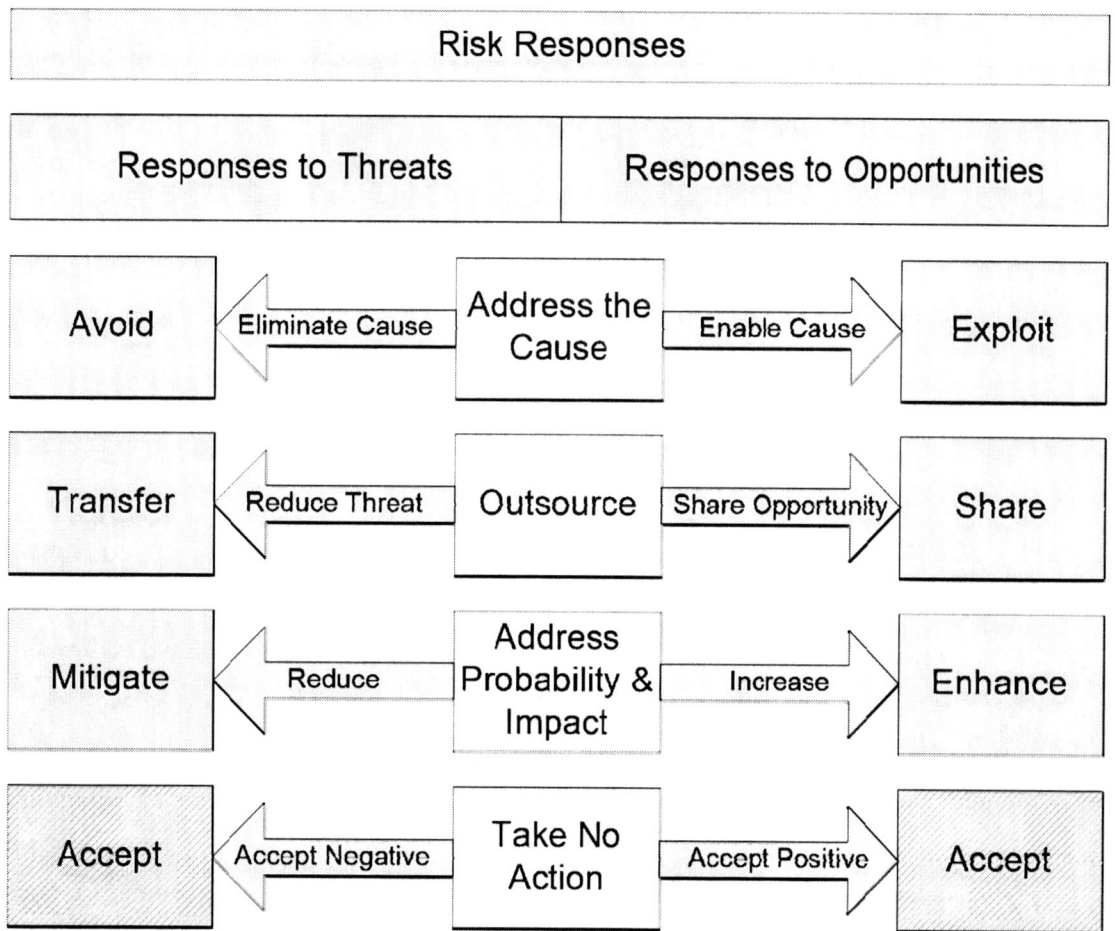

As you can see, there are seven potential responses to risk. Three responses address negative risks or threats. Three responses address positive risks or opportunities. One response addresses either positive of negative risks. Here is a quick breakout of these potential responses to improve your risk knowledge base.

- **Avoid and Exploit:** Avoid and Exploit strategies assume we can do something about the risk cause. Let's look at some examples.

    o **Avoid:** Let's say you have a troublesome team member you need to replace. You may be able to avoid the risk by eliminating the cause. You replace the team member, and the cause is avoided. If you have no choice but to keep the troublesome team member on your team, then avoid is not a response option.

    o **Exploit:** Your leadership team is ecstatic about the new project you are managing. You can exploit the cause by maintaining the level of excitement for the project in many ways. Perhaps you can share the wins with flair. Perhaps you can invite managers to milestone celebrations or ask for their involvement in recognizing top performers on your team. By doing so, you may reap the additional benefits this high level of leadership passion can provide.

- **Transfer and Share:** These two response strategies are all about third-party or external support. Here are two examples to show how this strategy pair works.

    o **Transfer:** The risk cause is lack of skills. Sadly, there is no way to eliminate the cause prior to your project hitting the fast lane. You transfer the risk to a third party by hiring a vendor who has the skills you need. Insurance is a very common transfer response. For example, you may not be able to afford the costs of an automobile accident if one of your fleet drivers is involved in a mishap. So you transfer the risk of payment to the insurance company—for a fee, of course.

    o **Share:** Alex and Peter both need a special widget to complete their respective projects. Peter needs 100 and received a quote from the supplier of $1000 each. Coincidentally, Alex needs the same number of widgets. Alex calls the supplier and asks if they would be willing to offer a discount for an order of 200 widgets rather than the 100 he needs. Good news, the supplier says the will discount each widget by $50 for a larger order. When the deal is done, Peter and Alex get the widgets they need at a cheaper price, and "share" the benefits. Peter and Alex both reduced their project budgets by $5000 each.

- **Mitigate and Enhance:** Mitigate and Enhance strategies are used to reduce the probability and/or impact of a risk that has a cause that nothing can be done to avoid or exploit. Here are a few examples.

    o **Mitigate:** In our avoid example, we shared the troublesome team member. As it turns out, this individual is the only resource available. To reduce the probability and negative impact potential this team member poses to the project, we assign him to a project activity where there are mature individuals who will not be swayed by his negative attitude, and may be able to serve as role models to turn him around. Here's another example. I live in Seattle, which is a lovely city. Unfortunately, there are many rainy periods during all but four months of the year. If my project is potentially impacted by bad weather, I need to mitigate the impact of the bad weather by developing workaround plans to keep the project moving during the bad weather periods.

    o **Enhance:** You are very fortunate. You work in an organization that has extremely skilled individuals. There is no purpose in exploiting these skills. You don't have to worry about sustaining the high skills, and the high skill situation will stay as is, regardless of how you manage your project. But here is the problem—there is no guarantee that high skills will relate to project success. Your job is to enhance the probability, and positive impact of leveraging these high skills for your project. You may want to create an incentive program so that if the team finishes early they may receive some kind of reward. Do what it takes to ensure the high skills in the organization benefit your project.

- **Accept:** There may be times when you need to simply accept the potential for a threat or opportunity to occur. One reason may be that the Risk Score for the opportunity or threat may to too low to justify spending time on a more detailed response. Another reason may be that you simply have no Contingency or Fallback Plan you can develop that will work.

**Note:** If your risk response has the potential to do more damage to your project if it fails to work than the impact of the actual risk itself, forego the response and accept the risk. On the other hand, you may develop a risk response that incorporates multiple strategies. For example, you may want to bring in a Subject Matter Expert to overcome a lack of skills (Transfer), to reduce the probability of encountering technology risks confronting the project (Mitigate).

So there you have it. We have arrived at the "PIER." We now need to get to PIER-C. To satisfy that goal, let's begin our explanation of the final PIER-C phase—Control.

## PIER-C Step 5: Control

The Control phase of risk management is critical. During this phase, you maintain the Risk Register and reassess risks, update the Risk Register as needed, share status with stakeholders, and respond to risks should they occur. Remember—risk management begins on day one of the project and is not finished until final project close out or transition. Don't give up now, you've come a long way.

Project management is both science and art—a familiar theme we have shared in this book. Let's begin with an overview of the risk control process—a bit of science if you will-- as depicted in Figure 9.12.

## Figure 9.12 Project Risk Management Control Process

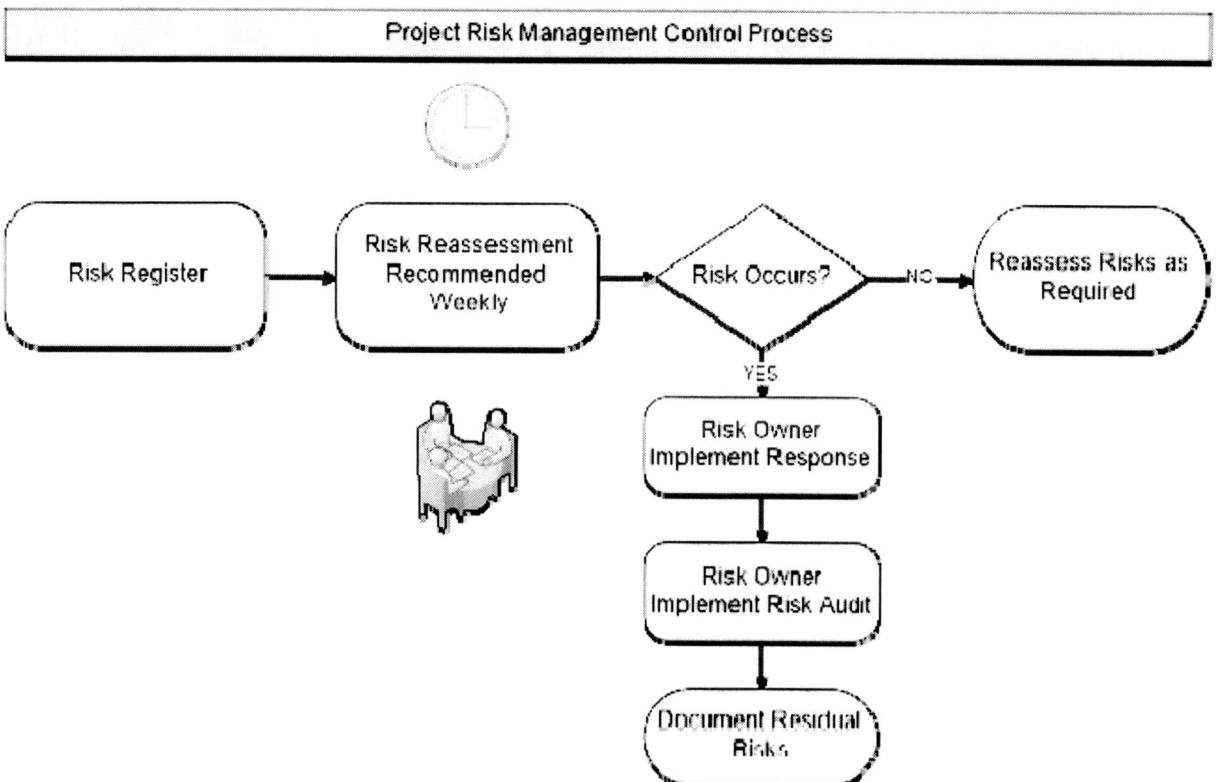

- **Risk Reassessment:** The Risk Register should be reviewed on a steady basis. For most projects, weekly is generally a good interval. Determine if any risk probabilities or impact changed. If so, update the Risk Register accordingly and take required actions dictated by the new Risk Score. If risks are no longer probable, eliminate them from the Risk Register. Risk Owners should be ready to share any changes.

- **Risk Occurs:** The Risk Owner leads execution of the risk response should a risk occur. A negative risk that occurs is referred to as an "issue." A positive risk that occurs is referred to as a "benefit."

- **Risk Audit:** A Risk Audit should be conducted every time a risk response is executed. The Risk Audit is a simple Lessons Learned activity. You determine what went well, what you could do better if a like risk occurs in the future, and document your improvement ideas.

- **Residual Risks:** There may be times when you implement a risk response and the result does not meet expectations. There may be other times when the response changes the risk Metalanguage definition. Risks that remain after a response is executed are referred to as "Residual Risks." These risks need to be annotated and reevaluated on the Risk Register to determine an appropriate response strategy.

The Control phase is critically important. Stay on top of risks, execute responses as planned, and evaluate how well the response worked. The entire project will benefit. We want to share one last tool used in the Control Phase before we summarize the chapter. Check out Figure 9.13.

### Figure 9.13 Risk Management Matrix

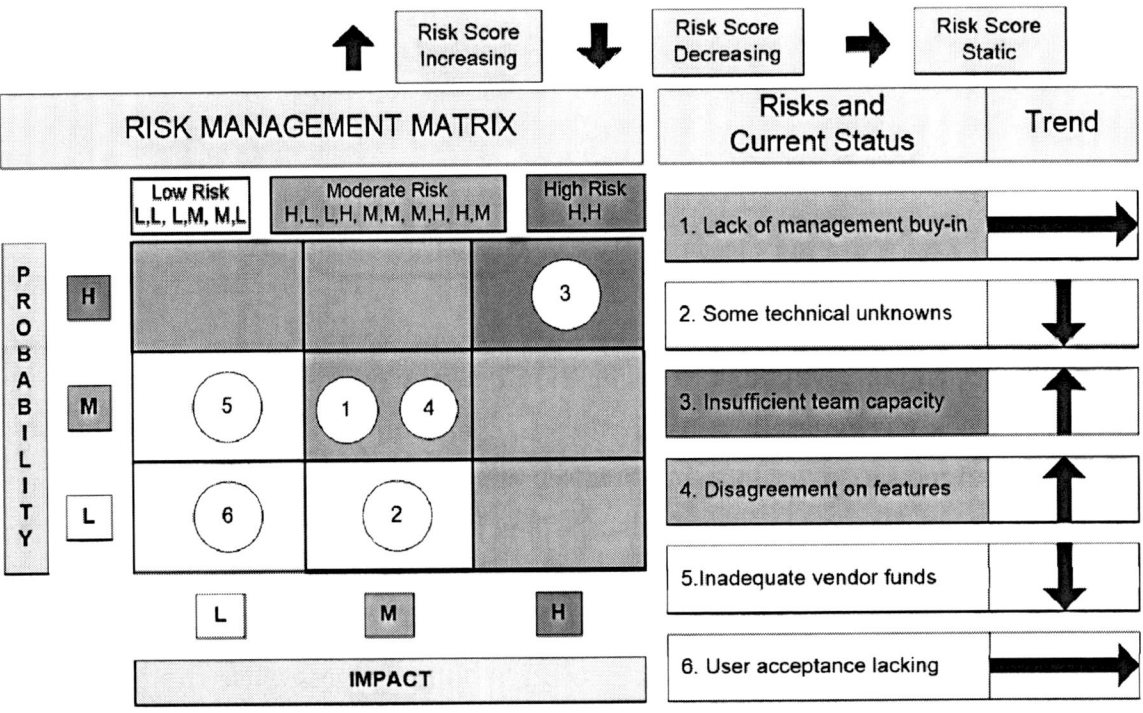

The Risk Management Matrix can be used to show the status of selected risks on a single page. Select those risks that you believe stakeholders need to know about. You are limited to six risks. However, you can add and subtract the risks you share as conditions change. Here are some main features of the Risk Management Matrix:

- **Arrows:** Dark colored arrows depict changing risk score conditions. You can show if the risk score has increased, remained stable, or decreased since the last status report.

- o   Arrows headed up will always grab the attention of the stakeholders, which is one of the primary purposes of the matrix.

- o   You may use downward trending arrows as a way to say thank you to the project team members or stakeholders who contributed to the downward change.

- **Risk Status:** Status of each risk is visually shown on the matrix. If using a five point scale as we suggest, low risk scores are 1 and 2, moderate are 3 and 4, and high is a 5. We shaded this matrix so you can view it easily in the book. Many project managers color code low risks as green, moderate as yellow, and high as red. If you use this coding, label the matrix sections to accommodate those who may be color blind.

- **Risk Identifiers:** Ensure the risk status is specific and easily understood by all. An ambiguous description may negate the effect of the matrix.

## Chapter 9 Summary

We hope you enjoyed our trip to PIER-C. More importantly, we hope this all makes sense. We reserve the right to repeat key concepts—"manage risk or it will manage you."

We will now move forward to a short but important chapter on Project Planning—Putting it all together. We have provided many different tips, tools, and techniques. Now that you feel you have a solid project plan, how do you present the plan to a prospective Sponsor to gain approval to move forward, or more challenging, recommend the project be delayed, altered greatly, or even cancelled?

Peter has some words of wisdom for you in his corner. In addition, we have some food for thought that you can ponder. Thanks all for staying with us through this important chapter. We are delighted you are along for what we think is a very important ride!

> *"Project Managers are the most creative pros in the world; we have to figure out everything that could go wrong, before it does." -- Fredrick Haren*

# Peter's Corner:  Chapter 9 Edition

A project manager is a risk manager.  Think about it – risk to schedule, risk to scope, risk to budget, risk to quality, and more.  One could say that risk management is about one-half of a project manager's job.  Really good project managers take project risk seriously, and use a disciplined approach to risk.  In this chapter, Dan has laid out a simple, comprehensive, and effective way to manage risk.  I strongly encourage you to adopt and adapt it to your projects.

**Some proven tips:**

Delegate risk management using the project WBS.  Assuming your project has a few persons leading major branches (also known as work streams) of your WBS (e.g., Dev, Test, and Release as Level 2 WBS "boxes)--try to delegate ownership for ALL of the risks in each WBS branch to the person leading that branch.  After all, shouldn't those closest to and most knowledgeable about the risks own the risks?  The WBS branch leader can delegate down the branch as appropriate.  This way each team member will own a handful of risks.  Besides freeing up the project manager to manage and lead other areas of the project, this results in everyone using the same risk management process, the same terminology, and the same register, matrix, etc.  Standardization of risk processes and management throughout the project will provide for a much more successful project.

Preventing an issue is much cheaper than resolving an issue.  You have no doubt heard that it is many times cheaper to prevent a bug than to fix a bug.  This same thinking applies to issues.  Recall that an issue results from a negative risk that "happens".  Issues are the main reason that projects fail, or partially fail to meet their success criteria.  What if we could reduce the number and severity of issues?  This is obviously where risk management comes into play.  More effective risk management will reduce the number and severity of issues.  Q.E.D. (Look this up!☺  Or, if totally stumped, here is a hint: Glossary.)

Risk is an ongoing "sport" throughout the project.  Continue to identify new risks from Day 1 to the end of the project.  Risk identification is not a "one and done" endeavor.  Some project managers identify risks during planning and think they are done.  Big mistake!

Consider inserting five minutes for identifying new risks into recurring project team meetings – go from unknown to known risks.  Put new risks on the Risk Register and assign Risk Owners.  This is especially effective during the execution phase of a project when team members get "surprised" by new issues. They would not be surprised and have to deal with new issues if they had made the time earlier to identify and manage the new risks. Consider offering incentives for team members to identify new risks. Make risk a forethought rather than an afterthought. In this way, risk as a forethought will become part of the project team's culture – a proactive rather than a reactive culture.

Your risk tolerance may be different than the risk tolerance of the Project Sponsor and Customers. Let's assume that you, as project management, have a high tolerance for risk. "Bring it on, we'll deal with the issues as they arise." Let's assume that the Project Sponsor and/or Customers have a comparatively low risk tolerance. They are rather risk averse. Let's further assume that during the project planning phase, you plotted all of your project's risk on to the Risk Management Matrix, and the risks tend to cluster toward the top right of the matrix – a risky project. You are comfortable with this project risk profile, but the Project Sponsor and/or Customers are not. What should you do? The project manager and their team are the "delivery vehicle." They deliver the project outcomes per the agreements and with an acceptable level of risk. The acceptable level of risk is determined by the Project Sponsor and Customers. The project manager is obligated to use risk response strategies to move the risks in the Risk Management Matrix to the left and down until the profile aligns with the risk tolerances of the Project Sponsor and Customers.

# Chapter 9 Food for Thought

1. How does your organization plan for risk? Are the methods used effective? Why? Are they ineffective? Why?

2. A senior manager impacted by the project you are managing believes risk management is overkill. He advises you to begin executing the project and to worry about risks when and if they occur. How would you respond to this request?

3. Has there ever been an opportunity in your life that passed by before you could grasp it? What was the opportunity lost, and if possible, what could you have done better to capture it?

4. A team member is looking at the Risk Register you just produced and asks why it is needed. What is your response?

5. Think about risks that are impacting your life today. Is there a risk that scores a 25 based on probability × impact? What is this risk? How might you respond?

6. Recall three or four risks that impacted a project you or your organization was working? How did they respond to these risks? Stretch yourself to use the seven strategies we shared in your explanation. In addition, stretch yourself one more time. Can you also add a positive risk reflection?

7. We stated that "you can manage risk or risk will manage you." Did we make a believer of you? Why or why not?

8. Peter's Deep Thought Challenges:

*Reflections*

   Imagine a situation where as a condition of a mortgage loan, the bank requires you to carry flood insurance. You do not want to carry flood insurance. You would prefer to bear the risk yourself. How does this situation relate to project risk? (Hint: recall risk tolerances of different stakeholders/stakeholder groups).

   - Recall a project that did not go well. What were the main reasons that it did not go well?

   - How many of these reasons did you or your project team foresee?

- How many of these reasons *should* you or your project team have foreseen?

- Most projects do not go well because of insufficient risk management. What will you do differently in your next project?

The Sydney Opera House was a fascinating and risky project.[30] It was completed in 1973, ten years late and 1,457% over budget in real terms. Skim its history at the link in the footnote and especially review the "Design and Construction" section. From what you now know about this project, was it a successful project (overall)? If you had been the project manager on this project, how would you have approached risk? How would you have communicated risks to your key stakeholders?

---

[30] https://en.wikipedia.org/wiki/Sydney_Opera_House

# Chapter 10: Project Planning: Putting it all Together

Over the past nine chapters, we have walked you through a number of proven techniques you can use to build a simple and effective project plan. Preparation is critical. Preparation gives you what you need to win the day. Presentation is critical as well. Presentation is the action that takes you to the winner's circle.

In this chapter we want to accomplish two goals. First of all, we want to tie together everything we've shared to ensure your preparation is adequate. We've given you a lot to think about. But when you look at the whole package and take a step by step approach to planning your project, it's not overly difficult.

With that said, having a solid project plan is not enough. How you share the plan with stakeholders to influence the right decision is challenging. That brings us to our second goal in this chapter. We want to share HOW to present your project plan so you can win the day. We can say that solid preparation gets you in the door. A solid presentation keeps you there.

Figure 10.1 provides a step by step approach to planning that covers everything we have shared in the first nine chapters. We'll share the figure first, then summarize and discuss each step.

> *Project Management Tip: When presenting a project plan, follow the rule of ABC. Ensure what you share is Accurate, Brief, and Concise.*

# Figure 10.1 Project Initiation and Planning Sequence

| Project Initiation and Planning Sequence | | |
|---|---|---|
| Step | Deliverables | Desired Results |
| Step 1: Initiating | 1. Project Charter<br>2. Stakeholder Register | 1. Approve, Kill, or Delay<br>2. Stakeholder Agreement<br>3. Pre-Baseline |
| Step 2: Stakeholder Planning | 1. Stakeholder Management Plan | 1. Stakeholder Current and Desired States<br>2. Commitment Strategies<br>3. Stakeholder Risks |
| Step 3: Scope Planning | 1. Requirements Feasibility & Prioritization Matrix<br>2. Scope Statement<br>3. WBS & Dictionary | 1. Defined Scope<br>2. Expectations Managed<br>3. Scope Risks |
| Step 4: Time & Cost Planning | 1. Project Schedule<br>2. Project Budget | 1. Schedule & Budget<br>2. Trade-offs Determined<br>3. Expectations Managed<br>4. Schedule & Budget Risks |
| Step 5: Support Planning | 1. Staffing Management Plan and RACI<br>2. Communications Management Plan<br>3. Change Management Process | 1. Project Team and Roles Established<br>2. Communications Strategy<br>3. Transparent Change Management Process |
| Step 6: Risk Planning | 1. Risk Management Plan<br>2. Risk Register | 1. End-to-End Risk Program<br>2. Risk Owners on Board |
| Step 7: Project Planning | 1. Project Management Plan | 1. Approve, Kill, or Delay<br>2. Stakeholder Agreement<br>3. Baseline Presentations<br>4. Approval & Acceptance |

## Step 1: Initiating

The initiating process group was covered in Chapter 2. During this step, we created two critical documents. The Project Charter is the first document completed. This document describes the project at a high level. If approved, the Project Charter drives the project planning. The Stakeholder Register lists key stakeholders impacted or interested in the project. The Stakeholder Register is started at the same time as the Project Charter but not completed until the Project Charter is approved. Goals in Initiating are listed below.

- **Approve, Kill, or Delay the Project:** Remember, not all projects should be approved. The purpose of the Project Charter is to ensure the right projects are approved and to kill or delay projects that for whatever reason should not be implemented.

- **Stakeholder Agreement:** The Stakeholder Register needs to be shared with stakeholders who you believe are impacted and interested in the project. Do not simply develop a Stakeholder Register; distribute it, and assume everyone is on board. Follow up and gauge the level of agreement and commitment of the stakeholders on the list.

- **Pre-Baseline:** Approval of the Project Charter is referred to as Pre-Baseline. This does not mean the project is ready for execution. Pre-Baseline authorizes a project manager to move to the planning stage. It should also provide an adequate level of sponsorship, and allow the project manager to form a project management team.

## Step 2: Stakeholder Planning

We shared a Stakeholder Management Plan in Chapter 2. Once Pre-Baseline is achieved, this is your first planning order of business. This is *your* plan. Unlike the Stakeholder Register, the Stakeholder Management Plan allows you to gauge levels of commitment, and develop strategies to align stakeholders where you believe they need to be.

- **Stakeholder Current and Desired States:** Stakeholders need to be committed at the level required to support the project. The project manager must determine current versus desired commitment states, and develop strategies to get stakeholders to the level they require.

- o Every stakeholder does not need to be listed on the Stakeholder Management Plan. Select specific stakeholders whose commitment levels are critical who may not be where they need to be, or who need "tender loving care" to keep them where they are.

- **Commitment Strategies:** Every stakeholder is unique. In Chapter 2, we shared McClelland's 3 Needs Theory. This is one example of developing a specific strategy to gain the commitment of everyone on the Stakeholder Management Plan. You may need to sell achievement to some stakeholders. Others may be swayed by the desire to support the team, or affiliation. Others may need assurances that their voice will be heard. The bottom line in terms of developing strategies is that truly, one size does not fit all. We will share some insight on commitment using the Emergenetics model later in this chapter.

- **Stakeholder Risks:** Identifying and documenting risks is not "finalized" until Step 6. In reality, however, identification of risks began in Step 1. Identify potential risks as you go through each step of the planning process. At this point, annotate any "stakeholder" risks you may identify. Add to the Risk Register as you go.

## Step 3: Scope Planning

Developing the project baseline begins with scope. This is the primary purpose of a project—to satisfy a customer need. Schedule and budget are important. However, there is no need for a schedule or budget if there is nothing of value to deliver. Get scope, schedule, and budget right—on time, within budget, and what the customer needs remains your mantra. Scope, however, is the gift that keeps giving long after the project is closed.

We shared some critical tools and techniques in Chapter 3 that we hope you will use. The Requirements Feasibility and Prioritization Matrix allows you to determine what should— and should not—be included in project scope. It allows for a method to quantify your rationale in a way that leads to prioritization of all requirements. The Scope Statement allows you to organize project deliverables in a way that details everything you need to accomplish— and provides a chronological timeframe to complete them. The WBS and WBS Dictionary build on the Scope Statement, and provide a detailed overview of all activities that must be accomplished, along with the order of accomplishment, to satisfy the project.

At the end of scope planning, there are a number of critical objectives you need to meet. There are many reasons why projects fail. Poor scope definition and management as we shared in Chapter 1 is one of the big ones.

- **Defined Scope:** You need to ensure that the scope of the project is defined. In addition, you need to ensure what is *not* in scope is defined and clear to all stakeholders. Strive to include the total scope required to meet the needs of the Project Charter. Scope planning is not the time to start looking for trade-offs and making concessions. That will occur when you build your schedule and budget, review constraints, and determine what scope can be accomplished within the time and budget you have.

- **Expectations Managed:** Don't catch stakeholders by surprise. Let them know what the project will produce, and be ready to share why some stakeholders may not get everything they asked for. It is imperative that all stakeholders understand the scope of the project, and buy-in. Buy-in does not necessarily mean everyone is happy. Buy-in means that they "get it" and will support the project as-is.

- **Scope Risks:** It is time to break out the Risk Register. There are a number of potential scope risks you will likely identify during this step. Capture them now before you move forward.

<u>Note 1:</u> There may be times when you can't gain agreement on what is in scope, and what is not. When this occurs, you need to schedule a meeting with the Sponsor who approved the Project Charter and explain the situation. You may need the Sponsor to act as an arbitrator to determine what gets done—and what doesn't.

<u>Note 2:</u> Decision making is a key interpersonal skill that all project managers need to excel on to the greatest extent possible. Peter shared a decision making model with me called "OARP." Stay tuned for Chapter 11—we will highlight and share this method. This may be a model you need to use if you can't gain agreement on scope.

## Step 4: Time and Cost Planning

Scope planning drives these next two planning areas. In the real world, time and cost planning happen concurrently. Build a schedule and budget that meets the needs of the project scope. Initially, strive for a "perfect" schedule and budget. This perfect scenario may not support the stated project constraints. When that is the case, conversations need to be had and adjustments need to be made. Here are some key success factors to strive for by the end of time and cost planning.

- **Schedule and Budget:** Develop a schedule and budget that meets the needs of the project. We discussed "bottom up" estimating in Chapter 5. Use your WBS as a means to determine time and cost requirements for each activity. This ensures you have covered all project activities in your Schedule Baseline and Cost Baseline that you will ultimately put in your final project plan.

- **Trade-Offs Determined:** There may be times when the schedule and budget do not support the stated objectives for the project in the Project Charter. When this occurs, you need to once again engage in conversation with the Project Sponsor and discuss trade-offs. There are a number of options you can present as follows:

    o **Accelerate Schedules:** You can accelerate schedules in two ways. First, reduce the scope. Look at the WBS and determine what can be cut to save time. Secondly, add budget and resources to increase work capacity needed to deliver the project and scope on time.

    o **Reduce Resources and Costs:** You can reduce resource requirements and costs in two ways. First, reduce the scope. Once gain review your WBS to determine which activities can be cut to save the resources and budget you need. Second, extend the schedule. Oftentimes, spreading out a schedule reduces resource requirements and yields cost savings.

    o **Document the Risk:** If you can't cut scope, extend schedules, or add budget, then you need to document the potential risks that may prevent the project from being successful if you pursue the original scope, time and cost constraints dictated. The Risk Register becomes part of the overall approved project plan. By documenting the risks, you can at least show "I told you so" if the project runs into problems. Remember your options to respond to negative risk include avoid, transfer, mitigate, or accept. Use these definitions to your advantage.

- **Expectations Managed:** At the end of this step, all stakeholders should be aware of the scope, time, and cost objectives you will share in the project plan. In addition, they need to be aware of the risks associated with this plan. It is a best practice to have "meetings before the meeting" with key stakeholders so they won't be surprised when you present the final project plan for their acceptance.

- **Schedule and Budget Risks:** It's time to update the Risk Register again. Document the risks associated with the schedule and budget you will propose.

## Step 5: Support Planning

Once scope, time, and cost are determined, you need to complete some key support plans to ensure the needs of the project are met. In Chapter 6, we shared a project change management process that is a must if you truly want to influence causes that lead to change. In Chapter 7, we presented a Staffing Management Plan and RACI tool that allow you to ensure the right project team members are on-board when the project needs them, and that their roles and responsibilities are defined. In Chapter 8, we shared the methodology to develop and staff a Communications Management Plan. Remember, you can manage communications or communications will manage you. Shut down the grapevine as quickly as you can. Your support planning needs to yield the following results:

- **Project Team and Roles Established:** Remember our quote earlier from Andrew Carnegie? People are your most important resource. You need to ensure that all project team members understand expectations of them. Share their role, and when they will be required to accomplish that role. In addition, ensure you provide as much advance notice as possible to Functional Managers who manage the team members you need.

- **Communications Strategy:** Development and sharing your Communications Management Plan is an important step you need to take to control project communications and ensure the right information gets to the right people at the right time. Share the plan, ensure stakeholders understand the communications rhythm you are trying to create, and commit to supporting the plan. If you believe there may be issues, identify the potential problems and develop strategies to overcome them. We said it before, "Communications is 90% of everything a project manager does."

- **Transparent Change Management Process:** Speaking of the Communications Management Plan—ensure a change management process is included. Develop the process, share the process, and to the best of your ability—enforce the process. Reward those who conform—and address those who do not. Partner with your Sponsor and enlist their support to evangelize your process.

## Step 6: Risk Planning

Summarize all risks you have recorded through the planning process. Then, use the RBS or some of the other risk identification tools we introduced to ensure you capture as many risks as possible. Don't forget that risks come in two forms—positive and negative. Strive to capture both types.

Chapter 9 was one of our longest in this book. There's a reason. Risk management IS that important. You are nearing the end of planning as you implement this step. Here is what success looks like:

- **End-to End Risk Program:** Ensure you develop a Risk Management Plan that defines "how" you will manage risk. This document needs to be shared with all stakeholders. The primary tool that identifies and qualifies project risk is the Risk Register. Develop it, share it, update it, and use this as a means to control risks. Your Risk Register is best organized by having three sections. Section 1 is for Threats. Section 2 is for Opportunities. Section 3 (Risk Register Dictionary??) is for more detailed responses by the numeric designator you assigned to each risk. You have been provided with some proven tools and techniques. Use them!

- **Risk Owners on Board:** Remember, the project manager isn't required to do everything. The more a project manager is in the "weeds", the more they lose sight of the big picture and what is happening around them. Try to enlist support of Subject Matter Experts who have the skills needed to effectively manage individual risks. Share the importance of this job, and reward those Risk Owners who go above and beyond. We shared earlier that "thank you" is powerful.

## Step 7: Project Planning

You are now ready to share your plan and your recommendations. Up to this point, you have invested time and effort to effectively analyze and plan the project. The good news is that you've not spent any funds or used personnel resources to begin development of the proposed product or service. It is worth repeating again—only recommend that the right projects move forward. Does your project satisfy this criterion? Here is your challenge before presenting the project plan to Sponsors and other stakeholders.

- **Approve, Kill, or Delay:** It's cut and paste time from Step 1. Remember, not all projects should be approved. The purpose of the project plan is to ensure the right projects are approved, and to kill or delay projects that for whatever reason should not be implemented. Just because you have a project plan doesn't mean that the project should move forward. The time you invested in planning is a small investment when compared to the cost of executing a poor project.

- **Stakeholder Agreement:** Planning a project is like climbing a mountain. You develop the project plan one step at a time. Consider each planning step as arriving at a base station on a mountain. At each base station, check in with stakeholders. Let them know where you are on the journey. Revise and redirect as necessary to ensure everyone agrees that the mountain is still worth climbing. The time to bring stakeholders on board—to have the meetings before the meeting—is during the planning process. If you wait until the end of the planning process, the likelihood of receiving lots of negative feedback or resistance is high.

- **Baseline Presentations:** You may need to make multiple presentations as you complete each planning phase. The one that counts is when you go in front of the Sponsor and make your go or no-go proposal. Our next section in this chapter will share best practices in presenting both a Project Charter and Project Management Plan. More repetition but worth sharing—preparation PLUS presentation wins the day.

- **Approval and Acceptance:** The Project Baseline by definition is the approved and accepted Project Management Plan. Approval comes from the Project Sponsor. Acceptance comes from the stakeholders. A project Kick-Off Meeting is intended to share the final approved plan with stakeholders to gain their acceptance and commitment and formally kick-off the Executing Process Group. Again—*key concept*—no surprises here. Grease the skids, so to speak, by sharing early and often during the planning process. Don't allow the Kick-Off Meeting to become a "kick you" event.

A lot of work goes into project planning. However, if you follow this plan and stay the course, the execution of the project will go much more smoothly. Some project managers fail to proactively plan up-front. In the end, they react to issues along the way, are in a constant state of re-planning, and actually spend more time on planning in the end with less than stellar results. Failing to plan is truly planning to fail.

We now turn our attention to the Pre-Baseline and Baseline Presentations. Tip number one: *don't* read the entire Project Charter or project plan. Tip number two: summarize the what, why, and who factors. Minimize the "how." Figure 10.2 provides an overview of how to conduct these important presentations simply and effectively.

> *Project Management Tip:*
> *Fail to plan and plan to fail.*
> *The time you spend planning*
> *is truly time well spent.*

# Figure 10.2 Five-Step Presentation Process

| Five-Step Presentation Process |
|---|
| **Step 1. Attention**<br><br>Develop a compelling "What is the project?" statement. Strive for action and result. Avoid long explanations and combat ambiguity. |
| **Step 2. Motivation**<br><br>Provide a quick value proposition for the proposed project. "Why is this project needed now?" Think "Balanced Scorecard." |
| **Step 3. The Body**<br><br>Focus on four areas for a Project Charter or Project Management Plan review. Your Project Management Plan information will be at a more definitive level than your Project Charter presentation.<br><br>• Scope: Provide a brief overview of the product or service the project provides.<br>• Schedule: What are the planned milestones?<br>• Costs: What is the cost impact to the firm compared to the benefits? Consider adding both direct and indirect costs.<br>• Risks: What potential risks may impact time, cost, and scope? Cite both threats and opportunities. |

| Five-Step Presentation Process Continued |
|---|
| **Step 4. Remotivation**<br><br>Here is the first part of your summary. Repeat your conviction that the project should or should not be approved. Here is a great place for any "testimonials" you may have. This may seem repetitive. However, sometimes repetition is a plus to influence the right decision. |
| **Step 5. Closure**<br><br>This is where you ask for something. What is your end goal? You might seek approval to move to planning, disapproval, delay the project, etc. If you can't get a commitment, strive to at least solidify next steps. Don't leave with a "We'll get back to you," if at all possible. |

Let's review the highlights of this presentation model. Successful presentations require preparation and organization. They are also crisp, and to the point. Don't be like the salesperson who talked so long they lost the sale.

- **Step 1: Attention Step:** Many presenters dive right into the details without providing context. The first question you want to answer in the listener's mind is "what" you are proposing. There are two ways to accomplish this. You may provide a boring "what" or a compelling "what." Here are a few tips on opening with a compelling "what."

    o **WII-FM:** Share the objective, action and result, in a way that resonates. Peter earlier alluded to WII-FM. It works. Do your homework and present your project objective in a way that motivates the listener. For example: "Customer satisfaction scores dropped 10 percentage points last quarter. This is a problem we need to address now, and we have a plan."

- o **Rhetorical Questions:** Rhetorical questions work well as attention steps. For example, "I believe we can all agree that continuing declines in customer satisfaction is not an option. Is that an accurate assumption?" No one needs to answer. The answer is obvious—and you made your point.

- o **Visuals:** Sometimes a graph can be an effective attention step. For example, a graph that shows customer satisfaction plummeting in the last quarter after being steady for years is a very compelling attention step.

- **Step 2: Motivation Step:** Answering the "what" question gets you in the door. Addressing the "why" question keeps you there. Strive to show why the project needs to be done now. In our previous example where customer satisfaction plummeted, you need little motivation. However, some projects may not have a clear value proposition.

  - o **Balanced Scorecard:** We shared the balanced Scorecard model in Chapter 2. Revisit this model. If you can show that the project has either financial, process, customer, and employee benefits, then you can win the day. The more of these four areas you can map project value to—the more compelling your case for project approval.

  - o **No Value?** On the other hand, if a project does not provide value in any of these four areas, or if the value is minimal, you may have the support you need to kill or delay the project. I know we keep reminding you—but this concept is important. Not all projects should happen.

- **Step 3: The Body:** The project manager's mantra is on time, within budget, and providing the product or service the customer needs. This standard makes "The Body" portion of your presentation easy.

  - o **Scope:** Provide a brief overview of the product or service the project will provide. Be able to show that this product or service meets the needs of the organization—you should be able to link the project to some organizational goal or directive. In addition, be able to share who needs this product or service and why. A little "name dropping" here never hurts if you can link your project to a key customer/user base.

- **Schedule:** Develop a simple milestone chart that tracks to the phases you built into your WBS. If you are using a PDCA model, show when the planning, execution, and follow up activities of the project will occur according to the plan.

- **Costs:** Share the costs of the project. Break out the costs into direct and indirect costs to show the total cost of the project. If there are economic or monetary benefits, share these as well. Typically, benefits fall within two categories; hard benefits and soft benefits.

    - **Hard Benefits:** Hard benefits are sometimes referred to as "bookable" benefits. Management loves hard benefits. Examples of hard benefits include additional revenue, real cost savings that reduce a budget, and cost avoidance. Cost avoidance is the elimination of an approved budgetary item that will not be needed if the project is approved.

    - **Soft Benefits:** Soft benefits are those that do not equate to an immediate measurable budgetary impact. Examples include increased customer satisfaction, increased production, improved morale, etc. However, these benefits are very real and should be included when applicable.

- **Risks:** We talked about the Pareto Principle in Chapter 9. Share the potential threats that may impact the project negatively. Make sure, however, you also show a little love to the opportunities as well. I know we revisit key points over and over again—and it's time to do it again. Not all projects should be approved. This is the area of the presentation you can use to your advantage if you believe the risks outweigh the benefits.

- **Step 4: Remotivation Step:** I was fortunate to attend the Air Force's Academic Instructor School. One of the first lessons I learned in effective presenting was this model: Tell them what you are going to tell them, tell them, and tell them what you told them. This is the essence of the Remotivation step—"tell them what you told them."

Project Planning: Putting It All Together

- o **Repetition:** It is said that people remember the first and last things they hear. This step is one of the last things you will share. If the project is good, reiterate the value. If the project shouldn't happen, reiterate the rationale for non-approval.

- o **Testimonials:** Testimonials work great during the Remotivation step. If the project team says a project is good, the recommendation carries a certain amount of weight. If someone outside the team says the project is a must, this often carries more weight. If a project adds value, or if a project needs to be killed or delayed, enlist the support of external stakeholders to share their stories and rationale.

- **Step 5: Closure Step:** Have you ever noticed that some people hate to present? At the end of a presentation, they cannot exit the room fast enough. Unfortunately, this is not a good strategy for Step 5. At minimum:

- o **Share Your Recommendation:** Is this a project that needs to happen or not? Have support for the recommendation in your back pocket so to speak.

- o **Next Steps:** You may not always get a decision during the first presentation—and that is ok. Make sure you define the next steps. As we shared in Figure 10.2, don't accept a "we'll call you." Walk out of the room with a plan.

## Five-Step Presentation Process: Final Thoughts

Presenting is difficult. The process we just shared works! *Do not* perform a Pre-Baseline or Baseline Presentation without preparation and a plan. Be organized, be confident, and win the day. This process works in other areas as well. In Chapter 11, we'll introduce effective meeting management. If you need to provide any presentation—project related or not—give this methodology a try. You may be very pleasantly surprised with the outcomes.

We have one final topic before we end Chapter 10. We all have had some introduction to diversity. Different genders, cultures, races, etc. all contribute to the need to use situational leadership and adapt our strategies. I want to briefly introduce you to the Emergenetics model in Figure 10.3.

Emergenetics is a measurable, proven way to recognize and apply thinking attributes and behavior patterns people use regularly. These were identified by reviewing research from a wide body of academic literature covering personality, psychology, and neuroscience. These results were then subjected to rigorous statistical analysis.[31]

Different people are motivated by different things. If you are presenting to a "people person," you need to address the people issues. If you are addressing someone who is a "stickler for the rules," you need an organized approach. Emergenetics provides proven data on how people think and behave. As a project manager—as a presenter—you need to adapt your presentation to meet the needs of your audience to gain approval and commitment.

## Figure 10.3 Emergenetics Approach to Gaining Project Approval and Commitment

| Emergenetics Approach to Gaining Project Approval and Commitment ||
|---|---|
| Thinking Attribute | Preferences |
| Analytical 68% | • Have all facts and figures—provide ahead of time<br>• Take a direct and to-the-point approach<br>• Clearly define the objective or problem<br>• Clearly show the project value proposition |
| Social 61% | • Develop rapport—strive to create a relationship<br>• Show who is "on board" with the idea or project<br>• Stress the "people" impact—how the project affects others<br>• Allow people to provide feedback—thank them for their input |
| Structural 55% | • Present a well-defined, step-by-step approach<br>• Highlight how predictable results will be achieved<br>• Answer how, when, and where questions<br>• Have all the details available, if needed |
| Conceptual 51% | • Present your case visually—show the big picture<br>• Allow for brainstorming and questions<br>• Show how the idea or project fits into the overall vision<br>• Share various options and possibilities |
| Note: Percentages indicate percentage of the overall population with a preference in a specific Thinking Attribute. For example, 68% of all people have an Analytical preference. ||

---

[31] www.Emergenetics.com

Emergenetics measures people based on their preference for one of four Thinking Attributes. Some of us have measured preferences in one or more of these Thinking Attributes. Here is a brief overview of the four Thinking Attributes and how you can effectively motivate each and potentially gain commitment to support your project.

## The Analytical Stakeholder

According to Emergenetics, 68% of the many millions who have taken an Emergenetics assessment have an Analytical preference. The primary question the Analytical stakeholder wants answers to is, "Why?"

What does this information mean to you? In essence, project decision makers need what we shared in Figure 10.3. Have your support data ready, cut to the chase, be clear and concise, and show the value. Include an analytical "pitch" in your attention or motivation statement if possible. There are three key questions you want to address in every presentation. Incorporate these questions where they make sense in the presentation process we shared earlier.

- Do I have the pertinent facts?
- What provides the most value?
- Will this solution resolve the problem?

## The Social Stakeholder

Approximately 61% of those who have taken an Emergenetics assessment have a Social preference. The primary question the Social stakeholder wants answers to is, "Who?"

If you are curious about the math here, individuals often have multiple preferences. According to Emergenetics statistics, 6% of the population has a single preference, 58% of the general population has two preferences, and 36% have three preferences. About 1/10 of 1% actually have preferences in all four areas.

When presenting to someone with a social preference, work to develop a relationship and ensure you can clearly state who is committed to the project, which stakeholders the project impacts, who you have collaborated with, and any pertinent feedback you received. A great place for this is during the scope overview. If you highly suspect the key decision maker is social, then lead with a social "hook" in your attention or motivation step. Here are three questions you need to be able to answer:

- How will the project affect others?
- How can we do this project together?
- Are the right people committed and involved?

## The Structural Stakeholder

Approximately 55% of those who have taken an Emergenetics assessment have a Structural preference. The primary questions the Structural stakeholder wants answers to are, "How, When, and Where?"

If you presenting to a stakeholder with a Structural preference, provide the details, share your process, focus on predictable results and outputs, and show examples if possible. Do not add too many details to your presentation. If needed, sprinkle them into the body without going too deep. Do, however, have the details available in the Appendix of the presentation and be able to access them if needed. The Structural stakeholder also has three questions that are near and dear. They include:

- How can we get the project done?
- What is the implementation process and timeline?
- Who is in control and what is my role?

## The Conceptual Stakeholder

Our final Thinking Attribute is Conceptual. Approximately 51% of all individuals have a preference in Conceptual thinking. Conceptuals are concerned most about the "What?" questions regarding the project fit, big picture, and context considerations. They are often very creative and enjoy thinking out of the box.

When presenting to a Conceptual, address key areas of the project, such as options considered and how the project fits with the organization's vision. Try to use visuals wherever possible, and allow time for brainstorming and questions. The primary Conceptual questions include:

- Have we looked at all the possibilities?
- What is the big picture?
- How can we take this to a new level?

## Identifying the Emergenetics Attributes

We realize you don't have access to your stakeholder's Emergenetics profile unless you work for one of the many firms that have embraced Emergenetics as a standard means to determine their employees' preferences. Fortunately, oftentimes each of the preferences are revealed by the phrases people use in their everyday lives. For your reference, here is a list of key phrases by Thinking Attribute.

Understanding the primary Thinking Attributes of those around you will enhance your ability to more effectively make statements and ask questions that have meaning to the individual you are trying to communicate with, and better target your communications. Here are lists of phrase and/or questions appropriate for each of the four Thinking Attributes.

### Analytical Phrases

1. Please get to the point.
2. Let's cut to the chase.
3. What is the cost/benefit ratio?
4. This doesn't seem rational to me.
5. I've been analyzing the situation.
6. What's the bottom line?
7. I'll skip the details and give you the Executive Summary.
8. If it isn't logical, it isn't right.
9. What does the research say?
10. I need to see the data.
11. This doesn't seem credible.
12. What is the problem we are trying to solve?

## Social Phrases

1. How are you feeling about this?
2. Respect and dignity above all else.
3. I'm concerned about how others will react.
4. I'm sure you want to be involved in the discussion.
5. Have all the right people been included?
6. How will this affect customers?
7. Are we administering the policies fairly to all?
8. Let's work through this together.
9. How does that grab you?
10. I am hurt. You haven't returned my call.
11. How does this appear in writing? I want to make everyone feel better.
12. I really love your contribution to this team.

## Structural Phrases

1. We've always done it this way.
2. If it isn't broke, don't fix it.
3. I need more details.
4. We don't need to reinvent the wheel.
5. A place for everything, and everything in its place.
6. Slow down. Let's take this one step at a time.
7. What does the policy say?
8. Are we on schedule?
9. The results are fairly predictable.
10. Let's take an inventory.
11. Let's get down to business.
12. Efficiency is the key.

## Conceptual Phrases

1. I have this wild idea.
2. Let's brainstorm new ways to solve this.
3. This routine stuff is so boring.
4. What is the big picture here?
5. Let's not rein ourselves in.
6. How does this connect to the vision?
7. I'll play around with this and come up with ideas. (Peter's favorite ☺)
8. This has the right flow.
9. Let's look at all the options.
10. Let's take this to the next level.
11. We need to think out of the box.
12. I treasure your ingenious ideas.

## Chapter 10 Summary

Understanding how to develop a project plan in the proper sequence will help you become more successful. One more time—remember that all projects should not be approved. Use your project plan to your advantage to elicit the right decision.

Preparation is critical. However, great preparation can be wiped out by poor presentation. Embrace and review the five-step presentation methodology we shared. It is simple, effective, and yields good results.

A key to presentation success understands the preferences of those you deal with. A "one size fits all" presentation will likely not yield desired results. We were delighted to introduce you to Emergenetics. Diversity goes beyond the person you see on the outside. We can make a great case that the greatest diversity consideration is how all human beings think. If you develop a presentation that resonates with the whole brain, then a greater chance of being successful will follow.

In Chapter 11, we will provide best practices for executing, monitoring and controlling, and closing the project. Effective meeting management is essential for the project manager. Status reporting is critical as well. We will also introduce a methodology you can use to make the critical decisions that will be required during the course of a project, and discuss the criticality of conducting Lessons Learned.

So there is more to come. But not without a trip to Peter's Corner and some additional food for thought about what we shared in this chapter.

## Peter's Corner: Chapter 10 Edition

**Be realistic. Tell it like it is.** Some project managers present the scope, schedule, and budget that others want or expect to see – and pay dearly for this mistake for the rest of the project.

Recall the project triangle, the triple constraints. The triangle is a means to prioritize scope, schedule, and budget. It tells the project what is a fixed constraint. Let us assume that the project finish date is fixed. Let us further assume that the project team developed a "most likely" schedule (recall PERT in Chapter 4) that calculates a project finish date 15% later than the fixed or mandated finish date. What should the project manager do? First, review what it would take to finish the project when mandated. Add resources? Cut scope? Reduce quality? Let us assume that these options have been exhausted, and the calculated project finish date remains later than the mandated date. Again, what should the project manager do? *Bring risk into the conversation* Recall that a project manager is a risk manager. *A schedule is a model, not reality.*

Many assumptions go into a schedule, some of which will not prove true. The project manager needs to remind the Sponsor and other key stakeholders that no scheduled project finish date is 100% probable. So if you have done everything possible with the schedule to try to meet the mandated finish date, and you are still coming up short, what do you do? I think you know the answer. The best you can do is to say that the team will do their best to make the date. What we know today is that the date is very unlikely (put a probability on it – say, 10%). If your schedule baseline must be the fixed or mandated date, then accept the mandated date *with your caveats* – 10% probability, and here is why. Tell the Project Sponsor and key stakeholders that you and the team will do everything possible to make the date, *and* that you will keep them informed throughout the project, *and* that you will most likely need their help along the way. If you choose to insert some humor, ask them "when was the last time you witnessed a miracle?" So try your best, and keep them informed throughout the project. Recall our Chapter 8 on communications.

The above discussion should bring to mind negotiation and conflict, two similar yet different things. The project manager should develop schedule scenarios, calculate the schedule with these different scenarios – in short, be prepared to thoroughly discuss options and tradeoffs with the Sponsor and key stakeholders – ideally before the baseline presentation. Recall the "meetings before the meeting". The objective is to resolve most if not all of the differences before the baseline meeting. Otherwise, the baseline meeting becomes a "war zone" with the probable outcome being an impasse, and the need for another meeting. Come to the baseline presentation with most if not all of the real and perceived differences resolved, and the baseline meeting will go smoothly. It is beyond the scope of this book to delve into negotiation and its close cousin, conflict resolution. Project managers need to be very competent in both of these areas. Dan and I go into these, as well as other soft skills, in our book on project leadership.

The main point of the above discussion is to do your homework, be realistic, bring risk into the conversation, negotiate, and be sure that everyone understands what is being agreed to, with the caveats. This applies to any and all parts of the baseline presentation, including schedule, scope, budget, etc. I like to say that the project manager and their team is the "delivery vehicle" – along the way they must "tee up" information for decision making – lay out the options, with pros and cons and, perhaps, your recommendation. Let the decision maker(s) decide, then you and your team carry out the decision – keep them informed along the way and ask for help when necessary. Here are a few more things to think about.

**Agree Change Management.** This bears repeating. By or at baseline, make sure that all key stakeholders understand and agree to abide by the change management process, including their role or roles in the process. Now is the time to get this agreement, not later when changes start coming in. Tell them you will hold them accountable to their agreement to abide by the process.

**Know your audience.** Communication is a two-way street. We default to the way we see things – the way we like to tell things. However, this is *usually not the way others see things and want to hear things.* So get to know how your Project Sponsor and other key stakeholders prefer to receive information. The last part of this chapter gives you phrases and questions, or cues, that will help you to size up your audience *before* you design and develop your presentation. *Begin with your audience in mind.* Try it. It will work in presentations, in conversations, on the job, and in life.

# Chapter 10 Food for Thought

1. Why do you need a structured approach to putting together a project plan? Can you share five reasons?

2. The Stakeholder Management Plan is the first plan you develop after approval of the Project Charter and completion of the Stakeholder Register. Why is this so?

3. Have you ever seen a great presentation? If so, what made it great?

4. Reflect on a presentation that didn't go well. As you look back, how could you have improved it?

5. In the Emergenetics model, which Thinking Attributes do you believe reflect your preferences and motivations? Why?

6. Choose an Emergenetics Thinking Attribute that does not reflect your preferences. If you were giving a Baseline Presentation to someone whose preferred Thinking Attributes were not like yours, what would be your strategy? Choose one attribute that is not a preference for you.

7. Peter's Deep Thought Challenges:

*Reflections*

- Recall a project where the project manager agreed at Baseline to finish the project by a very aggressive, mandated, and unrealistic date. How did the project play out? Reflect holistically, and include relationships and the health of the project team. Think about how it may have been different if the project manager had applied the approach provided in Peter's Corner for this chapter.

- Recall a time when you gave a presentation. How did it go? Did it exceed your expectations? Why or why not? Okay, now that you are warmed up, let's get to the hard part. Ideally, you, as presenter, are fully *present* and *aware* throughout your presentation. This means that you are aware of everything that is going on with your audience, including reading their body language and deeply listening to what they say. To do this, you must be totally comfortable in yourself, as well as with the content of your presentation. This frees you up to be aware of and manage the relationships of you and others, and others with others. Have you done this before? Have you seen others do this? What were the results? How did it feel?

# Chapter 11: Project Executing, Monitoring and Controlling, and Closing: Achieving Results

There are so many topics we could share here! However, we will stick with some basics. We will start the chapter by sharing best practices and tips to ensure your project is executed and closed as planned. We will then turn our attention to decision making. This is one of the key skills needed by a project manager to succeed. There is a decision making model called "OARP" we think you'll appreciate.

Status reporting is critical to project success as well. It is important to ask for the right amount of information at the right time and share current status with the stakeholders of the project. We will share a status report template that works.

Meetings are a fact of life in a project manager's life. When I first became a project manager, I quickly found out that an alternative definition of the PM acronym was "Perpetual Meetings." ☺ We will share some key meeting management tips, and share a sample agenda template that works. We'll also share a proven meeting minutes template that works as well.

We'll include some discussion on managing stakeholders effectively. As a project manager, it is imperative you effectively influence stakeholders to move them in the direction needed to satisfy the project.

Finally, we'll end with a brief overview of Project Closure. There are actions that must be planned and executed to ensure closure is completed properly. Lessons Learned are a key success factor to support future projects.

## Project Execution, Monitoring and Controlling, and Closing: Scope, Time, and Cost

Having a great plan is one thing. Turning the plan into reality is another. Here are some tips to be aware of as you execute your project.

### Managing Scope

As we shared earlier, you have to get the scope right. Scope is the gift that keeps on giving long after the project has closed out. Keep these tips in mind:

- **Check In Incrementally:** Check in with your team at various stages during execution. Make sure the team is aware of all approved changes and working on the latest version of the plan. Keep your eyes open for any "Scope Creep" and prevent it to the greatest extent possible. Be available for any questions your team may have, and provide guidance as needed.

- **Validate Scope:** Share deliverables with the customer on a periodic basis when it makes sense. Share your progress with customers as you progress and solicit their input. If changes are required, work with the customer to process them. This step is often referred to as User Acceptance Testing (UAT).

- **Fail Fast:** Let the team know that if something doesn't work to share the status and enlist support of all to develop a Plan B. Create a culture where it is ok to fail, as long as the failure is analyzed, corrected quickly, and Lessons Learned are annotated.

- **Say Thank You:** Celebrate success. Share phase completions with key stakeholders and reward top performers contributing to the project. Let management know who excelled as well. Your team will appreciate it.

- **Conduct Lessons Learned:** Document what went well, what you can improve upon, and what you should change next time you execute a like project. Share best practices with others. Share issues that developed that negatively impacted the project. This will allow future project managers to hopefully avoid those issues. Lessons Learned should be accomplished at the end of each phase while recent events are fresh in your team's minds.

## Managing Time

Scheduling is critical. You may produce great scope, but if the product or service does not meet the scheduling needs of the customer, it may be too little too late.

- **Update the Network Diagram:** We hope you took our advice to keep your WBS manageable. If so, you should have a network diagram that is manageable as well. Update your network diagram as changes are approved, and as work packages are completed. Compare the actual versus planned and note variances. Share changes with all key stakeholders, and don't forget, your team is a key stakeholder group too.

- **Compression Techniques:** Use Fast Tracking and Crashing as a means to compress the schedule when it makes sense. Remember that Fast Tracking may increase risk, and Crashing may increase costs.

- **No Surprises:** Let stakeholders know when there are issues that may impact schedule completion. Don't be afraid to code status as "yellow" and ask for help early.

- **NO "No Problem":** Remember that acceleration of schedules comes at a cost. Do not blindly agree to accelerate schedules without sharing the impact on scope and cost.

## Managing Cost

Manage the Cost Baseline. It is impacted by your scope and schedule, and any adjustments must be balanced. Here are a few tips to remember when managing the budget.

- **Cost Risks:** As we just mentioned, risk impacts budget in both a negative and potentially positive way. Keep an eye on risks. When they occur, there will likely be an effect.

- **Earned Value Management (EVM):** EVM has become a popular way to determine a project's schedule and budget status. More and more organizations are adopting EVM methods as a way to determine planned versus actual results, identify variances, and course correct before it is too late. Figure 11.1 provides an overview of EVM methodology.

## Figure 11.1 Tracking Schedule and Budget Using EVM Methodology

| Tracking Schedule and Budget Using Earned Value Management |
|---|
| Your project has a total budget (BAC) of $100,000<br>Your project is 60% complete (EV)<br>You had planned to be 70% complete by this time (PV)<br>To this point, you have used 50% of your available budget or $50,000 (AC) |

| Key EVM Terminology | Budget at Completion (BAC) | Earned Value (EV) | Planned Value (PV) | Actual Cost (AC) |
|---|---|---|---|---|

| Key EVM Calculations | |
|---|---|
| | Cost Variance (CV) = EV – AC<br>In this project, you are 60% - 50% = 10% under budget |
| | Schedule Variance (SV) = EV – PV<br>In this project, you are 60% - 70% = 10% behind schedule |
| | Cost Performance Index (CPI) = EV/AC<br>In this project, you are 60%/50% = 1.2 This is good<br>You are getting $1.20 of value for each dollar you spend |
| | Schedule Performance Index (SPI) = EV/PV<br>In this project, you are 60%/70% = .85 This is not good<br>You are 85% of where you should be. You are behind schedule |
| | Estimate at Completion (EAC) = BAC/CPI<br>In this project, the EAC is $100,000/1.2 = $83,333<br>Good news—if current trends continue you come in under budget |

The EVM process requires you to quantify three key project metrics. You need to know how much of the project you have accomplished. This is called Earned Value, or EV. Next you need to determine how much of the project should be complete at the time of the status sample. This is called Planned Value, or PV. Last, you need to calculate how much of the project budget has been used at a given point in the project. This is called Actual Costs, or AC.

The most challenging piece of EVM is the EV calculation. Many projects do not lend themselves to calculating a precise percentage complete. If you are making 100 widgets, and you have completed 60, this is an easy calculation. Your EV is 60%. However, not all projects have outcomes that are easily quantified. If you are improving a key process for example, calculating an exact percentage complete could be challenging.

In Chapter 3, we introduced a method of calculating a project's completion percentage called the 50/50 method. This is a way to determine the EV so you can use EVM. Let's revisit this method as shown in Figure 11.2.

## Figure 11.2 Calculating Earned Value (EV) Using 50/50 Progress Reporting Method

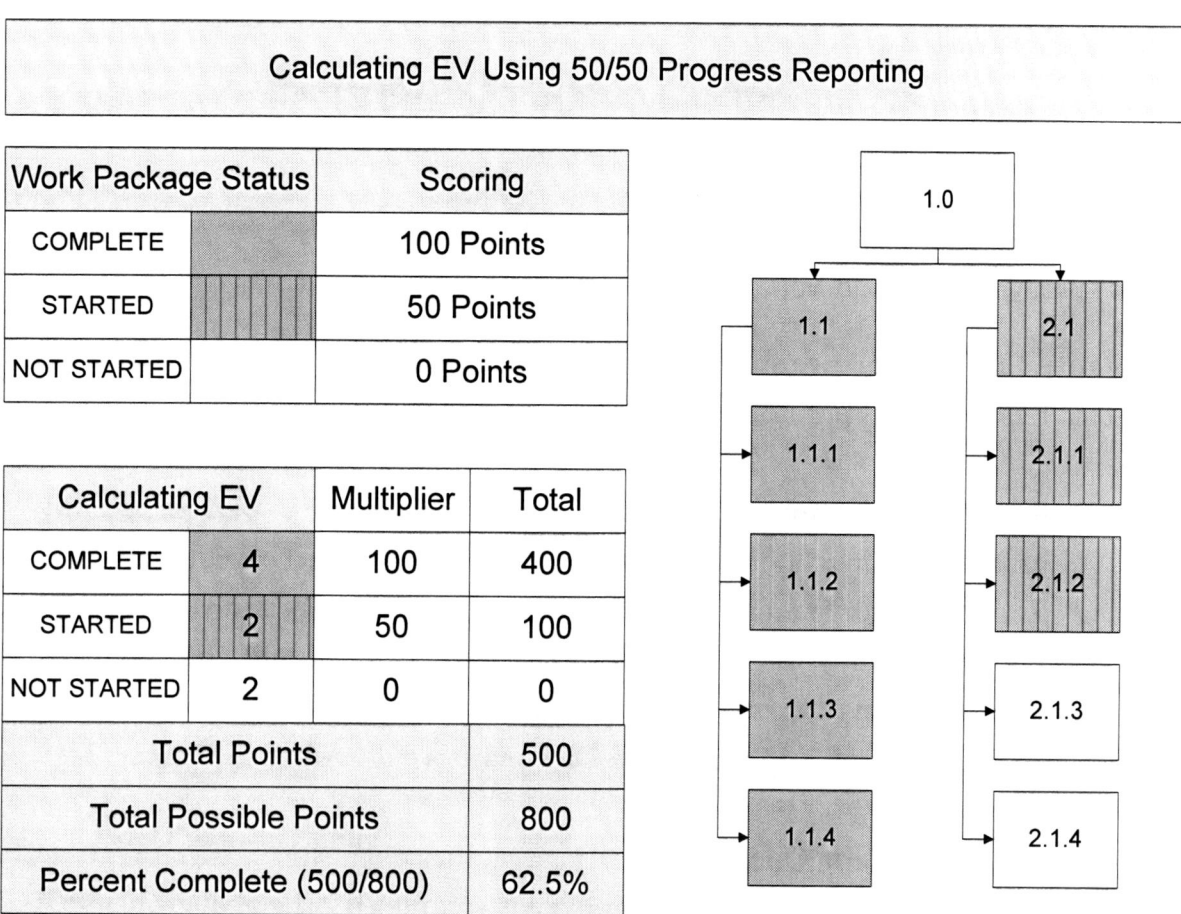

Using the 50/50 progress reporting method is relatively easy if you have a WBS. Determine how many work packages are completed, started, and not started.

- A work package that is complete receives 100 points for 100% complete. In the example we have eight work packages. Four are complete. The calculation is 4 × 100 points = 400 points.

- A work package that is started is scored 50 points. It receives the final 50 points when complete. In the example there are two work packages that have started but are not yet complete. The calculation is 2 × 50 points = 100 points.

- Two Work Packages have not started. They receive zero points. The calculation is 2 × 0 points = 0 points☺.

- This project scores a total of 500 points. Total points available are 8 work packages × 100 points or 800 points. Calculate 500/800 to attain a percentage complete of 62.5%. This is your EV.

## Project Execution, Monitoring and Controlling and Closing: The Support Plans

There are multiple activities to accomplish to support your time, cost, and scope baselines. Here are a few additional tips to keep in mind:

- **Quality:** In Chapter 3, we shared the definition of quality—"conform to requirements and fit for use." This phrase should become a rallying cry for project managers.

    o **Conform to Requirements:** Work time into your schedule to perform Quality Assurance (QA) functions. QA is performed during project execution. The goals are to ensure that your team is following the standards described in your project planning documents. In addition, try to be proactive in identifying and preventing potential problems that may surface in your project. A great place to annotate required QA activities is in the WBS Dictionary we described in Chapter 3.

    o **Fit for Use:** Perform Quality Control (QC) at the conclusion of each phase, and in particular, whenever a project deliverable is completed. The goal of QC is to inspect deliverables, validate conformance to the project planning documents, and correct any problems you discover before you present your product or service to a customer. Again, build QC activities into your project, allot required time to accomplish inspections, and annotate activities in the WBS Dictionary.

    o **Customer Acceptance:** The project's customer must accept the project deliverables before the project can be closed. We briefly discussed "Validate Scope" in Chapter 10. The concept is worth repeating. Perform User Acceptance Testing (UAT) with your customers often during the project execution phase. Allow them to look, touch, and feel what is being developed. It is better to fail fast and change direction before it is too late rather than waiting until the end of a project and realizing then that the deliverables fell short of expectations.

- **Human Resources:** We devoted Chapter 7 to human resource management. It was worth a chapter. Here is your list of "things to do."

    o **Build the Team:** Remember team building is not a one and done. If you recall the Tuckman Model, it is very difficult to get to the "Perform" stage. Conversely, your team, or selected members, can fall back into the "Storm" in a matter of minutes. Watch your team like a hawk! Maintain high levels of motivation and commitment, and the project will take care of itself.

    o **Maintain Relationships with Functional Managers:** Functional Managers provide the human resources you need. Check in with these critical stakeholders on a periodic basis. Let them know how their people are performing. Work personnel issues early. Thank them for their continued support.

    o **Staffing Management Plan:** Build it, share it, use it, and update it. It will change as the project progresses. Do your best to let team members and Functional Managers know who is required, when, and for how long. Don't catch people by surprise. Work issues early and often. And again—don't forget to say thank you.

- **Communications:** As we have stated on a number of occasions, this is the glue that holds the project together. We also shared that communications is 90% of the project manager's job. With that, this is one area you want to get right.

    o **Manage the Grapevine:** Rumors will happen. Keep your eyes and ears open! Clarify the reality of the project with stakeholders as early and often as possible.

    o **The Communications Management Plan will Change:** Update the plan as required. Use version control. Remember this plan should be shared, validated, and used.

o **Address Challenges:** Some stakeholders will not comply. Address issues as they occur. The primary reason why stakeholders do not comply is because they are unaware of the expectations you have for them. Educate your stakeholders, provide a heavy dose of WII-FM, and issues will be reduced.

- **Risk:** Remember PIER-C. Don't forget the "C." Control risk, or it will control you. Here are the tips to remember.

    o **Share and Update the Risk Register:** Ensure all project stakeholders have access to the Risk Register. Ensure periodic status of risks is provided to those who need to know. Review Figure 9.13. A Risk Management Matrix works! Update the Risk Register as required and highlight important changes.

    o **Assign Risk Owners:** The project manager doesn't need to know or do everything. Assign the right people to the right job when you have the luxury of SMEs on your team. Use the "C" in RACI.

    o **Risk can be Opportunities**: Remember that opportunities are risks that can help mend a troubled project. Keep your eyes open and proactively look for opportunities to improve your schedule, budget, and scope deliverables.

    o **Perform Risk Reassessments:** Review risk on a periodic basis. Ensure risk reviews are part of your Communications Management Plan. Weekly is a recommended interval for most projects. Ignore risk and it will find you.

    o **Update the Risk Breakdown Structure:** We provided a generic RBS in Chapter 9. You can likely fin risks on our example that impact your projects and organization. Try to develop an RBS that is unique to your organization's projects. As new risks are discovered, update the RBS. In doing so, you will help future project managers to identify the risk you discovered early in the project rather than waiting for the risk to find them—often at the most inopportune time.

- **Update Key Planning Documentation:** You worked hard and long to develop a Project Management plan that will lead you to success. Keep it current. As changes occur, share them. Ensure everyone is working off the same version and has the right information at the right time.

## Decision Making: The "OARP" Model

Decision making is a key need during project execution. Failure to make a decision, or making the wrong decision, can greatly impact chances of success. The OARP model was developed as a means to assist project managers in making the right decision. It is a framework that can be set up to support any project, and any organization. It is best to include the OARP framework in your Communications Management Plan as an Appendix item if you suspect the need for multiple decisions will be required to support the needs of the project.

Figure 11.3 shares the OARP framework. Let's review the framework, and discuss how you can make OARP work for you.

### Figure 11.3 OARP: A Decision Making Framework

| \\ | OARP: A Decision Making Framework | |
|---|---|---|
| Component | Concept | Success Tips |
| O: Owner | • Generally the Project Leader or Project Manager. This is the stakeholder accountable for ensuring a decision is made | • Control the process<br>• Assign roles<br>• Formalize the process as necessary<br>• Present recommendations to Approver |
| A: Approver | • Generally a Project Sponsor or member of the organizational leadership team. Could be a respected Project Champion | • Strive for Approver who understands the project<br>• Optimal Approver is one management level above all project Stakeholders |
| R: Reviewers | • A group of select stakeholders most impacted by the decision. May include customers, users, project management team representatives, operations, etc. Recommended limit is 5 Reviewers | • Select one liaison to represent a given group<br>• Strive to select Reviewers who are most positive and committed to project success<br>• Establish the ground rules—they will be given options and must choose the most feasible<br>• Let Reviewers know there may not be a "perfect option" |
| P: Participants | • A group of stakeholders who are closest to the project, performing the work, responsible for deliverables, etc. Recommended limit is 10 Participants | • Strive to select Participants who are most positive and committed to project success<br>• Establish ground rules—Participants must develop options they deem as most practical, feasible, value driven, etc.<br>• Establish a tight timeframe for completion |

## The OARP Process

The OARP process is quite effective when the following steps are followed. Note that the Owner is in control of the overall process and needs to ensure all stakeholders understand the problem, decision required, and their roles. When a decision is reached, change management will likely be required to gain support for the decision reached. The steps:

- **Step 1:** The Owner frames the problem and guidelines for the required decision. Owner ensures that there is proper representation in the reviewer and participant categories.

- **Step 2:** Owner presents problem to the Participants. Owner defines ground rules, and sets a reasonable deadline for generation of options.

- **Step 3:** Owner presents participant options to reviewers with a reasonable deadline. Reviewers analyze Participant options, and select the most feasible. Reviewer options are then presented back to the Owner.

- **Step 4:** Owner presents reviewer options and recommendations to Approver for a decision. Owner shares decision with all stakeholders and takes next steps to execute the decision as required.

Decision making is both an art and a science. The OARP model is a mix of both that can be used as another tool in the project manager's toolbox to be successful. Another challenge encountered by a project manager is effective status reporting. We will tackle this challenge next.

## Status Reporting: How to Get It Right

Status reporting is also a combination of art and science. The science piece is having a process that is easy, realistic, understood, and yields results. The art piece is getting stakeholders to not only report status, but to report the "right" status.

Many project managers fail to develop a standardized status reporting process. When this is the case, status reporting may be random, non-standardized, and fail to produce results.

A project manager should begin by developing a simple status report format that is easy to understand, takes little time to complete, and provides information that is both required and used to effectively manage the project.

Figure 11.4 provides a simple report that Peter, Alex and I developed. It is one page, it takes little time to complete, and, most importantly, it works.

> *Project Management Tip: Keep your status reports simple. Only ask for information that you will use and share. Let status report contributors know how you will use the information.*

### Figure 11.4 Project Status Report Sample

| Project: | | |
|---|---|---|
| Name/Organization: | | |
| Overall Project Status of Deliverables ||| 
| Deliverable Status: (Red, Yellow, Green) <br> • Green: On track for completion as planned <br> • Yellow: Some risks and issues present <br> • Red: Will not achieve desired results | Objectives | Status |
| ^ | Scope | |
| ^ | Schedule | |
| ^ | Budget | |
| Help Needed: (Requirement and Sources) Describe as Must Have, Should Have, and Like to Have | | |
| Risk: New risks and changes since last report (Add, Change, Delete) | | |
| Issues: Risks that occurred or questions that need responses | | |
| Forecast: Outlook moving forward | | |
| Comments: | | |

## Status Reporting 101: The Report and More

The status report we shared was developed with two goals in mind. Goal one was functionality. Goal two was simplicity. The report shares all information needed by stakeholders to determine current project status, and it accomplishes this goal in a one- to two-page format. Here are the highlights you need to understand to use this tool.

- **Project/Name and Organization**: Multiple projects and multiple project managers are normally hard at work in an organization. Distinguish your project and yourself from others.

- **Overall Project Status of Deliverables**: Using "traffic light reporting" is quite common. Classify scope, time, and cost status as either green, yellow, or red. Here are some important clarifying notes:

  o Define what green, yellow, and red mean. Different people may have different interpretations. In addition, different types of projects may require a tweak of the definitions.

  o Encourage stakeholders to report yellow status and reward them for doing so. Some corporate cultures discourage yellow reporting. As a result, status often changes rapidly from green to red without warning. Yellow status reporting gives the project manager and team a chance to proactively address issues before they become red showstoppers.

- **Help Needed:** This section of the status report is critically important. An old adage states, "Never come to me with a problem unless you have a solution." This section is your opportunity to request the assistance needed to change a yellow or red status back to green.

  o Use Must Have, Should Have, and Nice to Have for your requests for assistance. If your status is green, you may still need some support to maintain that status. However, in most cases, this need will not be a Must Have requirement.

- o Project managers sometimes have a tendency to label all support needs as Must Haves. When you overuse this classification, stakeholders may have a tendency to not share your urgency. Everything can't always be Priority One. Don't be like the little boy who cried, "Wolf."[32]

- **Risks and Issues:** Refer back to Chapter 9, our risk management guidance. List any new risks that developed that are worthy of reporting. This section should be reserved for urgent risks that require management support to approve a necessary response, or issues (risks that happened) that are impacting scope, time, and/or budget status.

- **Forecast:** Use this section to share your vision of where the project is headed. For example, you may state that scope is currently green. However, if needed help is not obtained, then the next status report will likely reflect yellow or even red status.

- **Comments:** Here is your opportunity to share any pertinent thoughts you may have regarding the project. You can also use this section as an opportunity to applaud the efforts of key stakeholders contributing to the project and making a positive impact. Did you turn an opportunity (positive risk) into a benefit? If so, share it here.

> *Alex's Project Management Tip: Print the project schedule, issues, organizational charts, etc., on plotter paper and post it on your wall or cubicle. This simple step makes it look like you know what you are doing. It also leads to people stopping and asking questions, which allows you to evangelize the project.*

---

[32] Aesop's Fables

# Effective Meeting Management

When I first became a PM, I assumed the acronym stood for project manager. A supervisor shared that the acronym really stood for "Perpetual Meetings." I smiled at the time, but as I've progressed into my project management career, I realized that the joke was truly a reality. Project managers must have meetings. However, most stakeholders dread them.

Here is a quote from Psychology Today[33], "How often have you sat through a meeting and said to yourself, *What a waste of time, I could be doing something better!* If your answer is yes, you are not alone. Meetings take up an ever-increasing amount of employees', and particularly managers', time."

So what is the takeaway? Meetings are essential for a project manager. Most people dread meetings. So, if you are going to call a meeting, you better get it right. This section is devoted to "getting it right."

## Is a Meeting Necessary?

Many project managers have a tendency to call a meeting for everything. However, believe it or not, there are times when you shouldn't have a meeting. Figure 11.5 provides an easy-to-use checklist to determine if a meeting is required. Simply stated, if you answer no to all the considerations, then send an email☺.

## Figure 11.5 Meeting Determination Checklist

| Consideration | Yes | No |
|---|---|---|
| Must meet face-to-face | | |
| Information is complex/voluminous | | |
| Idea generation is key | | |
| Consensus and commitment are needed | | |
| A decision is needed | | |
| Non-verbal communications is critical | | |
| Want to build the team | | |
| Lots of stakeholders | | |

---

[33] Psychology Today, April 2012

### The Ten Commandments of Meeting Management

If you decide that a meeting is necessary, remember the Ten Commandments of Meeting Management. Alex shared these with me many years ago, and this guidance has stood the test of time. To quote Alex, "A project manager must get the most out of team meetings!" These best practices are provided for your reading pleasure in Figure 11.6.

## Figure 11.6 Ten Commandments of Meeting Management

| Ten Commandments of Meeting Management | Comment |
| --- | --- |
| 1. Determine the Outcome: Be Realistic | Every meeting should have a desired and measurable outcome that is of value to all attendees. You may need to sell the purpose to attend by sharing a value proposition of interest to everyone. |
| 2. Develop an Agenda: Rule of 48/24; Parking Lot | Send out an agenda 48 hours in advance. This allows stakeholders the opportunity to prepare. Send out meeting minutes within 24 hours of the meeting. This practice allows meeting attendees to review next steps and reduces the chance of "selective amnesia." Defer all non-value conversation in the meeting to a "Parking Lot." The Parking Lot annotates subjects not essential to the meeting and provides the promise to revisit at a later date. |
| 3. Communicate the Purpose: WII-FM | Peter shared this acronym earlier: What's In It For Me? Create a value proposition for each attendee. Let them know that attending the meeting will provide valuable information and will not be time wasted. |
| 4. Share Materials and Pre-Work | Do you recall our discussion of Emergenetics in Chapter 10? Analytical and Structural thinkers prefer information ahead of time so they can review, analyze, and develop discussion points. Accommodate these attendees, or be ready to spend time in the meeting allowing some stakeholders to ramp up while other attendees wait and become frustrated. |

| Ten Commandments of Meeting Management, Continued | Comment |
|---|---|
| 5. Assign Facilitator(s): Avoid One-Man Show | Nobody likes to listen to a single individual speak while everyone else in the room listens. Assign roles and discussion opportunities for all. Engage the audience in the discussion. The "One-Man Show" violates many of the meeting considerations we shared in Figure 11.5. Rotating meeting ownership keeps everyone invested. |
| 6. Hire a Scribe | Non-verbal communications are far more revealing than the verbal communications shared in a meeting. Don't be a project manager whose head is down writing notes during the entire meeting. While you write, others are sharing key non-verbal communications you may miss. |
| 7. Assign Owners to Action Items | Some project managers expertly define meeting takeaways. The mistake is assuming everyone knows what they've been tasked to do. Assign action items to individuals. *And*, verify their commitment to accept the action item and run with it. |
| 8. Practice Non-Attribution: No Bad Ideas | The best meetings occur when there is a free exchange of ideas, regardless of agreement or disagreement. Set the meeting ground rules early: what is shared in the meeting, stays in the meeting. There will be time at the end of the meeting to formulate minutes that state the meeting takeaways adequately but *do not* violate the non-attribution rule. |
| 9. Publish Minutes | Two "Always" rules are associated with meetings. *Always* have an agenda. And *always* publish meeting minutes. Ensure the minutes are timely (remember the Rule of 48/24). In addition, ensure action items are clearly stated and assigned to owners. A great practice is to have attendees acknowledge receipt and validate ownership of action items. Voting buttons work well. |
| 10. End Early if You Meet Objectives | Many project managers feel obligated to extend the one-hour meeting to an hour, even if the amount of material covered does not justify the time. Don't be afraid to end a meeting early. If you've covered everything, give the meeting attendees some valuable time back. |

**The Meeting Agenda**

The meeting agenda is your ticket to success. It should state precisely what the meeting is about, what the required outcome of the meeting is, state the subjects to be discussed, and assign ownership to each item. Your minutes are the record of the discussions and decisions made at the meeting. You need to get both of these steps right.

Figure 11.7 provides a meeting agenda format and Figure 11.8 shares a meeting minute's template that has served Peter, Alex, and me well over the years. Feel free to give them a try!

## Figure 11.7 Meeting Agenda Templates

| Meeting Agenda Template |
|---|
| **Step 1: Goal** State the goal of the meeting. What feedback do you want to attain by the meeting's end? Remember that the goal of a meeting is to:<br><br>• persuade<br>• inform<br>• entertain |
| **Step 2: Overview** The overview should track to specific objectives of the meeting. These are the areas you will discuss with some quantifiable result desired.<br><br><u>Note</u>: Objectives should have value to the attendees. |
| **Step 3: Body** The "Rule of Three" works well. Try to limit a meeting to three key objectives of discussion areas.<br><br>The areas should have synergy. You should be able to link the objectives back to the goal. As a hint for success, build your agenda items as follows:<br><br>• Objectives<br>• Responsible Team Members<br>• Expected Result of Discussions<br><br>Example: Review project budget expenditures. Responsible: Amy, John, and Bill. Result: Show planned versus actual expenditures to date. Provide recommendations and comments. |

**Step 4: Summary**

1. Review what you accomplished and didn't accomplish
2. Discuss next steps
3. Ask everyone for comments or to restate their takeaways

**Notes:**
- Ensure everyone at the meeting has a role. If a meeting attendee has no role, there is no need for their attendance
- Each member should summarize their takeaways. Don't assume a member understands and accepts responsibility for tasks until they say so
- Use a Parking Lot to stay on track. If a member wants to discuss something outside the agenda, note this as a Parking Lot item to discuss later
- Observe the Rule of 48/24. Publish the agenda 48 hours prior. Publish minutes within 24 hours of the meeting

*Project Management Tip: Stephen Covey stated, "Start with the end in mind." This is so true for planning effective meetings. Define what you want to accomplish, why it is important, and invite only those individuals who need to be there.*

## Figure 11.8 Meeting Minutes Template

| Meeting Minutes Template |
|---|
| **Date and Subject of Meeting:** Share the date of the meeting and provide a brief overview of the primary subject matter discussed. |
| **Meeting Attendees:** List the individuals who participated in the meeting. |
| **Meeting Objectives and Results:** List the measurable objectives from the meeting as follows: |

| Meeting Objective | Owner | Discussion Results |
|---|---|---|
|  |  |  |
|  |  |  |
|  |  |  |
|  |  |  |

| |
|---|
| **Parking Lot Items:** List items that were put in the Parking Lot. Add a plan to address them. |
| **Key Commitments and Next Steps:** Add a list of key action items and validate commitment of key stakeholders to address them. End with next steps. |

## Managing the Meeting

As we mentioned earlier, send the agenda out at least 48 hours before the meeting. In addition, send out minutes within 24 hours of completing the meeting when possible. The agenda and meeting minute's formats we shared provides a great overview of what is required so there is no need to rehash that here. However, there are a few points worth sharing and repeating. Peter came up with a great list, and I will "add on. Here it is.

- Introduce everyone, including why they are here (start with the people – *who*). This will ensure the Social stakeholders feel welcome, and acknowledge the necessity of their feedback. The Analytical stakeholders will better understand the value proposition each member brings to the meeting.

- Share *why* we are here. Begin with the end in mind. We are here to accomplish X, Y and Z. Ensure your outcomes add value (Analytical), and are organized (Structural). Have the "meeting before the meeting," and share the objectives ahead of time to gain early consensus, if necessary.

- Share the *how* – go over ground rules (meeting norms). Ensure everyone understands how the meeting will be run. This is a requirement for Structural stakeholders. Provide time in the meeting for Conceptual stakeholders to brainstorm, share ideas, and tap into their creativity. In particular, ensure everyone in the meeting, whether attending in-person or virtually, realizes their feedback is essential and required. Assign roles, be a great listener, and be inclusive.

- Share *the what and when*. Review the time-boxed agenda, and agree on the agenda (Structural). Show the value (Analytical), and gain buy-in (Social) from all. Ensure you include time to explore the possibilities (Conceptual).

- Appoint a time keeper and a note taker, if possible. Your job as the meeting facilitator is to keep your finger on the pulse of the meeting. You can't do that when you are concentrating on time and documentation.

- Keep a Parking Lot and ensure after meeting actions in the Parking Lot are addressed in a timely manner.

- Review actions, owners and due dates at the meeting's end. Don't assume that everyone is committed to the decisions made in the meeting. Strive for a verbal acknowledgement during the meeting, and follow up this acknowledgement with timely minutes. Together, this two-step approach will combat a lack of follow-through, and, at times, selective amnesia.

- Practice non-attribution in the meeting. Create an environment where all attendees feel they have the freedom to share their thoughts honestly, regardless of agreement or disagreement.

- Be a great facilitator. This subject is another key success factor that could be written as a stand-alone publication. That is not the intent of this book. However, we will provide some tips that will help your facilitation techniques in our next section on managing stakeholders.

## Managing Project Stakeholders

Managing stakeholders effectively encompasses far more than identification, classification, and assigning roles and responsibilities. While these things are important, there are other aspects of stakeholder management you need to consider. This section will provide some ideas and tips and essentially provide a summary of key tools and techniques provided.

- **Dust Off the Project Charter:** The excitement that generally supports new projects has a tendency to lessen as the project progresses. Team member commitment begins to wane, and oftentimes sponsorship is not at the level it needs to be. Periodically revisit the Project Charter and remind stakeholders why this project is important. Try to regenerate a bit of that initial enthusiasm that was present when the project was born.

- **Update the Stakeholder Register and Management Plans:** Stakeholders will come and go as the project progresses. In addition, current and desired states for stakeholders will change as well. Continually update and share the Stakeholder Register as changes occur. Welcome new stakeholders to the project and ensure they are aware of their roles and responsibilities. Keep an eye on commitment levels as well. A stakeholder who is "Supportive" may suddenly become "Resistant" for a number of reasons. If this occurs, you need to be aware and take action to develop strategies that will allow you to regain the level of commitment you need.

- **Manage Scope Closely:** Continually reiterate the product or service that the project will provide. Keep people excited. In addition, share changes to scope as soon as they are known. Some stakeholders may see a positive change from your standpoint as a negative. Change management is needed to let the stakeholders understand why the change was necessary. Celebrate success. Let all stakeholders know when a major phase is complete, and send kudos to all responsible for the success.

- **Manage Time Closely:** In most projects, events will transpire that impact the planned schedule. Use your Project Network Diagram to your advantage. Track work packages that are completed and determine the impact on the overall schedule. When changes are requested, use the Project Network Diagram to show cause and effect. Ensure all stakeholders understand that the "triangle needs to be balanced." If schedule acceleration is requested, the need for less scope or increased resources may be called for. If scope reductions and increases in resources cannot be accommodated, ensure the new risk the project will incur is shared.

- **Manage Costs Closely:** Meet with your team periodically and review the planned versus actual resources required for each work package once completed. Our advice on balancing the triangle shared above pertains here as well. Encourage team members to think out of the box and come up with ways to perform project activities more efficiently and effectively. Reward those who come up with great ideas, as well.

- **Manage Change:** Ensure the project change process and the status of pending changes is visible and understood. Ensure all new stakeholders are informed of the process as part of their onboarding. Process changes when received, perform a thorough analysis, and let all stakeholders know the results of pending change requests immediately upon approval or rejection. If a change is rejected, work with the submitter one-on-one and provide a thorough explanation of why the change was not accepted. Failure to approve changes is a primary reason why some stakeholders go from "Supportive" or "Leading" to "Resistant."

- **Guard Your Number One Resource—People:** Support your stakeholders, and they will support you. We introduced MBWAT in Chapter 7. This is critical. The best project managers use the opportunity to meet with their team early and often to ensure commitment levels are where they need to be. Use the Staffing Management Plan and update it as needed. Remember the Tuckman Model and employ some team building activities to get the team into the "Norm" or "Perform" levels. Ensure virtual team members are included and feel part of the team. Manage personal issues that develop, provide training opportunities for growth, and build those relationships.

- **Communicate, Communicate, Communicate:** Use your Communications Management Plan to create a "Rhythm of the Project." Update the plan as required, and validate each new version. Analyze what is working and what is not working, and develop strategies for improvement. Feedback is a gift; encourage input, express appreciation, and take action, regardless of the positive or negative nature of communications you receive.

- **Manage Risk:** *Do* revisit risk on a periodic basis. Add new risks that develop and prioritize them. Assign Risk Owners to each new risk when you have the luxury to do so. Eliminate the risks that are no longer applicable. If a risk occurs, track the issue through completion, and share status with stakeholders as applicable. Remember to guard against threats, but also look for opportunities. Risk is not always negative. Finally, include all stakeholders in risk management and reward those who identify risks and develop value added responses that make a difference.

- **Treat Each Stakeholder as a Unique Human Being:** We shared a brief overview of Emergenetics in Chapter 10. In addition, we shared a few additional motivational techniques throughout the book. Strive to become a situational leader. Remember a one-size-fits-all management style will likely not provided the results you desire. Try to learn as much as you can about each key stakeholder and interact in a way that will improve collaboration, understanding, and commitment.

## Project Closure

Project Closure is a great opportunity to transition a new product or service into operations, celebrate success, and share what you learned with your stakeholders and future project managers. In this section, we will provide a few keys to ensure your project closure is completed without issues. We will end this section with a very important obligation each project manager has to the organization and to future project managers, performing Lessons Learned.

- **The Customer Is Always Right:** The customer has the final say when it comes to acceptance of the project's deliverables. Include the customer in project execution and control early and often. If possible, adopt a phased approach to designing, building, and testing deliverables and include the customer in each phase. A "Worst Practice" is waiting until the end of a project to perform your customer demo. Requirements and needs change over time. A requirement that met the customer's needs six-months ago may not be what is needed today. Include the customer during the executing journey and adopt changes as needed to ensure at the end of the project the customer is delighted.

- **Ensure Contract Deliverables Are Complete:** Perform a Procurement Audit with the vendors or sellers involved in your project. A Procurement Audit checks the contract requirements against what was delivered. The project manager is the organization's primary representative responsible for ensuring you only pay for what you get. Don't pay 100% unless you get 100%. In addition, perform the Procurement Audit regardless of whether the customer is accepting project deliverables or not.

- **Transition Deliverables:** In Chapter 3, we discussed the need to build transition planning into your scope documentation. Now is the time to implement the plan. You need to delight your customers. At the same time, you need to satisfy the needs of the operations team that will support and maintain the project deliverables after the project is complete. The same advice we shared for collaboration with customers applies to the operations as team as well. Include operations during the executing journey and adopt changes as needed to ensure at the end of the project operation's needs are met.

- **Closure Is Not a "One and Done" Activity:** Project closure is best accomplished using a phased approach. Close out small project phases as you complete them. Include the customer and operations personnel in the interim phase closures and gain their concurrence to move forward. A new term becoming common in project management is to "fail fast." Closing out a project by phases allows you to realize earlier in the project if you are headed in the wrong direction. Course corrections become much more difficult and complex as the project moves closer to completion.

## Conducting Lessons Learned

Lessons Learned is a small-time investment that yields big results. Lessons Learned is also referred to as the "Post Mortem." Lessons Learned allows the project stakeholders to evaluate a project in terms of what worked and what didn't. This also allows an organization to better prepare for future projects by embracing best practices and avoiding pitfalls. Here are some great reasons to conduct Lessons Learned:

- **Assist Future Project Managers:** We often repeat the same mistakes over and over again. Lessons Learned point out common mistakes and provide an opportunity for future project managers to learn from you how to best avoid those pitfalls. In addition, new ideas that provide value are often discovered during the execution of a project. Sadly, many of these great ideas are not shared and are lost. Lessons Learned provides a great opportunity to share the wealth.

- **Validate Stakeholder Satisfaction:** Lessons Learned allows the project team to interact with customers, users, leadership and other key stakeholders to determine what worked and what needs improvement from their standpoint as well. As a case in point, let's say a customer who worked with you throughout the project was very supporting. At the end of the project, their needs were not met. Lessons Learned allows you to determine what went wrong from this customer's standpoint and perhaps address these issues in future projects. If you don't address the issue now, support from this customer may be less than optimal on future projects.

- **Next Steps:** Oftentimes, a single project is a journey that leads to new ideas and opportunities to go from good to great. Use Lessons Learned as an opportunity to discuss what you learned and identify opportunities to take that next step while the project is still fresh on your mind.

Lessons Learned are easy to conduct. Figure 11.9 provides an easy-to-follow template on how to maximize your Lessons Learned.

## Figure 11.9 Lessons Learned Template

| Question | Comments |
|---|---|
| 1. What went well? | <ul><li>Always begin with a positive question. People love to share how they were successful.</li><li>Search for new best practices, great ideas, potential opportunities, etc., that resulted from the project.</li></ul> |
| 2. What can we improve? (note the wording) | <ul><li>*Do not* ask what went wrong. People are very resistant to share where they feel they may have failed or come up short.</li><li>*Do* ask how we can improve. Address this question from a "Good to Great" standpoint.</li><li>Let people know they did well, but allow stakeholders to offer suggestions on what to improve next time.</li></ul> |
| 3. How can we improve? | <ul><li>This section is a continuation of Question #2. For each improvement idea, spend some time determining how you can turn the great idea into reality.</li><li>Try to pick one or two things to apply to the next project. Have the team commit to these improvements.</li></ul> |

## Chapter 11 Summary

Chapter 11 provided a few hints on how to successfully implement your project plan. We covered a lot of ground! We showed how EVM is a great way to quantitatively show the status of your schedule and budget. Determining EV by applying the 50/50 progress reporting method is a way to classify percentage complete on projects that do not easily lend themselves to traditional completion reporting.

You will need to lead the decision making efforts in support of the project. We encourage you to adopt OARP. In addition, status reporting is an area where many projects are deficient. Keep your status reporting focused on what really matters, and simple. If you ask for information from stakeholders, use it, and let the providers know how their input provided value.

Meetings happen! As a project manager, you need to make your meetings meaningful and only hold meetings when they are necessary. Patrick Lencioni wrote a great book entitled *Death by Meeting*.[34] If you have a chance, it is well worth your investment and time to read.

Poor stakeholder management is one of the primary reasons projects fail. We used this section as an opportunity to show how the tools and techniques provided in this book can help you to "herd the cats" in a way that can potentially lead to project success.

Finally, we provided some key information on project closure. It is more than a quick handshake and goodbye. We *highly* encourage you to adopt a Lessons Learned cadence in your project management function. The benefits you gain are far greater than the costs of your time and effort.

---

[34] *Death by Meeting*, Patrick Lencioni

## Peter's Corner: Chapter 11 Edition

**Scope Creep and the End of the Project.** Almost invariably, the project manager permits some unplanned scope to creep into the project. Almost invariably, the project team runs out of time, resources, or money toward the end of the project, and they must deliver the remaining project scope to a deadline. Sometimes the customer makes "unreasonable requests" for changes or new scope very near the end of the project. This is the time to say, "Would you like us to deliver what we agreed by the deadline, or delay the project and/or increase the cost if we even *consider* (estimate) your request?" There comes a time where even considering a request will delay a project. Another scenario is where the team cannot deliver the agreed scope by the agreed deadline. It is much easier to ask for more time, resources, and/or money if you can show that you have provided several, or many, unplanned scope changes for free. This is easy to do if you have kept a log of *all* of the changes, both the approved changes *and* the unplanned and not formally approved changes that were implemented. The customer is likely to be more flexible if you can show that you and your team have been flexible and have already provided more scope than planned and agreed. Just make sure that the Scope Creep had value for the customer.

**Planning and Processes: Optimize.** During Planning, you set forth, to the best of your ability, the processes that you thought would best serve your project and your team. As you begin to execute your plans, you should assess how the processes and associated templates are working. Do you need more, less, or different processes and/or templates? The idea is to learn along the way, and make adjustments as needed. One size does not fit all. Get feedback, evaluate it, and act on it, as appropriate. This will help the project and the team, as well as boost your credibility.

**Meetings Are Very Expensive.** People complain all the time that there are too many meetings. I agree. So get creative. Figure out how to have fewer meetings, shorter meetings, and meetings with fewer participants. Be ruthless, yet respect the politics (I sincerely hope you do not have much politics in and around your project). And, perhaps above all, get really good at leading and facilitating meetings. This will "rub off" on participants and they will lead and facilitate meetings better as they copy you. This will result in huge and positive ripple effects for your project, not to mention other projects and your team members' careers.

**Decision Making.** Be very clear about decision rights and processes on your project team and elsewhere in your project. Who gets to decide what? What are the decision making processes or styles from which the leader may choose? See what happens when you become proactive with decision rights and processes; you may be very pleasantly surprised by the effects upon motivation and morale and how much more quickly and effectively the project progresses.

**The Unsupportive Stakeholder.** An unsupportive stakeholder or naysayer can do more damage to your project than ten supportive stakeholders. Throughout the project, you must identify and engage with problematic stakeholders to win them over. This may take all of your influencing, negotiation, and conflict resolution skills. It is vital during Execution for the team to be heads down and focused. Your job as project manager is to minimize distractions while enlisting the support needed by the project and its team. Processes and tools are unlikely to win over stakeholders; rather, it will take your people skills.

Thank you for reading this book. On behalf of Peter, Alex, and me, we enjoyed sharing. In the Appendices that follow, we provide examples of many of the tools and techniques we highlighted through a simple project scenario. In addition, you will find a combination Glossary of Terms and Index should you need a quick definition or reference.

One more time—you can access all of the tools and techniques in this book at www.P17Group.com. May all your projects be successful. And enjoy the Appendix scenario!

# Chapter 11 Food for Thought

1. A manager asks you for your opinion on EVM. What will you tell him?

2. How does your organization make decisions? Do you believe the OARP method has merit? Why or why not?

3. You have been asked to provide a brief overview of effective meeting management. You elect to share your top five tips to succeed. What are the five tips you will share and why?

4. What are the top three attributes of an effective project status reporting function? Justify your answers.

5. Managing stakeholders is essential. List three methods that will help you become successful. List three things to not do or avoid.

6. Your project implemented a new vacation planning process approved by the HR lead. How should you close this project? Walk us through the steps.

7. Peter's Deep Thought Challenges:

*Reflections*

We live in a fast-paced world, and everyone is too busy. No sooner does a project end than we are off to other urgent or important projects or other endeavors. We don't make the time and put forth the effort to assess what we really learned and how we developed and grew. What new skills and capabilities did we acquire during the project we just completed?

Titles are becoming less important and less useful as we venture into this faster-paced and faster-changing world. A portfolio of skills and capabilities is becoming more relevant and valuable than the pursuit of a higher title or a career track. In fact, many career tracks are vanishing.

Reflect upon how to apply the above to the just-completed project and, importantly, to the next project. What new skills and capabilities did you learn? Did team members learn? Take an inventory of these. As you look at the next project, how will you continue to develop and grow your skills and the skills of your team members? Personal development is the new currency. Use it for everyone's benefit.

## Website Access Code for Templates and Examples

When you go to our website, www.p17group.com, our templates and examples are waiting for you. Please use the code below for access.

> Access Code:
>
> 060110

# APPENDIX A: A Portfolio Approach

Here is an overview of a company who developed a portfolio to improve the Customer Partnership Experience.

- The company broke their portfolio into four programs. Programs were prioritized by program number.

- The portfolio shown assumes full use of available resources and capacity.

- Each project is categorized under an appropriate program. If a project is cancelled, the effect on the program can be measured.

- If new programs or projects are proposed, management will need to look for trade-offs in the current portfolio. In this case, new program needs would result in the elimination or downsizing of Program 4, the "Implement New Products Program".

Appendix A

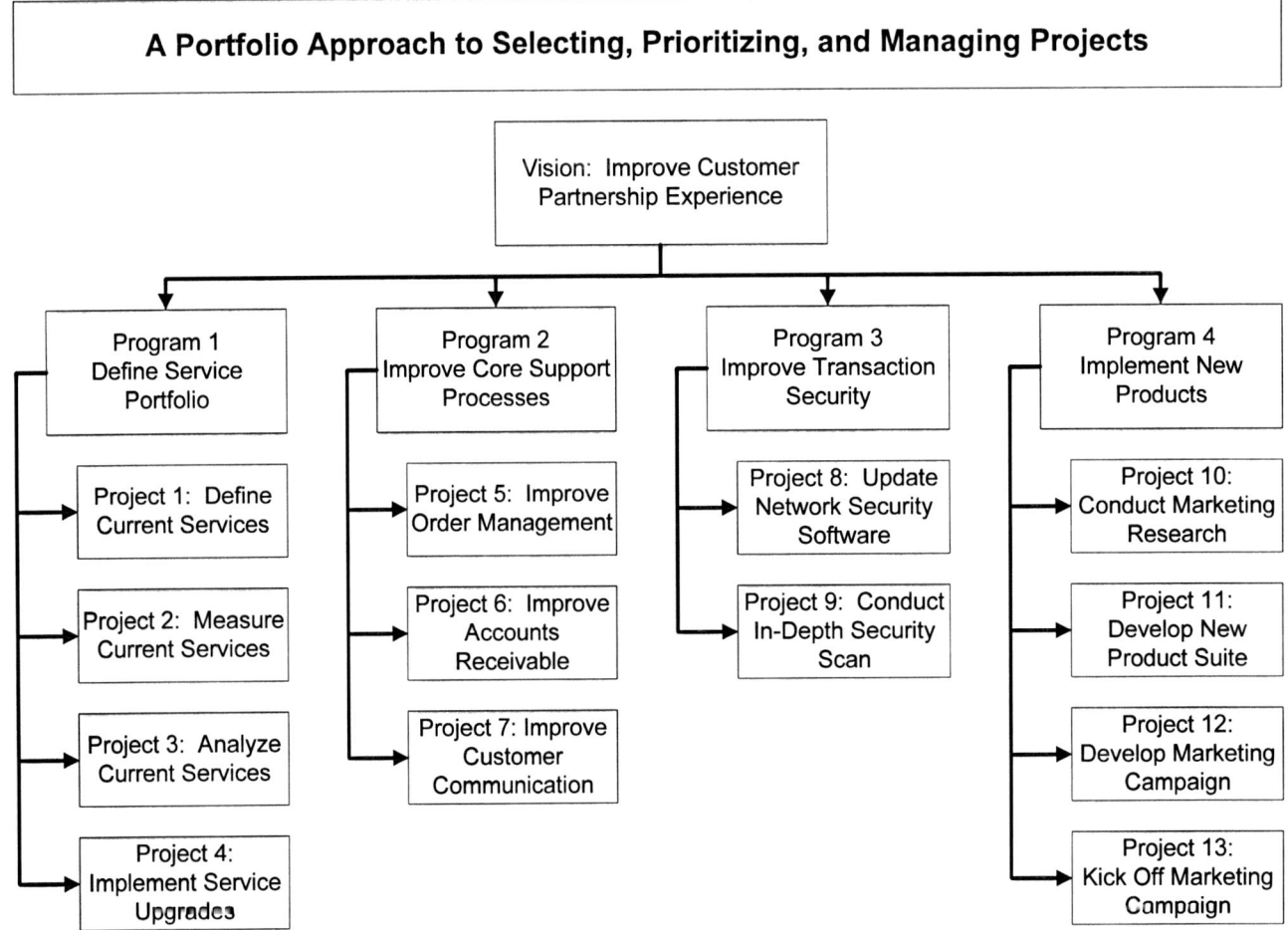

Notes:

1. Prioritize programs from left to right. Program 1 is higher priority than Program 2, etc.

2. Prioritize projects from top to bottom. Project 1 is implemented before Project 2, etc.

# APPENDIX B:  Project Charter Example

Welcome to Appendix B.  We have developed a sample project to show you how to use each of the tools and techniques provided in the book.  We begin with the first step you need to take, the development of a Project Charter.

Our scenario is simple.  Rogers Shipping is a firm that specializes in worldwide distribution of time-sensitive materials to an international clientele.  Last year, the Rogers Shipping customer satisfaction rate dropped from 95% to 85%.  Deadlines are being missed.  Shipments are incomplete.  And some customers have cancelled orders due to Rogers' inability to plan and meet deadlines.

CEO Alex Wright is unhappy, to say the least.  He tasked Lisa Sears to come up with a training solution.  Lisa is a strong believer in project management and wants to propose a companywide training program that will standardize the way Rogers plans and implements their shipping contracts and customer interface.

So enjoy the ride, as Lisa plans and implements her vision for Rogers.  Peter, Alex, and I talked about this sample project and decided that there will be a happy ending when the project is completed ☺.

Appendix B

| Charter Item | Comments |
|---|---|
| Project Name | Develop a formal project management training program for Rogers Shipping Inc. |
| Project Goal | Develop a standard project management training curriculum to train all key management positions within the firm. |
| Project Value Proposition and Benefits | Finance: Revenue is lost on an annual basis due to late shipments, incomplete shipments, or lost business due to our inability to meet key customer schedules. We need to define and improve our processes.<br><br>Process: Our current project management processes are undefined. Project management employs "tribal knowledge," which results in no standardized approach to managing projects.<br><br>Customer: Our last customer satisfaction survey showed a decrease in customer satisfaction from 95% to 85%. Many comments reflected the dissatisfaction with our shipping deficiencies. We need to formalize our "Voice of the Customer" collaboration methods.<br><br>Employee: Many managers have requested formal project management training to improve performance. |
| Problem or Opportunity Statement | Alex Wright, CEO of Rogers Shipping, stated that a key success factor in the next FY is to improve our overall management capabilities. He is highly disturbed with the reduction in customer satisfaction. |

| | |
|---|---|
| Proposed Solution(s) | Solution recommendations are as follows:<br><br>1. Pursue alternative, non-project management related, and training solutions.<br>2. Contract out project management training.<br>3. Develop an in-house project management training solution.<br><br>We recommend adoption of Solution #3. |
| Project Priorities | #1 Time: CEO Wright wants a near-term solution to the problem of dropping customer satisfaction.<br><br>#2 Scope: We need a solution that meets the real-world needs of Rogers Shipping.<br><br>#3 Resources: To quote the CEO, "Do whatever it takes to turn around this problem." |
| Return on Investment (ROI) | According to last quarter statistics, late shipments, incomplete shipments, and cancelled orders resulted in over $80,000 of lost business. We estimate it will cost approximately $10,000 to develop a project management training program at Rogers. This is an 800% ROI, if we can avoid the lost revenue. |
| Project Schedule | Our recommendation is as follows, pending approval of this Project Charter:<br><br>- Analyze Needs: 15 Mar, 2017<br>- Define Training Objectives: 30 Mar, 2017<br>- Develop Training Curriculum: 30 Apr 2017<br>- Implement Training: 15 May – 31 Jul 2017 |

| | |
|---|---|
| | • Evaluate Training and Next Steps: 15 Aug 2017 |
| Assumptions or Constraints | Assumptions: Assume that management will support this training as a means to improve overall corporate performance.<br><br>Constraints: We will need to tailor this training to resonate with managers from all departments. |
| Risks (Potential) | Lack of buy-in—may result in poor attendance and minimal results<br><br>Lack of qualified trainers—may result in less-than-effective end results<br><br>Partner buy-in—may allow us to partner with key customers to enhance the training experience |
| Resources Required | The following roles are key:<br><br>• Project Manager<br>• Course Developers<br>• Project Management Trainers<br>• Logistical Support Personnel<br>• IT |
| Project Manager | Recommend Project Manager be Lisa Sears |
| Approval Authority/Sponsor | Recommended Sponsor is Chief Operating Officer Jose Rodriguez |

# APPENDIX C: Stakeholder Register and Management Plan Examples

Lisa gave a brilliant Pre-Baseline presentation, and Jose approved the Project Charter with Lisa's recommendation to develop an in-house project management training solution for Rogers Shipping. Lisa had purchased a copy of this book and knew stakeholder identification and management were critical to success. She created her initial Stakeholder Register.

| Stakeholder Segment: | Rogers Shipping Leadership Team | | | | | | |
|---|---|---|---|---|---|---|---|
| Name | Organization | Role | R | A | C | I | Comments |
| Alex Wright | CEO | Leadership Team | | | | X | Share agreed upon steps to address CSAT issue |
| Jose Rodriquez | COO | Sponsor | | X | | X | Sponsor training project--solicit funds and approve |
| Erika Yeomans | Marketing | Supportive | X | | X | X | Solicit input--ensure curriculum works for Marketing |
| Laura Rogers | Operations | Supportive | X | | X | X | Solicit input--ensure curriculum works for Operations |
| Bob Winkler | Finance | Supportive | X | | X | X | Solicit input--ensure curriculum works for Finance |
| Peter Rogers | SME | Course Development Advisor | X | | X | | Provide advice on curriculum--support curriculum development |
| Lisa Sears | Operations | Project Manager | X | X | | | Manage end to end project--accountable for results |

| ROLE | DEFINED | |
|---|---|---|
| R | Responsible for doing work on the project | Version: 1 |
| A | Accountable for outcomes | |
| C | Consult as a Subject Matter Expert (SME) | |
| I | Inform as the project progresses | |

Next, Lisa identified a few stakeholders that she needed to manage closely. She developed a Stakeholder Management Plan as well.

Appendix C

| Stakeholder Management Plan Format ||||
| Name | Current State | Desired State | Strategy |
| --- | --- | --- | --- |
| Peter Rogers | N | L | Peter wants to concentrate on a 100% Agile curriculum. Need to show Peter that Waterfall is still viable. |
| Bob Winkler | R | S | Bob feels training is a waste of money. May need executive level support to move Bob to support. |
| IT | U | S | IT is not aware of their role. Need to meet with IT lead, assign IT lead for project, and determine requirements. |
| Jose Rodriguez | L | L | Jose is willing to take on active sponsorship role. Need to keep Jose engaged. He stated he is a "hands on guy." |
|  |  |  |  |

| Recommended Level of Commitment Designators | U | Unaware: Stakeholder is unaware of the project. |
| --- | --- | --- |
| | N | Neutral: Stakeholder has yet to determine level of support. |
| | R | Resistant: Stakeholder does not support the project. |
| | S | Supportive: Stakeholder agrees with the project. |
| | L | Leading: Stakeholder is supportive and actively engaged in project. |

**Note:** Lisa will continually update these documents throughout the course of the project. Version control will be used to ensure stakeholders access the latest Stakeholder Register.

# APPENDIX D: Scope Planning Tools Examples

Lisa got her team and key stakeholders together with the goal of answering perhaps the most critical planning question, "What is this project?" She included Erika, Laura, and Bob to discuss the training option from their standpoint, and after much discussion, gathered their input. She brainstormed potential requirements, did her best to clarify all SMARTWAY criteria, and developed a Requirements Feasibility and Prioritization Matrix. She categorized requirements using the project types outlined in Figure 3.1.

| Requirements Feasibility and Prioritization Matrix | | | | | | | | | | |
|---|---|---|---|---|---|---|---|---|---|---|
| Requirement | Type | S | M | At | R | T | W | As | Y | Score |
| Develop Project Charter | Bus | 2 | 2 | 3 | 3 | 2 | 3 | 2 | 3 | 20 |
| Identify & Manage Stakeholders | Stake | 2 | 2 | 3 | 3 | 2 | 3 | 2 | 2 | 19 |
| Define Scope & Time | Sol | 2 | 2 | 3 | 2 | 2 | 3 | 2 | 2 | 18 |
| Maintain Courseware | Trans | 2 | 2 | 3 | 3 | 2 | 3 | 1 | 2 | 18 |
| Define Change Management | Bus | 1 | 2 | 2 | 3 | 2 | 3 | 2 | 2 | 17 |
| Support Planning: Communications and Risk | Bus | 1 | 2 | 2 | 3 | 2 | 3 | 2 | 2 | 17 |
| VILT Course Version | Stake | 3 | 3 | 1 | 1 | 1 | 1 | 1 | 1 | 12 |
| Automated Tools | Sol | 1 | 1 | 2 | 2 | 1 | 1 | 1 | 1 | 10 |
| Agile Overview | Bus | 1 | 1 | 1 | 1 | 1 | 1 | 1 | 1 | 8 |

**Notes:** Lisa knew that she would be limited to a one-day offering of her new project management training solution. After much discussion of the SMARTWAY criteria, and numerous clarifying conversations, the final requirements list was presented.

- The project will feature Project Charter development, stakeholder management, scope and time, change management, and communications and risk planning. A key transition requirement will be to ensure a plan of attack is developed to maintain courseware.

# Appendix D

- The stakeholder team determined that a Virtual Instructor Lead Training (VILT) course was out of scope. In addition, they determined that automated tools would not be featured in the initial version of the course.

- Peter fought valiantly to feature an Agile project management curriculum. However, the team felt the time was not right for this shift at this point. Peter is sly however. Don't be surprised if he submits a change request during the course of the project to add something on Agile.

- Bob is still not excited about a training class, but stated he is willing to give it a try.

Lisa's next step was to develop a Project Scope Statement. Her goal was to identify all activities that would allow her to satisfy the end-to-end requirements of the project. Lisa organized the project using the ADDIE method. As we shared in Figure 3.6, this is a common method used to develop course curriculum for training.

| Project Scope Statement ||||||
|---|---|---|---|---|
| Phase | Phase | Phase | Phase | Phase |
| Analyze Needs | Define Curriculum | Develop Courseware | Implement Training | Evaluate and Update Courseware |
| Deliverables by Phase (List in Chronological Order) |||||
| 1. Determine audience | 1. Develop initial course outline | 1. Develop course workbook | 1. Set beta training date | 1. Collect feedback |
| 2. Define training needs | 2. Validate outline | 2. Finalize activities | 2. Prepare classroom | 2. Analyze feedback |
| 3. Validate needs | 3. Finalize outline | 3. Publish initial courseware | 3. Conduct initial training | 3. Determine next steps |
| | | 4. Perform course walkthrough | | |
| | | 5. Update courseware | | |

Lisa's final step was to develop a Work Breakdown Structure (WBS) using the Scope Statement she developed. She was careful to ensure the WBS included all activities defined in the Scope Statement and provided a process to implement the total scope of requirements she identified earlier.

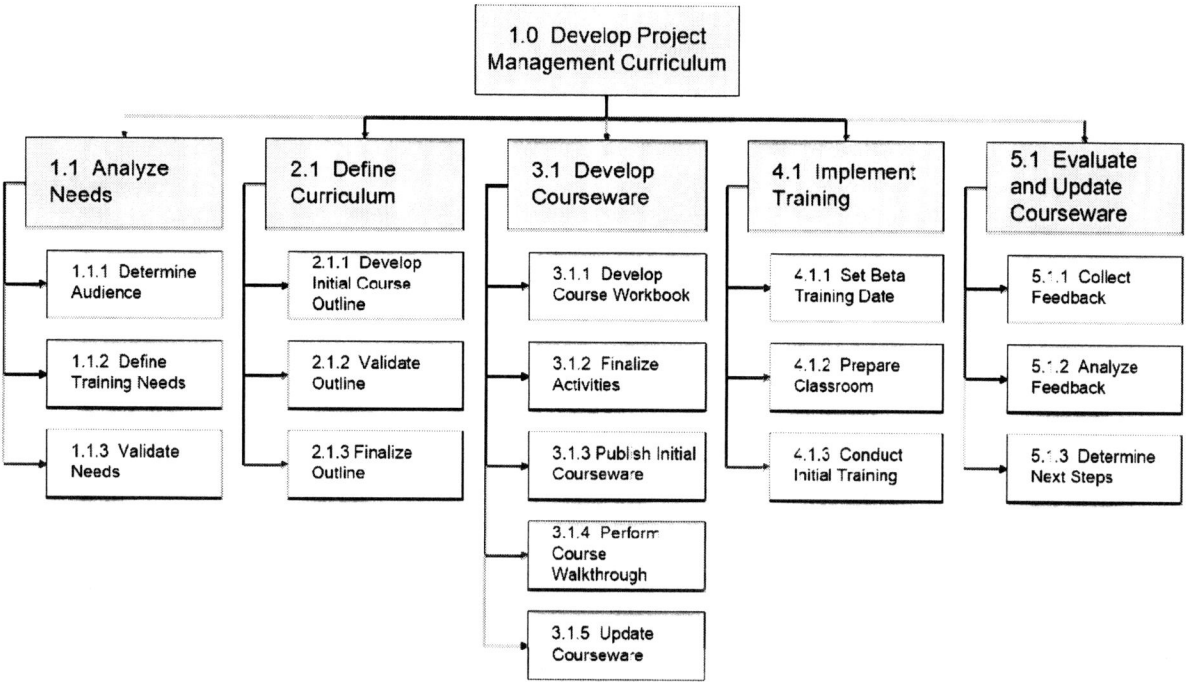

# APPENDIX E:  Schedule Planning Tools Examples

Lisa's next step was schedule development.  The team used the project WBS to develop a Project Network Diagram.  They found that without delays, the project will take approximately three months to complete.  Initial forecasts predicted a five-month cycle.  Good news!

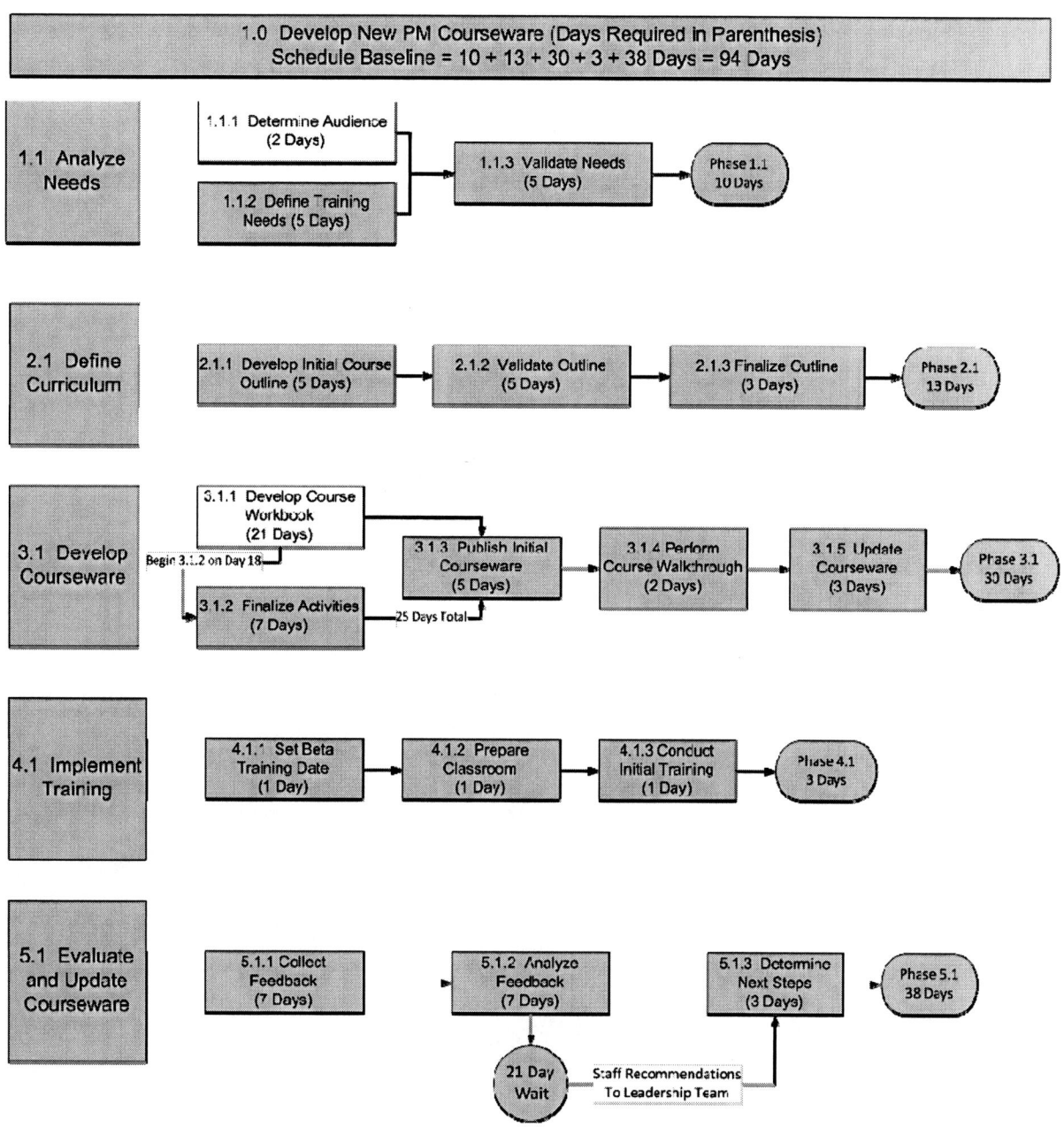

# APPENDIX F: Budget Planning Tools Examples

Lisa's next step was budget development. The team used the WBS to develop a Project Budget. The direct costs to build this class are $7,100. This is good news, as $10,000 was approved to support any project direct costs in the Project Charter. Some indirect costs are also incurred. These costs are primarily internal labor costs to develop the curriculum and the cost of the student's time when they attend training.

| Estimated Direct Costs | Estimated Indirect Costs | Total Project Costs | Category (Direct/Indirect) | Quarter Needed/Comments |
|---|---|---|---|---|
| $5,000 | $0 | $5,000 | Courseware Support | 2017 Q2 |
| $0 | $24,000 | $24,000 | Indirect (200 hours *$120) | 2017 Q1,Q2, Q3 |
| $0 | $0 | $0 | Direct | |
| $2,000 | $0 | $2,000 | Direct | $1000 per quarter Q1/Q2 |
| $100 | $0 | $100 | Direct | $50 per quarter Q1/Q2 |
| $0 | $0 | $0 | Direct | |
| $0 | $0 | $0 | Direct | |
| $0 | $24,000 | $24,000 | Indirect (25 Students) | 2017 Q2 Student Costs |
| $0 | $0 | $0 | Direct | 2018 Q4 |
| $0 | $0 | $0 | N/A | |
| $7,100 | $48,000 | $55,100 | | |
| Contingency Reserves | | | | |
| 10% Cost Basis | $710 | $7,810 | | |
| 5% Cost Basis | $355 | $7,455 | | |

Lisa did consider risk. She determined that the risk of this project was relatively low and determined that a 5% Contingency Reserve would be adequate. Her total budget ask in the end will total $7,455.

The team mapped out project funding requirements over a three-quarter period. This is a small price to pay to achieve quality project management training.

253

Appendix F

| Direct Budget Requirements | 2017 Q1 | 2017 Q2 | 2017 Q3 | 2017 Q4 | TOTAL |
|---|---|---|---|---|---|
| Personnel (Vendor) | | $5,000 | | | $5,000 |
| Personnel (Indirect-Internal) | | | | | $0 |
| Equipment | | | | | $0 |
| Materials | $1,000 | $1,000 | | | $2,000 |
| Supplies | $50 | $50 | | | $100 |
| Development/Construction | | | | | $0 |
| Travel | | | | | $0 |
| Training (Indirect-Internal) | | | | | $0 |
| Support | | | | | $0 |
| Licenses/Permits | | | | | $0 |
| TOTAL | $1,050 | $6,050 | $0 | $0 | $7,100 |

# APPENDIX G: Project Communications Management Plan Example

It was now time to build a Communications Management Plan that would ensure all project communications were accomplished in a timely manner. The goal was to get the right communications to the right person at the right time. Here is a copy of the initial Communications Management Plan, Version 1, that Lisa and her team developed.

| Communications Management Plan for Project Management Training Development Project ||||||
|---|---|---|---|---|---|
| Communications Item (What) | Owner (Who-Sender) | Audience (Who-Receiver) | Timing (When) | Medium (How) | Purpose (Why) |
| Weekly Project Status Reporting | Project Manager | Sponsor, Leadership Team, All key stakeholders | Weekly-Thursday Afternoon | Post to Project SharePoint | Consolidated status report for entire project |
| Course Development Review | Course Development Team | Marketing, Operations, Finance, Trainers | Every second Thursday | Meet in Conference Room 4A from 1:00PM to 2:00PM | Review course development throughout all phases. Solicit feedback |
| Weekly Status Meeting | Project Manager | Sponsor, Leadership Team, All key stakeholders | Weekly-Friday morning | Meet in Conference Room 4A from 9:00AM to 10:00PM | Review status reports, discuss issues, make decisions, inform stakeholders |
| Sponsor 1 on 1 Meet | Project Manager | Jose Rodriguez | Weekly- Friday morning | Meet in Jose's office. 8:00AM to 8:30AM | Discuss changes, blockers, and help needed. Prepare for weekly status meeting |
|  |  |  |  |  |  |
|  |  |  |  |  |  |
|  |  |  |  |  |  |
| Version: 01 |  |  | Date: 28 Feb 2017 |  |  |

**Note:** Lisa is aware that this plan will change as the project progresses. Note how she dated the plan and is using version control to ensure everyone is working off the current version.

# APPENDIX H: Project Risk Register Example

Lisa and the team documented initial risks on a Risk Register. They took time to identify both opportunities and threats. This example is dated. Remember that the Risk Register is a living document that is updated as the project evolves.

**Project: Project Management Training Development Project**

| # | Cause | Event | Impact | Risk Owner | Category | Probability | Impact | Risk Score | Trigger | Response |
|---|---|---|---|---|---|---|---|---|---|---|
| 1 | Lack of Agreement | Delay Course Completion | May not meet milestones | Lisa Sears | Threat | 3 | 4 | 12 | Late Reviews | Iron out disagreements early. |
| 2 | IT Support | SharePoint Development Issues | May delay curriculum sharing | Lisa Sears | Threat | 2 | 4 | 8 | None | Meet with IT upon project approval. Create awareness. |
| 3 | Funding | Funds Withdrawn | Kill or postpone project | Jose Rodriguez | Threat | 1 | 5 | 5 | None | Maintain enthusiasm for project. |
| 4 | Leadership Support | Overcome objections | May allow exceeding schedules | Jose Rodriguez | Opportunity | 4 | 4 | (16) | None | Keep CEO Wright up to date on progress. Share wins. |
| | | | | | | | | | | |
| | | | | | | | | | | |
| Current as of: 28 Feb 2017 | | | | | | Total Risk Score | | 25 – 16 = 9 | | |

**Note 1:** Note the Total Risk Score. A common practice is to add up all threat scores—in this case 25—and subtract all opportunity scores—in this case 16. The total risk score is nine. For a larger project, you may want to consider two separate tabs. Use one for negative risks and one for positive risks.

**Note 2:** Lisa plans on performing Risk Reassessments on a weekly basis. She will incorporate this activity into her weekly status meetings every Friday morning.

# APPENDIX I: Project Plan Pitch Sample

We shared a key concept in Chapter 10. Here is an example of Lisa's pitch using the five-step process we introduced.

| Project Plan Pitch |
|---|
| **Step 1. Attention Step**<br><br>Customer satisfaction dropped from 95% to 85% this past year. We are missing deadlines, shipments are incomplete, and customers are cancelling orders. |
| **Step 2. Motivation**<br><br>The problems we are facing have been created by inconsistent customer interface methods and shipping processes. We need to implement a standard project management approach to regain our excellence. |
| **Step 3. The Body**<br><br>Here is a brief overview of what this project proposes:<br><br>• Scope: We plan to develop standard project management training curriculum to train all key management positions within the firm.<br>• Schedule: We are confident we can train all managers by 15 Aug 2017 or earlier.<br>• Costs: Cost to implement this key curriculum is minimal. We can roll out this project for a bit over $7000.<br>• Risks: There are minimal risks as long as this project is funded and all key leadership groups commit to support this effort. |

Appendix I

---

### Step 4. Remotivation

We highly encourage approval and implementation. We have an opportunity to reverse the negative customer satisfaction trend and create a project management skill set in the company that will benefit everyone.

---

### Step 5. Closure

Request approval and funding of the Project Management Plan.

---

Peter, Alex, and I are all about happy endings! Lisa's Project Management Plan was approved by the Sponsor, Jose, and accepted by all stakeholders to include Bob and Peter! As a result, project management training became a reality at Rogers Shipping. CEO Wright was at the Baseline presentation and told Lisa he was impressed by her work.

# APPENDIX J: Project Status Report Sample

Let's fast forward to the end of the project. Lisa did a great job as project manager, and the project is well in the Executing phase. There are a few issues, but nothing that can't be worked. Here is the June 30, 2017, status report for the project.

| Project: Project Management Training Development Project | | |
|---|---|---|
| Name/Organization: | Lisa Sears/Project Manager | |
| Overall Project Status of Deliverables | | |
| Deliverable Status: (Red, Yellow, Green)<br>• Green: On track for completion as planned<br>• Yellow: Some risks and issues present<br>• Red: Will not achieve desired results | Objectives | Status |
| | Scope | Yellow: Still need to determine Agile objectives |
| | Schedule | Green: Project tracking 1 month ahead of schedule |
| | Budget | Green: Actual expenses forecast at $6,500 |
| Help Needed (Requirement and Sources) Describe as Must Have, Should Have, and Like to Have | Must have decision on contrasting Agile versus Waterfall in the curriculum based on an approved change request. Peter Rogers lead. | |
| Risk: New risks and changes since last report (Add, Change, Delete) | Delete IT Risk #2. SharePoint issues resolved on June 15th. | |
| Issues: Risks that occurred or questions that need responses | No new issues | |
| Forecast: Outlook Moving Forward | Positive. Confident we can work the Agile objective issues in next week. | |
| Comments: | Thanks to all for great support and hard work on this project. | |

# Glossary of Terms and Index

| Term | Chapter | Definition |
|---|---|---|
| 7 Qs | 3 | Seven key questions that must be addressed to ensure your scope is adequately defined |
| Accept | 9 | Response to either a negative or positive risk. No action is prescribed, should the risk occur |
| Actual Costs (AC) | 11 | Used in Earned Value Management. Depicts budget you have spent to date |
| ADDIE | 3 | A logical means to plan a project and place into phases. Best for course development and training. Stands for Analyze, Define, Develop, Implement, Evaluate |
| Analytical | 10 | An Emergenetics Thinking Attribute. People energized by facts, value propositions, and fast problem resolutions. Key question is, "Why?" |
| Approver | 11 | OARP Entry. Generally, the Sponsor who is accountable for project results |
| Assumption | 2 | Something we believe to be true but have yet to validate. All assumptions are potential risks until evaluated as true or false |
| Avoid | 9 | Response to a negative risk. Seeks to eliminate a negative cause |

## Glossary of Terms and Index

| Term | Chapter | Definition |
|---|---|---|
| Balanced Scorecard | 2, 10 | A model that shows the four aspects of a business that must be satisfied to be successful. Includes financial, process, employee, and customer considerations |
| Bottom Up Estimating | 4, 10 | Method of estimating that determines costs and time requirements for each work package. Once calculated, all work package costs and time estimates are aggregated |
| Budget at Completion (BAC) | 11 | Used in Earned Value Management. Depicts dollar value of total project budget |
| Buffer | 4 | The term for the waiting time when you use a lag between the completion of a predecessor activity and start of a successor activity |
| Business Requirements | 3 | Project requirements generated from any internal organization such as Finance, Operations, Marketing, Information Technology, etc. Normally the primary driver or purpose of a project. |
| CAPEX | 4 | CAPEX funds are used to purchase buildings, equipment, or other assets with a long life |
| Change Control Board (CCB) | 6 | A board consisting of a Project Sponsor and senior leadership convened to review and approve/reject change requests impacting the Project Baseline. CCB is managed by the project manager |
| Change Request Form | 1, 6 | Form that defines key information required to process a change request, and allow for the right approval or rejection decision to be made |

## Glossary of Terms and Index

| Term | Chapter | Definition |
|---|---|---|
| Change Timeline | 6 | A four-step process all individuals must go through when change is encountered. The four phases include stability, doubt, hope, and capability |
| Closing | 10, 11 | The fifth and final step in the project management framework. Transition deliverables to operations, close out all contracts, and gain acceptance |
| Code of Account Identifier | 3, 7 | A numbering system that ensures each activity or work package in a WBS has a unique numeric designator |
| Collocated Environment | 9 | Environment where all project team members work in the same general location |
| Communications Blocker | 8 | Anything that can limit the effectiveness of your communications. Sometimes referred to as "Noise Factors" |
| Communications Channels | 8 | A Project Management Institute term. Depicts the number of individual conversations that can occur within a team based on the number of team members |
| Communications Management Plan | 1, 8, 10, 11 | Plan that sets stakeholder communications expectations and addresses potential communications challenges |
| Communications Model | 8 | A model that shows the flow of communications between sender and receiver and points out challenges a project manager must address |
| Compression Techniques | 4, 11 | Methods used to accelerate a project schedule or prevent delays on the Critical Path. Common methods include Fast Tracking and Crashing |

## Glossary of Terms and Index

| Term | Chapter | Definition |
|---|---|---|
| Conceptual | 10 | An Emergenetics Thinking Attribute. People energized by out-of-the-box thinking, creative solutions, and the big picture. Key question is, "What?" |
| Constraint | 2, 8 | Situations/events that may limit a project, such as regulations, dependencies, economic conditions, capacity, etc. |
| Contingency Plan | 9 | The primary action planned to respond to a risk that occurs |
| Contingency Reserves | 4, 9 | Project funds set aside and managed to address known risks |
| Core Team | 2, 7 | *See* Project Management Team |
| Corrective Changes | 6 | Change requests submitted to correct actual problems |
| Cost Performance Index (CPI) | 11 | Earned Value Management calculation. Shows whether you are ahead of, equal to, or behind on budget. Displays result as a percentage |
| Cost Variance (CV) | 11 | Earned Value Management calculation. Shows whether you are ahead of, equal to, or behind on budget. Displays results as dollar amount |
| Crashing | 4 | Using resources from a work package with Float and applying them to work packages on Critical Path to prevent delays |

| Term | Chapter | Definition |
|---|---|---|
| Critical Path | 4 | The path of the longest duration on a Project Network Diagram. The Critical Path is a measure of how long the project will take |
| Customer/User | 2 | Uses product or service developed by the project. Both terms are used in this book |
| Decomposition | 3 | The process of dividing a Work Breakdown Structure into levels |
| Delphi Technique | 9 | A technique to identify risks that eliminates apprehension and fear. Inputs are solicited in a manner where submitters remain anonymous |
| Depreciation | 4 | Lost value of an asset that can be used to reduce overall taxes. A potential cost reduction in a project budget |
| Direct Costs | 4 | Any project cost that requires an actual expenditure of funds |
| Discretionary Dependencies | 4 | Discretionary dependencies can be broken. Discretionary dependencies are included during schedule planning to reduce risk |
| DMADV | 3 | A logical means to plan a project and place into phases. Best for creation of new products and services. Stands for Define, Measure, Analyze, Design, Verify |
| DMAIC | 3 | A logical means to plan a project and place into phases. Best for process development and improvement. Stands for Define, Measure, Analyze, Improve, Control |

## Glossary of Terms and Index

| Term | Chapter | Definition |
|---|---|---|
| Earned Value (EV) | 11 | Used in Earned Value Management. Depicts dollar value of work accomplished |
| Earned Value Management (EVM) | 1, 11 | A common method used to show current schedule and cost status for a project. |
| Earned Value Technique (EVT) | 1, 11 | *See* Earned Value Management |
| Emergenetics | 7, 10 | A methodology that defines the preferences of an individual or a team. Emergenetics breaks results into four Thinking Attributes and three Behavioral Attributes |
| Emotional Intelligence (EQ) | 7, 8 | A model that shows personal competence and social competence skills an individual must perfect to improve performance |
| Enhance | 9 | Response to a positive risk. Prescribes actions to either increase the possibility of a risk occurring, or heighten the positive impact if it occurs |
| Equanimity | 7 | Art of maintaining mental calmness, composure, and evenness of temper, especially in difficult situations |
| Estimate at Completion (EAC) | 11 | Earned Value Management calculation. Shows final budget requirement at project completion if CV and CPI trends continue |
| Executing | 10, 11 | The third step in the project management framework. Implement the Project Management Plan as written |

## Glossary of Terms and Index

| Term | Chapter | Definition |
|---|---|---|
| Exploit | 9 | Response to a positive risk. Seeks to accentuate and enable a positive cause |
| Extended Team | 2, 7 | Team members who are onboarded to perform specific work on the project |
| External Dependency | 4 | Dependencies generally driven by external factors such as policy, regulation, compliance, law, etc. |
| Fallback Plan | 9 | The secondary action planned to respond to a risk that occurs should the Contingency Plan prove to be no longer feasible or ineffective |
| Fast Tracking | 4 | The art and science of eliminating discretionary dependencies and starting work packages simultaneously |
| Finish to Finish | 4 | A successor activity cannot finish until a predecessor activity has finished |
| Five-Step Presentation Process | 10 | A five-step approach to conducting a Pre-Baseline or Baseline Presentation. Steps are Attention, Motivation, Body, Remotivation, and Closure |
| Fixed Constraint | 10 | A mandatory constraint with no deviation. Usually related to time, cost, or scope. For example, a fixed budget of $50,000 means there is absolutely no additional budget available |
| Fixed Costs | 4 | Direct costs required for initial set-up and long-term asset purchases that are subject to depreciation |

## Glossary of Terms and Index

| Term | Chapter | Definition |
|---|---|---|
| Float | 4 | Term that indicates you can extend the time required to complete an activity without impacting the Critical Path |
| Functional Manager | 2, 7 | Managers who provide authorized personnel resources you need for your project. Also referred to as a Resource Manager |
| Functionality | 3 | A FURPS component. Describes the behavior of the product or service being produced and applicable measures to ensure success |
| FURPS | 3 | A model conceived to define functional and non-functional project requirements. FURPS was developed for software projects, however, can be applied to all types of projects. Stands for Functionality, Usability, Reliability, Performance, Supportability |
| Grapevine Effect | 8, 11 | The reality that stakeholders create their own reality and rumors in lieu of a formalized communications methodology |
| Hard Benefits | 10 | Benefits that are "bookable" and have a tangible financial impact. Examples: Revenue increases, real cost savings, and cost avoidance |
| Indirect Costs | 4 | Costs incurred by a project that do not require expenditures of funds. Examples may include internal labor, utilities, etc., paid from other sources |
| Influencers | 2 | Stakeholders or others who can influence project results positively or negatively |

# Glossary of Terms and Index

| Term | Chapter | Definition |
|---|---|---|
| Initiating | 10 | The first step in the project management framework. Developing the Project Charter and Stakeholder Register are key deliverables |
| Issue | 7 | Any question or problem that is impacting a team member that must be addressed. A second definition is a risk that occurred |
| Issue Log | 7 | Logs developed by a project manager to track issues. Do not share the "people" Issue Log. Do share risks that occurred |
| Kick-Off Meeting | 10 | A meeting designed to present a completed Project Management Plan to stakeholders in an effort to gain acceptance |
| KISS | 8 | Acronym for "Keep It Short and Sweet" |
| Known Risks | 4, 9 | Risks identified and documented on a Risk Register |
| Lag | 4 | Delay the start of a successor activity after completion of a predecessor activity for a valid reason |
| Lead | 4 | Begin implementing a successor activity prior to completion of a predecessor activity |
| Leading | 2 | Highest level of commitment designator. Stakeholder supportive and actively engaged in a project |

| Term | Chapter | Definition |
|---|---|---|
| Lessons Learned | 1, 11 | Best practice where the project manager and team analyze what went well and what could be improved and recommend improvement changes over the course of a project. Best practice is to perform Lessons Learned at the end of each project phase |
| Management Reserves | 4, 9 | Project funds set aside and managed to address unknown risks |
| Mandatory Dependency | 4 | Mandatory dependencies are integral to the project's deliverables development and cannot be broken |
| MBWAT | 7, 11 | An acronym for "Management by Walking and Talking" |
| Mitigate | 9 | Response to a negative risk. Prescribes actions to either (1) reduce the possibility of a risk occurring or to (2) decrease a negative impact, if it occurs |
| Monitor and Control | 10, 11 | The fourth step in the project management framework. Ensure deliverables are produced as planned. Take corrective action if variances are identified |
| Negative Risk | 9 | Any potential threat that can negatively impact scope, time, and cost if it occurs or becomes an issue |
| Neutral | 2 | Level of commitment designator. Stakeholder has yet to determine level of support |

## Glossary of Terms and Index

| Term | Chapter | Definition |
|---|---|---|
| Noise Factors | 8 | *See* Communications Blockers |
| OARP | 1, 11 | Decision making model that establishes a solid process you can use to ensure all decisions are properly collaborated and implemented |
| One-Point Estimating | 4 | A method of estimation that considers the most likely estimate only. The pessimistic and optimistic estimate is not considered |
| Operations Manager | 2 | Incorporates project deliverables into operations |
| OPEX | 4 | OPEX funds are generally used to support the operational costs of running a product, business, or system |
| Owner | 11 | OARP Entry. Generally project manager who controls the process |
| Parametric Estimating | 4 | An estimation method that determines cost and/or time requirements by multiplying a unit times either time or cost required to complete the unit |
| Parking Lot | 11 | Method used to defer out-of-scope conversations at a meeting to a later time, while still acknowledging the importance of the conversation |
| Participant | 11 | OARP Entry. Generally team members and stakeholders closest to a problem tasked to generate multiple solution options |

| Term | Chapter | Definition |
| --- | --- | --- |
| PDCA | 1, 3 | Plan, Do, Check, Act. A methodology created by W. Edward Deming that provides a framework for Predictive project management models |
| PDEL | 1, 3 | Plan, Do, Evaluate, Learn. A methodology that supports Adaptive project management models such as Scrum |
| PEAK | 3 | A logical means to plan a project and place into phases. Best for sales campaigns. Stands for Prospect, Engage, Acquire, Keep |
| Performance | 3 | A FURPS component. Requirements to ensure desired speed, efficiency, throughput, capacity, etc. are achieved |
| PERT | 4, 5 | A form of three-point estimating that weights the optimistic, most likely, and pessimistic averages to calculate an estimate |
| PIER-C | 9 | A risk management acronym standing for the steps required to manage risk effectively. Plan, Identify, Evaluate, Respond, and Control |
| Planned Value (PV) | 11 | Used in Earned Value Management. Depicts dollar value of work you had planned to accomplish by a certain timeframe |
| Planning | 10 | The second step in the project management framework. Complete all planning documents and gain approval and acceptance of a Project Management Plan |
| Portfolio | 1 | Organizational vision created as a result of organizational strategic planning. States where the organization is, and where they need to be |

| Term | Chapter | Definition |
|---|---|---|
| Portfolio Manager | 2 | Responsible for high level governance of programs and projects |
| Portfolio Steering Committee | 2 | Committee responsible for developing and managing the company or organization project portfolio. Generally defines governance |
| Positive Risk | 9 | Any potential threat that can positively impact scope, time, and cost. If it occurs, it is referred to as a benefit |
| Post Mortem | 1, 11 | Another term for Lessons Learned |
| Pre-Baseline | 2, 10 | Term used to show a Project Charter was approved by a Sponsor. Allows project to move into Planning phase. |
| Predecessor Activity | 4 | An activity on a Project Network Diagram that occurs before the next activity referred to as the successor activity |
| Preventative Change | 6 | Change requests submitted to prevent potential problems |
| Probability Risk Matrix | 9 | Matrix that rates risk levels of urgency based on total risk score |
| Probability × Impact | 9 | Common method used to qualify risks |

## Glossary of Terms and Index

| Term | Chapter | Definition |
|---|---|---|
| Procurement Audit | 11 | A formal review of contract deliverables conducted at the end of a project to ensure deliverables meet the contract specifics |
| Program | 1 | Defines broad goals necessary to implement a portfolio. Managed by a program manager |
| Progressive Elaboration | 1 | The gradual definition of scope over the course of a project. Scope should be defined at a high level early in a project and "elaborated" or more detailed as project planning progresses |
| Project | 1 | Objectives required supporting a program. Projects are temporary, unique, and defined through progressive elaboration |
| Project Budget | 5, 10 | Finalized project budget that becomes the Cost Baseline in your Project Management Plan |
| Project Champion | 2, 11 | Possesses high levels of expertise and knowledge. Often provides key go or no-go input to decision makers |
| Project Change Log | 1, 6 | A document created by the project manager to log and track status of all project change requests |
| Project Change Management Process | 6, 10 | A five-step process to manage project change requests. Log the change, evaluate the change, determine options, make recommendations, and share the decision |
| Project Charter | 1, 2, 10, 11 | Important first step when a project is born. It defines, at a high-level, what the project will deliver |

Glossary of Terms and Index

| Term | Chapter | Definition |
|---|---|---|
| Project Chunking | 3 | Planning method that allows a complex project to be broken out into smaller, more manageable phases |
| Project Funding Requirements | 4 | Total funding requirements for a project broken out in timeframes or phases when funds are required |
| Project Management Body of Knowledge | 2 | Published by Project Management Institute (PMI). Provides generally recognized practices in project management and shares common vocabulary |
| Project Management Office (PMO) | 2 | An organization responsible for providing project management support throughout an organization. Directly or indirectly responsible for a project |
| Project Management Plan | 2, 10 | Finalized plan that is presented to a Sponsor for approval and stakeholders for acceptance. (Project Plan for short) |
| Project Management Team | 2, 7 | Develop key project management documentation. Manage team members. Provides project manager with the management expertise needed to effectively plan and manage a project. Sometimes referenced as the Core Team |
| Project Manager | 2 | Responsible for project deliverables and managing expectations. Controls the project processes |
| Project Manager's Triangle | 2 | Traditional goals of a project. Finish on time, stay within cost constraints, and provide the right scope |

| Term | Chapter | Definition |
|---|---|---|
| Project Network Diagram | 1, 4, 10, 11 | Uses the project's WBS to lay out a chronological plan to effectively complete all activities on-time |
| Project Requirements | 3 | Definitions of project scope, time, and cost objectives. Optimally, these definitions are placed in priority order |
| Project Schedule | 4, 10 | Finalized project schedule that becomes the Schedule Baseline in your Project Management Plan |
| Q.E.D | 9 | Abbreviation of the Latin phrase "quod erat demonstrandum; literally, "that which was to be demonstrated". Commonly used at the end of mathematical proofs to signify the proof is complete |
| Qualitative Risk Analysis | 9 | A method of qualifying risks by assigning probability and impact values to determine a Risk Score |
| Quality Assurance (QA) | 11 | Activities conducted during Executing phase to ensure the team is following the project plan, standards, processes, etc. Goal is to prevent problems |
| Quality Control (QC) | 11 | Activities conducted during Monitor and Control phase to ensure the deliverables conform to requirements and are fit for use. Goal is to correct problems |
| Quality Requirements | 3, 11 | Project requirements designed to ensure you conform to requirements and provide a product or service that is fit for use |

## Glossary of Terms and Index

| Term | Chapter | Definition |
|---|---|---|
| RACI | 2, 7, 10 | Methodology to define particular stakeholder roles such as Responsible, Accountable, Consult, Inform, or a combination of one or more |
| Reliability | 3 | A FURPS component. Requirements needed to minimize failure rates, ensure predictability, accuracy, etc. |
| Requirements Feasibility and Prioritization Matrix | 1, 3, 10 | Tool used to quantitatively analyze and score requirements. Allows for feasibility analysis, prioritization, and identification of key risks |
| Residual Risk | 9 | A risk that remains in some form after a risk response has been undertaken. Generally identified at a Risk Audit |
| Resistant | 2 | Level of commitment designator. Stakeholder does not support the project |
| Resource Breakdown Structure | 1, 5 | Tool that allows you to effectively estimate resources required to complete all project work using your WBS |
| Resource Manager | 2, 7 | *See* Functional Manager |
| Responsibility Assignment Matrix | 1, 7 | A document that shows actual responsibilities, execution guidelines, and approval requirements for the project team |
| Reviewer | 11 | OARP Entry. Generally key leaders, customers, or users accountable for final project results. Select options provided by Participants |

## Glossary of Terms and Index

| Term | Chapter | Definition |
|---|---|---|
| Rhetorical Question | 10 | A question posed to make a point or solicit a response that requires no answer. Example: How would you all like to be rich? |
| Risk | 9 | Any potential event that can impact a project either positively or negatively |
| Risk Audit | 9 | Review of a response taken to address a risk. Reviews how the response went, and annotates results for Lessons Learned |
| Risk Breakdown Structure (RBS) | 9, 11 | A hierarchical breakout of potential risks by category used during the risk identification process |
| Risk Management Matrix | 9, 11 | A matrix that visually presents the top risks impacting a project. Breaks out current risk status as low, moderate, or high. Shows how status has changed since the last Risk Reassessment |
| Risk Management Plan | 1, 9, 10 | A simple plan that provides guidance and information to members of the risk management team. This is a "how to" manage project risk overview. |
| Risk Metalanguage | 9 | A process to identify and document risks. First identify the cause. Then record potential events, and the impact of each event if the risk occurs |
| Risk Owner | 9, 11 | A team member assigned to monitor and manage a given risk. Risk Owner monitors status, and initiates responses if required |

## Glossary of Terms and Index

| Term | Chapter | Definition |
|---|---|---|
| Risk Reassessment | 9, 11 | Periodic review of all project risks. Generally accomplished on a weekly basis |
| Risk Register | 1, 9, 10, 11 | Essential project management tool to help identify, document and manage project risks |
| Risk Trigger | 9 | Any action or indicator that a risk is about to occur. Allows for early initiation of a risk response |
| Rule of 48/24 | 11 | Best practice that states you should share a meeting agenda at least 48 hours in advance and publish meeting minutes within 24 hours |
| Schedule Performance Index (SPI) | 11 | Earned Value Management calculation. Shows whether you are ahead of, equal to, or behind on schedule. Displayed as a percentage |
| Schedule Variance (SV) | 11 | Earned Value Management calculation. Shows whether you are ahead of, equal to, or behind on schedule. Displayed as a dollar amount |
| Scope | 1, 3 | The definition of the product or service that a project will provide. Scope is achieved through progressive elaboration |
| Scope Creep | 3, 11 | The process of adding scope to a project without going through a formal change process |
| Scope Statement | 1, 3, 10 | Document that defines a project's scope at the greatest level of detail. Allows for development of a Work Breakdown Structure (WBS) |

# Glossary of Terms and Index

| Term | Chapter | Definition |
|---|---|---|
| SDLC | 3 | A logical means to plan a project and place into phases. Best for computer software development. Stands for Software Development Life Cycle |
| Sellers/Business Partners | 2 | External partners who contribute in some manner or are dependent on the project |
| Share | 9 | Response to a positive risk. Seeks to find a third party to address a positive risk factor. |
| Situational Leadership | 7 | Model developed by Hersey and Blanchard that matches preferred leadership styles to levels of readiness |
| SIPOC | 3 | A common method used to map business processes. Stands for Supplier, Inputs, Process, Outputs, Customer |
| SMARTWAY | 3 | Method of analyzing requirements to ensure they are specific, measurable, attainable, relevant, target driven, worth doing, assignable, and yield results |
| Swim Lane | 3 | A process mapping methodology that shows how processes flow from function to function |
| Subject Matter Expert (SME) | 1, 2, 9 | A Stakeholder with high technical skills that provides technical guidance and advice as required |
| Social | 10 | An Emergenetics Thinking Attribute. People energized by how a project impacts others, teamwork, and ensuring commitment and buy-in. Key question is, "Who?" |

| Term | Chapter | Definition |
|---|---|---|
| Soft Benefits | 10 | Benefits that are not "bookable" and are difficult to quantify. Examples: Morale increases, productivity boosts, customer satisfaction, etc. |
| Solution Requirements | 3 | A detailed breakout of how project goals and objectives will be transformed into actual deliverables |
| Sponsor | 2 | Individual responsible for approving a project, allocating funding, and providing project manager authority |
| Staffing Management Plan | 1, 7, 10, 11 | Plan that uses the WBS to ensure you and all project stakeholders understand when human resources are required to support the project |
| Stakeholder | 1 | Any individual interested or impacted by a project. Can include sponsorship, customers, project team members, etc. |
| Stakeholder Change | 6 | A project change request submitted by any project stakeholder |
| Stakeholder Management Plan | 1, 2, 10, 11 | Tool used to classify stakeholder levels of commitment, and develop strategies intended to ensure they are committed at the proper levels |
| Stakeholder Register | 1, 2, 10, 11 | A tool that defines who the key stakeholders in a project are, along with expectations for each stakeholder |
| Stakeholder Requirements | 3, 10 | Project requirements that impact the various stakeholders of a project that must be considered. Includes customers, users, operations, etc. |

## Glossary of Terms and Index

| Term | Chapter | Definition |
|---|---|---|
| Start to Start | 4 | A successor activity cannot start until a predecessor activity has started |
| Status Report | 1, 11 | A document that reflects current status of a project. Most typical status reports share status on scope, time, and costs. |
| STP | 3 | A logical means to plan a project and place into phases. Best for marketing projects. Stands for Segment, Target, Position |
| Structural | 10 | An Emergenetics Thinking Attribute. People energized by predictable results, implementation and schedule guidelines, and control. Key questions are "How?, When?, and Where?" |
| Successor Activity | 4 | An activity on a Project Network Diagram that occurs after the prior activity referred to as the predecessor activity |
| Sunk Costs | 4 | Costs associated with feasibility studies or Research and Development. Sunk costs are not included in a project budget |
| Supportability | 3 | A FURPS component. Requirements that ensure an orderly transition of the project's product or service to operations |
| Supportive | 2 | Level of commitment designator. Stakeholder agrees with the project |
| SWOT Analysis | 9 | Strengths, Weaknesses, Opportunities, and Threats A method used to identify risks. Identify strengths that can lead to opportunities and weaknesses that can lead to threats |

# Glossary of Terms and Index

| Term | Chapter | Definition |
|---|---|---|
| Team Charter | 7 | Developed by and for the team. Defines meeting, working, leadership, communications, consideration, and continuous improvement norms for the team |
| Testimonials | 10 | Acknowledgement from external stakeholders that a project has merit. Used to "sell" the merits of a project |
| Three Needs Theory | 2, 7, 10 | Motivational model developed by David McClelland. States people are motivated by some combination of achievement, affiliation, and empowerment |
| Three-Point Estimating | 4, 5 | A method of estimation that considers an optimistic, most likely, and pessimistic scenario. Common methods are averaging and PERT |
| Trade Off | 10 | Negotiating final scope, time, and cost when initial estimates do not meet the stated objectives of management. Give and take |
| Traffic Light Reporting | 11 | Typical method used to report status using red, yellow, and green indicators |
| Transfer | 9 | Response to a negative risk. Seeks to find a third party to address a negative risk factor |
| Transition Requirements | 3 | Project requirements that plan for the transition of the project's product or service to operations for sustainment after the project is complete |
| Triple Constraints | 2 | *See* Project Manager's Triangle |

## Glossary of Terms and Index

| Term | Chapter | Definition |
|---|---|---|
| Ten Commandments of Meeting Management | 11 | Ten key concepts necessary to ensure effective meeting management |
| Tuckman Model | 7, 11 | A model that shows the four stages a team must go through to become high performance. Steps include Form, Storm, Norm, and Perform |
| Unaware | 2 | Level of commitment designator. Stakeholder is not aware of the project |
| Unknown Risks | 4, 9 | Risks that exist but have not yet been identified |
| Urgent List | 9 | Those risks with a high probability × impact risk score that require the most attention |
| Usability | 3 | A FURPS component. Requirements needed to enhance the user experience |
| User Acceptance Testing (UAT) | 3 | The process of bringing in a customer to inspect and accept project deliverables. *See* Validate Scope |
| Validate Scope | 10, 11 | The process of bringing in a customer to inspect and accept project deliverables. *See* User Acceptance Testing |
| Variable Costs | 4 | Direct costs associated with production. Includes materials, supplies, etc. |

| Term | Chapter | Definition |
|---|---|---|
| Verbal Contract | 2 | Verbal acknowledgement of expectations after completion of a real conversation with a stakeholder |
| Virtual Team | 1, 7, 8 | Members of a project team not co-located with the project manager or other team members. |
| Watch List | 9 | Those risks with a low probability × impact risk score that require the least amount of attention |
| WII-FM | 2, 10 | Acronym for, "What's In It For Me?" |
| Work Breakdown Structure (WBS) | 1, 3, 10 | Hierarchical breakout of a project's requirements using decomposition. The WBS defines all activities required to complete a project |
| Work Package | 3 | The lowest level activity annotated in a WBS |
| Work Breakdown Structure Dictionary | 1, 3, 10 | Supplements the WBS. Defines activity attributes to provide clarification of activities listed on the WBS |

CPSIA information can be obtained
at www.ICGtesting.com
Printed in the USA
LVOW09s0801260817
546479LV00027B/99/P

9 781457 549816